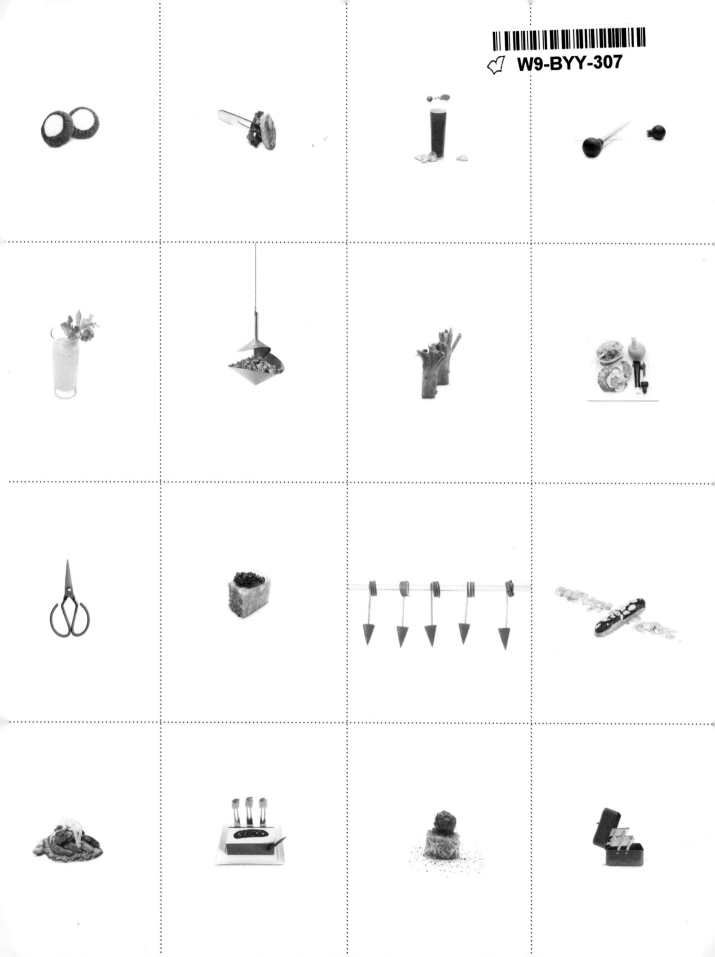

{ INSPIRED BITES }

INSPIRED BITES

Unexpected Ideas for Entertaining
from Pinch Food Design

TJ GIRARD and BOB SPIEGEL

with Casey Barber

Stewart, Tabori & Chang | New York

CONTENTS

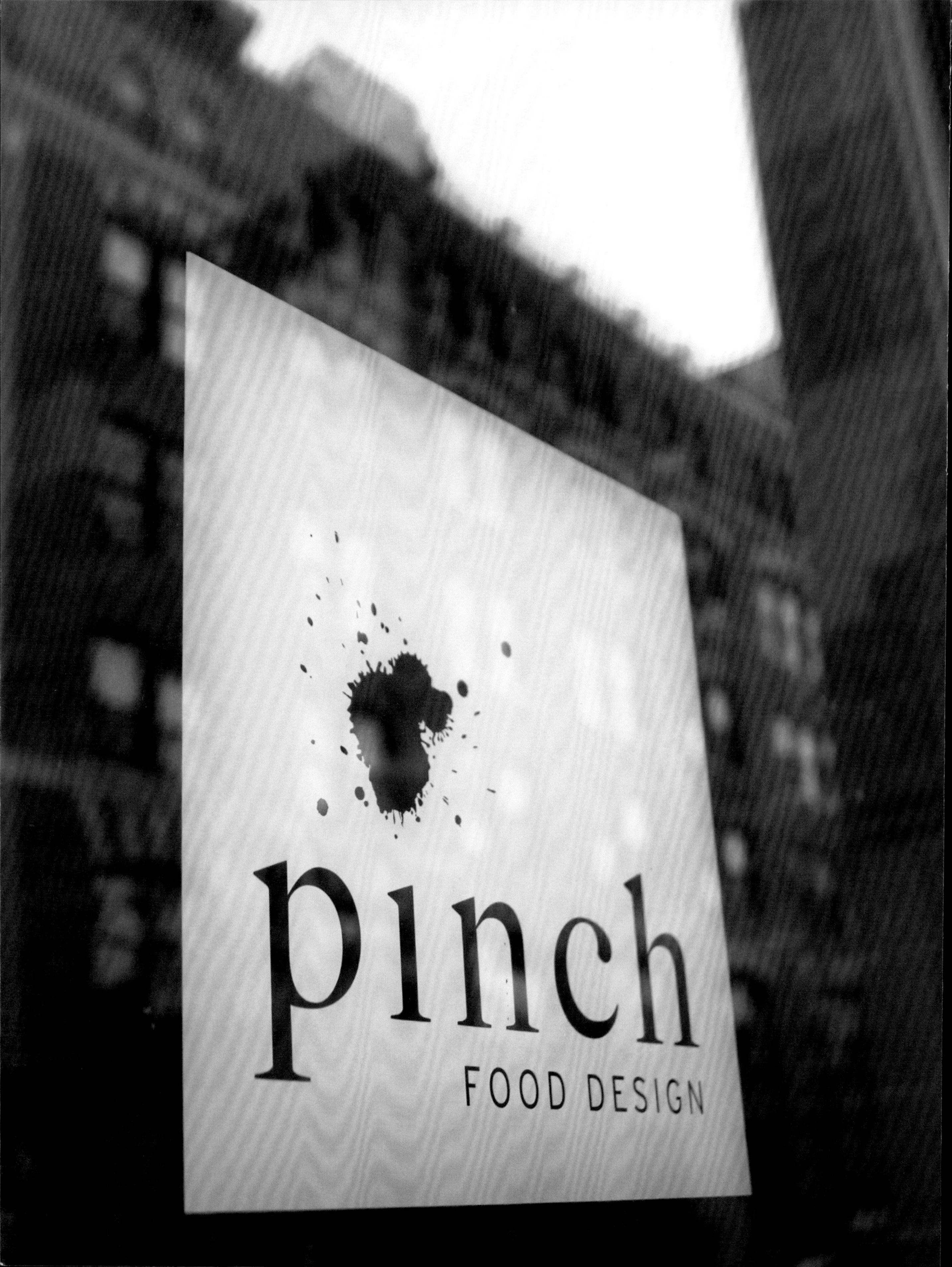
pinch
FOOD DESIGN

INTRODUCTION

··

GET PINCHED

Pinch (our definition):

    1. A small addition of an ingredient that makes an entire dish better: *A pinch of saffron makes bouillabaisse yellow and flowery.*

    2. A playful yet provocative squeeze between the thumb and finger meant to arouse awareness in the recipient.

    3. A turn of phrase evoking a memory of an unbelievable event: *Pinch me; was that a dream?*

This book is first and foremost an inspiration manual. Instead of telling readers there's only one way to do things, we want to show there are no constraints. There's no "right" way to serve an hors d'oeuvre or to entertain graciously. With this book, we hope party hosts feel free to start thinking creatively about how they present food at home. We want to help them venture beyond the kitchen and step away from the table. And most of all, we want everyone to have a good time.

Pinch Food Design was built on the idea of happy surprises and memorable moments. The word itself—*pinch*—conjures up a sense of provocation (a little squeeze that makes you say "oooh!"), a jolt that snaps you out of a reverie, or a small but important cooking instruction. Adding a pinch of something to a recipe, like a nonna might do with her favorite sauce, makes the entire dish taste so much better.

We have nothing against conventional catering and event design—it was what we lived, breathed, slept, and ate for decades, working at top-tier restaurants and production companies in New York City. But when we met in 2005, the words "food design"—placing equal weight on the food itself and the way it's served, creating a mouthwatering and visually stunning presentation—were a pairing we had yet to consider. Each of us was firmly ensconced in our roles: Bob as a chef and TJ as a designer. We had no idea how pivotal our relationship to each other was going to be.

Our backgrounds overlapped more than we initially thought. Bob's dad was a second-generation furniture store owner, and TJ grew up in a French-food-centric household. Through our roots, we had an appreciation for each other's craft. Not only that, but we both grew up in families who used food as the centerpiece of their community, where eating, cooking, and sharing food were central to a welcoming environment.

As we worked together more closely, we realized how much fun we had talking about the same dish from two different perspectives—not opposite, but like the lenses of a 3-D camera, just a few degrees apart. As we tried to one-up each other over ways to present something as simple as sliced salami, we influenced one another—Bob started thinking about how to design and assemble each bite to make it more functional, and TJ began considering ways to present each food based on its shape and composition. We saw the creative possibilities of a partnership, and Pinch Food Design was born.

Having worked in the catering and entertaining industry for decades, neither of us wanted to be part of just another catering company—we wanted to revolutionize catering. When we founded Pinch, we followed through on our mission to reinvent the way parties looked and felt, to change the way guests thought about parties, and to give them the same thrilling experiences they were getting from groundbreaking restaurants all over the world—as well as experiences that restaurants could never pull off. It's the dual perspective, the ability to see through the other's eyes, that's a crucial part of the Pinch philosophy. Looking at exceptional food from a different vantage point—whether physically staring up at pizzas hanging from hooks, watching beignets slide into a pool of honey, or just seeing a familiar dish presented in a new form—makes you not just hungry but also curious.

That curiosity extends through each page of this book. Here, we offer a revolutionary approach to entertaining that throws the same old dips and frozen mini quiches out the window. Instead, fun, inventive, and sophisticated recipes and serving options abound—all of which look incredible and professional but are completely approachable for the home cook. We've tailored our recipes to serve small cocktail gatherings and sit-down dinners for twelve or fewer people, with detailed instructions gleaned from our years of experience. We know it's more fun to be part of the action, so we've detailed how to prep a number of components in advance so you can still enjoy your own party.

In keeping with our vision, which places equal importance on food and design, this book also encourages the home cook to consider creative ways of presenting food beyond standard serving trays. DIY projects in each chapter explain how to re-create some of our signature serving pieces and elements at home and offer ideas for reusing and adapting simple household items for display and presentation. In the chapters that follow, feel free to either adopt our recommended presentation tactics, especially when you are hosting a more elaborate event, or just simply make the food for a casual gathering.

Some Italians might eat a form of macaroni and sauce almost every day, but because there are hundreds of different pasta shapes, every meal feels different. Though they're all made with flour and water, pastas offer infinite inspiration with their textural and visual variations. In the same vein, you don't have to use obscure ingredients or over-the-top preparations at your parties—you can serve your favorite meat loaf, if you want! But the minute you mix it up, by serving your familiar favorites on a cluster of lamp shades instead of the same old platters, or by adding an element of spontaneity, like making your guests squeeze their own dipping sauces from bags hanging overhead, suddenly the regular repertoire becomes exciting and new.

And we see that excitement from our guests when they immediately whip out their phones to take pictures of our food as they walk into the room—already excited by what we've presented—then close their eyes in blissful satisfaction when they take a bite. That's the ultimate return on investment: seeing the exhilaration and connection on our guests' faces. With this book, we're bringing the same sense of surprise and wonder to smaller-scale gatherings, so we can change how people entertain at home as well. You don't need to be at a multimillion-dollar event or a destination wedding to experience new and creative presentations: We can help you accomplish all of this in your own kitchen with your own equipment.

The act of cooking and entertaining, no matter if it's four people around your dining room table, twenty people in your backyard, or two hundred people in a reception hall, is intimate at its core. Though we don't personally know most of the people we've served at our events, we've touched their lives. It's an amazing

feeling to look around a party and realize how many people we've affected. Our end goal is to help people experience togetherness and have meaningful memories, and we hope that with this book we can help more people do just that.

But let's not get too emotional. After all, it's a party! Let's have some fun.

COCKTAILS AND BAR SNACKS

....

GETTING THE PARTY STARTED

We're incredibly grateful that handcrafted cocktails and mixology are reaching a wider audience. With the inclusion of vegetables and herbs in so many high-end specialty cocktails these days, bartenders are thinking like chefs, and vice versa. This inclusive thinking, where lines are blurred and expectations are turned upside down, is a crucial part of the Pinch way of looking at food and drink.

However, while it would be fabulous to have our bartenders custom-craft each drink to order, no guest wants to wait more than a minute to get a drink in hand. So we returned to the drawing board again and again, streamlining recipes that were too complicated in order to make "pre-batched" drinks that can be assembled in advance, but still taste like they were shaken and stirred fresh for each partygoer. Our simple, minimal-ingredient cocktails, like the ones you'll find in this chapter, are the result of familiar flavors that we've tinkered with and adjusted along the way. We believe a great party drink is something you can drink all night—it stimulates the senses, but doesn't compete with the food; it has a personality, enhancing the overall flavor experience.

Because we serve hundreds of people every five minutes, the drinks have to be able to come out quickly; for the home bartender and host, the pressure isn't as nerve-racking, but having batches of drinks at the ready means you can kick back and enjoy a cocktail alongside your guests when they arrive instead of sweating away with a cocktail shaker in hand.

We create curious serving presentations, from rolling coolers and ice mortars to hidden surprises within the drinks themselves, letting us personalize the cocktail experience even if we can't be crafting drinks one at a time. These pieces and drinks keep the interactive, good-time Pinch philosophy at the forefront, but at the end of the day, if you just sat down at a bar and ordered one of our drinks served individually, it would still be damn good.

The recipes that follow are cocktails that can be made in advance and served the more traditional way, in pitchers, or the Pinch way. As with all the recipes in this book, feel free to use our suggestions as inspiration to mix and match and create your own flavor combinations.

Each of the recipes can also be scaled down to make one or two cocktails instead of a pitcher's worth of drinks, so there's no reason you can't shake one or two up for yourself at the end of a long day. Likewise, our bar snacks are easily adaptable for larger or smaller numbers of guests, and all snacks and drinks are a snap to make in advance so you're not rushing around when the party starts.

THE PUNCH WALL IS AN INTERACTIVE DRINKS STATION THAT ELIMINATES THE NEED FOR A BARTENDER. GUESTS PLUCK GLASSES HANGING FROM THE WALL AND SQUEEZE THE COCKTAIL OF THEIR CHOICE INTO THEM WITH OVERSIZE BASTERS.

{ BASTERS }

A staple of everyone's Thanksgiving Day routine, a run-of-the-mill turkey baster can also be a really amusing (not to mention functional) way to serve cocktails. Everyone knows how to use one, but when placed in a new context, the baster makes people stop and think, and most likely smile in delight, as they squeeze themselves a drink!

One of our favorite ways to serve pre-made cocktails is in beautiful squat glass cylinders sitting on five vintage elevator stools attached to a freestanding wall covered with a grid of glasses hanging from hooks. Once the basters are in place, the Punch Wall, as we refer to it, becomes a self-manned drinks station for hosts who don't want to hire a bartender for the evening (see page 11). Even if we offer trays of pre-poured drinks near the Punch Wall, everyone ignores the trays and prefers to "baste" their cocktail! It's a much cooler, more adult way of self-serving than tapping and pumping a keg—and perfectly suited for small-scale gatherings at home.

Though our dream is to find glass basters, like oversize versions of the pipettes used in scientific laboratories, our basting equipment is nothing more than the clear plastic, black-knobbed kind you've seen a million times. We like the eighteen-inch basters that are slightly larger and more industrial than the supermarket models typically found near the aluminum roasting pans. They are commonly used in beer making, and now that home-brewing is so popular, they are pretty easy to locate online.

DIY

OUR DIY BAR CART, SHOWN HERE, IS EASY TO ASSEMBLE AT HOME. WE USE A PREFAB BUTCHER-BLOCK CART WITH S-HOOKS FOR HANGING GLASSES AND DRINK DISPENSERS FOR GUESTS TO SERVE THEMSELVES.

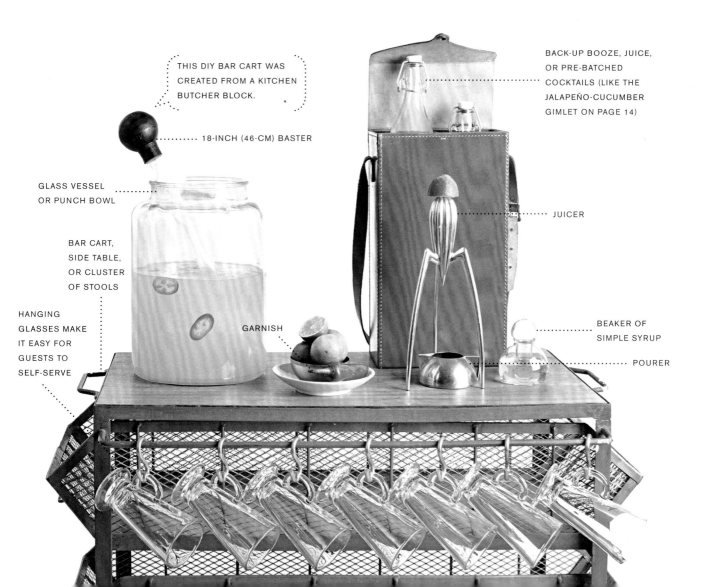

THIS DIY BAR CART WAS
CREATED FROM A KITCHEN
BUTCHER BLOCK.

BACK-UP BOOZE, JUICE,
OR PRE-BATCHED
COCKTAILS (LIKE THE
JALAPEÑO-CUCUMBER
GIMLET ON PAGE 14)

18-INCH (46-CM) BASTER

GLASS VESSEL
OR PUNCH BOWL

BAR CART,
SIDE TABLE,
OR CLUSTER
OF STOOLS

JUICER

HANGING
GLASSES MAKE
IT EASY FOR
GUESTS TO
SELF-SERVE

GARNISH

BEAKER OF
SIMPLE SYRUP

POURER

Jalapeño-Cucumber Gimlet

If you've never had St-Germain elderflower liqueur, then we are so jealous that you get to taste it for the first time. Its taste is hard to pinpoint: It's floral, it's fruity, it's strong yet delicate. The vegetables are the star of this drink, but the St-Germain lends an intriguing undercurrent. This was our first signature drink—so simple to mix, yet so addicting. Bet you can't have just one!

YIELD: Serves 12
SPECIAL EQUIPMENT: baster

3 cups (720 ml) New Amsterdam gin
1½ cups (360 ml) St-Germain elderflower liqueur
1½ cups (360 ml) fresh lime juice (from about 12 limes)
12 thin cucumber slices, for serving
12 thin jalapeño slices, for serving

In a 2-quart (2-L) punch bowl or other serving vessel, stir together the gin, St-Germain, and lime juice.

Garnish each of twelve ice-filled highball glasses with one cucumber slice and one jalapeño slice. Set the punch bowl, garnished glasses, and a baster on a tray or bar table and allow your guests to serve themselves with the baster.

MAKE-AHEAD/STORAGE
The gin, St-Germain, and lime juice can be stirred together up to 4 hours in advance and stored in an airtight container in the refrigerator until ready to garnish and serve.

Spicy Mango Margarita

The combination of mango and Sriracha in this margarita was inspired by TJ's trips to Mexico, where the lime- and chile-sprinkled fruit sold by street vendors left a memorable impression on her taste buds. Now these quintessential tastes come in cocktail form.

YIELD: Serves 12
SPECIAL EQUIPMENT: baster

1½ cups (360 ml) Milagro silver tequila
¾ cup (180 ml) mango puree or mango nectar
¾ cup (180 ml) Bols triple sec
¾ cup (180 ml) fresh lime juice (from about 6 limes)
¾ cup (180 ml) simple syrup
1½ cups (360 ml) club soda
Sriracha, for serving
1 teaspoon red pepper flakes
12 lime wedges

In a 2-quart (2-L) punch bowl or other serving vessel, stir together the tequila, mango puree, triple sec, lime juice, and simple syrup. Top with the club soda.

Fill twelve highball or margarita glasses with ice. Set the punch bowl, ice-filled glasses, and a baster on a tray or bar table and allow your guests to serve themselves with the baster. Garnish each drink with 5 to 7 drops of Sriracha, a sprinkling of red pepper flakes, and a lime wedge.

MAKE-AHEAD/STORAGE
The tequila, mango puree, triple sec, lime juice, and simple syrup can be stirred together up to 4 hours in advance and stored in an airtight container in the refrigerator. Stir in the club soda imediately before serving.

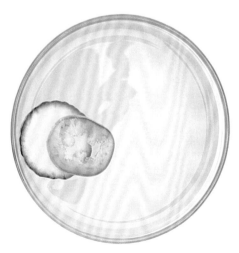

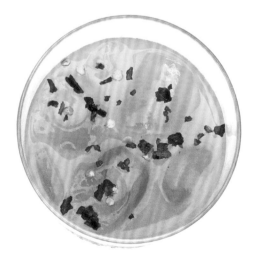

Celery-Cilantro Pop

The key ingredient here is the celery soda. When it's combined with the tang of the cilantro, images of a fragrant garden can't help but make their way into your brain. Though an unexpected pairing of flavors, celery and cilantro make a perfect late-summer quencher.

YIELD: Serves 12
SPECIAL EQUIPMENT: baster

3 cups (720 ml) vodka
1 (12-ounce/360-ml) bottle Dr. Brown's Cel-Ray
  celery soda
¾ cup (180 ml) fresh lime juice (from about 6 limes)
1 celery stalk, cut into brunoise (cubes no larger than
  ⅛ inch/3 mm)
1 teaspoon minced fresh cilantro leaves
Additional whole celery and cilantro leaves

In a 2-quart (2-L) punch bowl or serving vessel, stir together the vodka, celery soda, and lime juice.

Garnish each of twelve ice-filled highball glasses with the celery brunoise and minced cilantro. Set the punch bowl, garnished glasses, and a baster on a tray or bar table and allow your guests to serve themselves with the baster. Guests can add the whole celery and cilantro leaves as desired.

MAKE-AHEAD/STORAGE
Because of the carbonation in the celery soda, this drink should be made immediately before serving.

{COOLERS}

Maybe no one actually gathers around the office watercooler to gossip anymore, but they sure do congregate at bars for happy-hour camaraderie and conversation. Inspired by a German art exhibition called *Drink Away the Art*, where gallery guests were encouraged to serve themselves from wall-mounted glass aquariums filled with colorful liquor infusions, we wanted to offer another sort of interactive self-serve drink dispenser for our party guests. Our wheeled watercoolers are modern, streamlined versions that house gallons of refreshing beverages—from kimchi Bloody Marys to vodka-spiked juice—so guests can easily grab a glass and drink up.

DIY

GLASS AND CERAMIC DRINK DISPENSERS WITH POUR SPOUTS ARE READILY AVAILABLE FROM MOST UPSCALE HOME DÉCOR STORES AND CAN BE PLACED ON A WHEELED BAR CART OR FILING CABINET AS IN THE BAR CART DIY ON PAGE 12. USE THE SHELVES, DRAWERS, AND HANDLES TO STACK OR HANG GLASSWARE FOR YOUR GUESTS TO SERVE THEMSELVES.

AND IF YOU ALREADY OWN A WATERCOOLER AT HOME (AND ARE NOT FEARFUL OF VOIDING YOUR WARRANTY), YOU COULD REPLACE THE PLASTIC CONTAINER OF SPRING WATER WITH A STYLISH OVER-SIZE GLASS JUG, ALSO REFERRED TO AS A "WINE BALON," AND FILL IT WITH A COCKTAIL OR WINE OF YOUR CHOICE.

GLASS BALON FILLED WITH A COCKTAIL SUCH AS HUGO'S SPIKED HORCHATA (SEE PAGE 19)

SIMPLY INSERT BALON INTO A CERAMIC WATER DISPENSER TO CREATE A COCKTAIL COOLER.

Kimchi Bloody Mary

Kimchi is the new ketchup—it's such a ridiculously popular flavor now. It's also sour, sweet, and spicy, and these are three qualities of a good Bloody Mary. The smoothness of this drink will make it hard to go back to the traditional version. We use pickles or green bell pepper for garnish, but you can use cilantro, fennel, or daikon.

YIELD: Serves 12
SPECIAL EQUIPMENT: watercooler-style serving vessel (optional)

3 cups (720 ml) vodka
3 cups (720 ml) tomato juice
1½ cups (360 ml) kimchi brine, drained from 1 to 2 (16-ounce/480-ml) jars of premade kimchi (such as Mother-in-Law's)
2 tablespoons plus ¾ teaspoon soy sauce
Black Hawaiian sea salt (optional)
12 thin pickle spears, or 24 green bell pepper slices

In a watercooler-style serving vessel or 3-quart (2.8-L) pitcher, stir together the vodka, tomato juice, kimchi brine, and soy sauce.

Salt the rim of each of twelve ice-filled highball or Collins glasses, if desired. Garnish with pickle spears or 2 pepper slices and let guests serve themselves.

MAKE-AHEAD/STORAGE
The vodka, tomato juice, kimchi brine, and soy sauce can be stirred together up to 4 hours in advance and stored in an airtight container in the refrigerator until ready to garnish and serve.

Pear-Ginger-Thyme Cooler

This particular flavor combination hits home especially in the fall and winter. The juxtaposition of the savory herb and the sweet fruit works well in cooking applications, like turkey and cranberry sauce, and this drink will conjure up visions of crisp days and warm fireplaces. When we serve this, we use fresh pear puree, but bottled pear nectar can be substituted.

YIELD: Serves 12
SPECIAL EQUIPMENT: watercooler-style serving vessel (optional)

3 cups (720 ml) vodka
1½ cups (360 ml) pear puree
1½ cups (360 ml) agave nectar
12 fresh thyme sprigs
12 wafer-thin slices of fresh ginger
1 (12-ounce/360-ml) bottle ginger beer

In a watercooler-style serving vessel or 3-quart (2.8-L) pitcher, stir together the vodka, pear puree, and agave.

Garnish twelve ice-filled highball glasses with a sprig of thyme and a slice of ginger. Let guests serve themselves, and then float 1 ounce (30 ml) of the ginger beer individually into each glass.

MAKE-AHEAD/STORAGE
The vodka, pear puree, and agave can be stirred together up to 4 hours in advance and stored in an airtight container in the refrigerator until ready to garnish and serve.

Hugo's Spiked Horchata

Horchata is typically served at family gatherings and festivals, so we wanted to continue in that tradition. Some might mistake this creamy cocktail for a milk shake, but Pinch chef Hugo's version of the Mexican comfort drink is not as rich and filling. The rice is soaked, then pureed to make the horchata creamy and give it its unique taste. The evaporated milk gives the drink its sweetness, and the rum cuts the thickness and marries all the flavors perfectly.

YIELD: Serves 12
SPECIAL EQUIPMENT: watercooler-style serving vessel (optional)

For the horchata:
4 cups (400 g) uncooked white rice
8 cups (2 L) whole milk
1 (12-ounce/360-ml) can evaporated milk
2 tablespoons ground cinnamon
1 tablespoon pure vanilla extract

To assemble:
3 cups (720 ml) amber rum
12 cinnamon sticks
12 vanilla beans
Ground cinnamon

Make the horchata: Pour the rice into a large bowl and add enough water to cover it by 1 inch (2.5 cm). Cover and set aside to soak at room temperature for 4 hours.

Drain the rice and transfer it to a blender. Add the milk, evaporated milk, cinnamon, and vanilla and puree until smooth.

Strain the horchata through a fine-mesh sieve into a bowl or pitcher and chill.

Assemble the cocktail: In a watercooler-style serving vessel or 3-quart (2.8-L) pitcher, stir together 6 cups (1.4 L) of the horchata and the rum.

Garnish each of twelve ice-filled highball glasses with a cinnamon stick, and after guests have filled their glasses, let them add a dash of cinnamon.

MAKE-AHEAD/STORAGE
The horchata can be made up to 3 days in advance; store the strained horchata in an airtight container in the refrigerator until ready to use.

Honey Pot

Traditional simple syrup is made by combining equal parts granulated sugar and water, but substituting honey for refined sugar adds caramelized depth to the sweet liquid. Paired with the vibrant tropical flavors of pineapple and citrus, it makes for a surprisingly complex cocktail.

YIELD: Serves 12
SPECIAL EQUIPMENT: watercooler-style serving vessel (optional)

For the honey simple syrup:
¼ cup (60 ml) honey
¼ cup (60 ml) water

To assemble:
2¼ cups (540 ml) vodka
1½ cups (360 ml) pineapple juice
¾ cup (180 ml) fresh lemon juice (from about 4 lemons)
12 basil sprigs
1 (12-ounce/360-ml) bottle club soda

Make the honey simple syrup: Pour the honey and water into a small saucepan and stir over medium heat just until bubbles start to form around the edges of the liquid. Cool to room temperature.

Assemble the cocktail: In a watercooler-style serving vessel or 3-quart (2.8-L) pitcher, stir together the honey simple syrup, vodka, pineapple juice, and lemon juice.

Garnish twelve ice-filled highball glasses with a basil sprig. Let guests serve themselves and then splash about ¼ ounce of the club soda individually into each glass.

MAKE-AHEAD/STORAGE
The honey simple syrup can be made up to 1 week in advance; store in an airtight container in the refrigerator. The combined simple syrup, vodka, pineapple juice, and lemon juice can be stirred together up to 4 hours in advance and stored in an airtight container in the refrigerator until ready to garnish and serve.

{ ICE MORTAR }

If you don't want your guests to miss out on the luxury of having a drink made to order, you can still serve your cocktails in a creative way. Who needs a cocktail shaker when you've got a bowl made of ice to stir your martinis?

If you've ever sat at the actual oyster bar in the famous Grand Central Oyster Bar and watched the shuckers and prep cooks at work, you've likely been captivated by the old-timey metal stockpots that the cooks use to make oyster pan roasts and stews. These shallow cooking vessels, built on mechanisms that help them tilt the finished stew into a waiting bowl, were Bob's inspiration for the Pinch Ice Mortar and Pestle. We use this stunning carved block of ice to mix drinks, keep them cold, and pour them directly into our guests' glasses.

For us, the piece is a modern take on ice sculpture, a reimagining that banishes all thoughts of swans and monograms and takes the idea from cheesy to cool. After making a couple of our own attempts with a chainsaw and a giant block of ice, we decided to call on the masters. The only person we could trust to bring our Ice Mortar and Pestle to life was Shintaro Okamoto of the renowned Okamoto Custom Ice Studio in New York City, who's carved everything from handcrafted ice cubes to a giant ice Buddha displayed at the Rubin Museum of Art. While we called in the big guns to finesse our Ice Mortars, it's not as difficult as you might imagine to make a simple ice punch bowl at home.

TO MAKE YOUR OWN VERSION OF THE ICE MORTAR, TRY CREATING THIS ICE FUNNEL AND STAND.

PLUG UP THE HOLE AT THE BOTTOM OF A LARGE METAL OR PLASTIC FUNNEL WITH ABOUT A TABLESPOON'S WORTH OF MUSEUM GEL OR MUSEUM PUTTY, AND WRAP THE EXTERIOR OF THE FUNNEL WITH PLASTIC WRAP FOR GOOD MEASURE.

HEAT THE END OF A BRASS PIPE (WITH A SMALLER DIAMETER THAN THE FUNNEL'S HOLE) ON A STOVETOP BURNER AND USE IT TO MELT A HOLE THROUGH THE MIDDLE OF A PLASTIC DELI CONTAINER. PUSH THE PIPE INTO THE MOUTH OF THE FUNNEL AND SLIDE THE PLASTIC CONTAINER ONTO THE ROD UNTIL IT FITS SNUGLY INSIDE THE FUNNEL AND THE PIPE STANDS UP STRAIGHT. WEIGH THE CONTAINER DOWN WITH ROCKS OR BEANS AND FILL THE FUNNEL WITH WATER, MAKING SURE THE WATER FILLS THE SIDES BETWEEN THE FUNNEL AND THE DELI CONTAINER. FREEZE OVERNIGHT TO MAKE AN ICE FUNNEL, THEN REMOVE THE DELI CONTAINER, PIPE, MUSEUM GEL, AND PLASTIC WRAP.

SET A CRATE ON ITS SIDE AND DRILL A 3-INCH (7.5-CM) HOLE INTO THE "TOP" SIDE OF THE WOODEN CRATE. SLIDE A 3-INCH (7.5-CM) ROUND COOKIE CUTTER INTO THE HOLE SO IT ACTS AS A LINER BETWEEN THE WOOD AND ICE. PLACE A DRIP TRAY IN THE CRATE. PLACE THE ICE FUNNEL IN THE COOKIE CUTTER–LINED HOLE.

TO SERVE YOUR DRINKS, PLUG THE BOTTOM OF THE ICE FUNNEL WITH A CORK. POUR THE COCKTAIL INTO THE ICE FUNNEL AND STIR TO CHILL THE LIQUID. PLACE YOUR COCKTAIL GLASS UNDER THE FUNNEL AND QUICKLY AND CAREFULLY REMOVE THE CORK TO FILL THE GLASS.

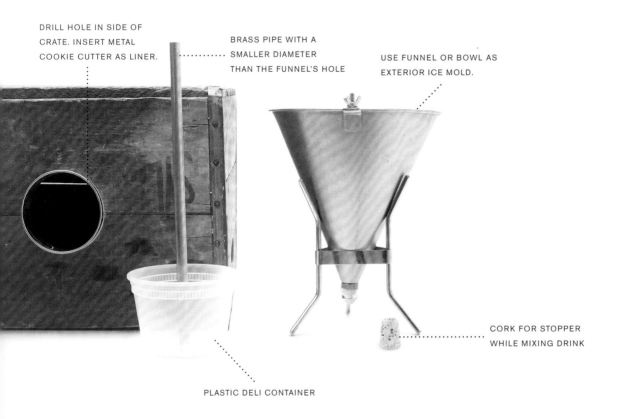

DRILL HOLE IN SIDE OF CRATE. INSERT METAL COOKIE CUTTER AS LINER.

BRASS PIPE WITH A SMALLER DIAMETER THAN THE FUNNEL'S HOLE

USE FUNNEL OR BOWL AS EXTERIOR ICE MOLD.

CORK FOR STOPPER WHILE MIXING DRINK

PLASTIC DELI CONTAINER

THIS ICE FUNNEL AND STAND
FORM THE DIY VERSION OF
THE PINCH ICE MORTAR.

REMOVE CORK ONCE
GLASS IS IN PLACE
FOR COCKTAIL.

FILL ICE FUNNEL WITH
INGREDIENTS FOR DRINK.

MAKE SURE THERE
IS A DRIP TRAY TO
CATCH EXCESS LIQUID.
FILL IT WITH RIVER
ROCKS OR PLANTS
LIKE MICRO SHISO.

Spicy Pickled Ramp Martini

Often described as wild leeks, ramps are a seasonal treat that appear in early spring and often fly off the farmers' market stands in what seems like the blink of an eye. To preserve this favorite green, with its natural hints of onion and garlic, for year-round enjoyment, people often turn to pickling. But as delicious as the pickled ramps are, the brine is liquid gold. Naturally, when we created a Pinch dirty martini, we decided to forgo the olive brine in favor of the delicious ramp pickling liquid.

NOTE: Got your hands on some fresh ramps? Pickle them yourself using the parsnip pickle recipe (see page 106) as a base.

YIELD: Serves 12
SPECIAL EQUIPMENT: Ice Mortar (optional)

7½ cups (1.8 L) vodka or gin
1½ cups (360 ml) pickled ramp brine
12 splashes dry vermouth
12 pickled ramps (see Note)
Red pepper flakes, for garnish

Fill twelve martini glasses with ice water to chill the glasses.

In an ice mortar or 3-quart (2.8-L) pitcher, stir together the vodka and ramp brine. If using a pitcher, stir in some ice to cool the mixture, then strain it out before serving.

Discard the ice water from the martini glasses and add a splash of dry vermouth to each glass. Let guests pour ramp vodka from the mortar (or pitcher) into each glass, then garnish each with a pickled ramp and a sprinkling of red pepper flakes.

MAKE-AHEAD/STORAGE
The vodka and ramp brine can be stirred together up to 4 hours in advance and stored in an airtight container in the refrigerator until ready to garnish and serve.

Yuzu Sake Krush

Sake seems to be taking the cocktail world by storm these days. Whether sweet and tangy or dry and floral, this spirit's versatile flavor profile lends itself well to mixed drinks. Inspired by the great lime-and-mint combo found in so many popular drinks worldwide, we decided to marry the sake with traditional Japanese flavors like citrusy yuzu and fresh shiso. The sweetness of the kumquat preserves ties it all together to create a delightfully crisp and refreshing "krush."

NOTE: Yuzu is an East Asian citrus fruit. While the fruit itself may not be readily available near you for fresh juicing, bottled yuzu juice is easily found online and in many Asian markets and grocery stores.

YIELD: Serves 12
SPECIAL EQUIPMENT: Ice Mortar (optional)

1½ cups (360 ml) sake
6 tablespoons (90 ml) bottled yuzu juice (see Note)
1 tablespoon kumquat preserves
3 cups (720 ml) white rum
12 whole kumquats
12 shiso leaves

In a pitcher, whisk together the sake, yuzu juice, and kumquat preserves.

Pour the sake mixture into the ice mortar, if using, or a 3-quart (2.8 L) pitcher. Add the rum, then swirl together.

Pour the sake-rum mixture into twelve highball glasses filled with crushed ice, and garnish each with a kumquat and shiso leaf.

MAKE-AHEAD/STORAGE
The sake, yuzu juice, and kumquat preserves can be stirred together up to 4 hours in advance and stored in an airtight container in the refrigerator until ready to garnish and serve. Re-stir before pouring into an Ice Mortar or pitcher and adding the rum.

Green Pepper Gimlet

This drink has become an instant classic at Pinch. The green bell pepper adds a lush, verdant color and a surprising crisp, sweet twist to the flavor of the traditional citrusy gimlet cocktail.

YIELD: Serves 12
SPECIAL EQUIPMENT: cocktail strainer, Ice Mortar (optional)

12 to 18 large green bell peppers, cored and seeded, plus 12 thin green bell pepper rounds
3 cups (720 ml) New Amsterdam gin
1½ cups (360 ml) fresh lime juice (from about 12 limes)
¾ cup (180 ml) simple syrup

Roughly chop twelve whole bell peppers, reserving a thin round from each; place in a blender or food processor and blend to make a smooth, juicy puree.

Chop and add the remaining bell peppers as needed to get 3 cups (720 ml) puree.

Strain the puree into an Ice Mortar, if using, or a 3-quart (2.8-L) pitcher. Then stir in the gin, lime juice, and simple syrup. If using a pitcher, stir in some ice to cool the mixture then strain it out before serving.

Pour the cocktail into each of twelve chilled martini glasses and garnish each glass with a green pepper round.

MAKE-AHEAD/STORAGE

The green pepper puree, gin, lime juice, and simple syrup can be stirred together up to 4 hours in advance and stored in an airtight container in the refrigerator until ready to garnish and serve. Re-stir before pouring into an Ice Mortar or pitcher.

{ENHANCERS}

At Pinch, we're always looking for additional ways to make the cocktail experience even more intimate and exciting for our guests, even when we're not mixing drinks to order.

We fill vintage glass atomizers and eyedroppers with everything from diluted extracts and bitters to flavored simple syrups and rosewater, and offer them up as add-ons that guests can dribble or spray into their drinks at their leisure. A quick spritz from a cool bottle is a fun way to let each guest personalize his or her drink with a fun flavor profile, and creates more opportunities for fellow partygoers to get to know one another as they trade tips and suggestions.

Start with a basic cocktail like a vodka or gin and tonic, and let guests add rosemary simple syrup, rhubarb bitters, or rosewater, marveling at how drastically and deliciously the drink can change. Then experiment with your own tried-and-true cocktail combinations—who knows, you might discover a new way to drink your favorite!

DIY

CREATE A BESPOKE COCKTAIL BAR WITH VINTAGE GLASSWARE FILLED WITH BITTERS, SYRUPS, AND A FEW FRESH SPRITZES OF CITRUS. A WORLD OF ATOMIZERS, BOTH MODERN AND VINTAGE, ARE WIDELY AVAILABLE, AS ARE BITTERS AND EXTRACTS IN EVERY FLAVOR UNDER THE SUN. SPRAYERS THAT ATTACH DIRECTLY TO LEMONS AND LIMES ARE NOW AVAILABLE ONLINE AND AT KITCHEN SUPPLY STORES. BUY A FEW AND TWIST THEM INTO THE FRUIT TO GIVE YOUR GUESTS A GARNISH THAT'S 100 PERCENT NOT-FROM-CONCENTRATE.

The Mademoiselle

Don't let the feminine name and color of this drink fool you: It is undiscriminatingly addictive. Everyone loves lemonade, but adding a splash of rosewater will utterly transport you to a Maghreb paradise.

YIELD: Serves 12
SPECIAL EQUIPMENT: atomizer

3 cups (720 ml) New Amsterdam gin
3 cups (720 ml) Poland Spring or other filtered mineral water
¾ cup (180 ml) fresh lemon juice (from about 4 lemons)
¾ cup (180 ml) Monin rose syrup
Rosewater
Edible rose petals (optional)

In a pitcher, mix together the gin, water, lemon juice, and rose syrup.

Fill an atomizer bottle with rosewater.

Pour the gin mixture into twelve old-fashioned glasses or stemless red wine glasses filled with ice, and top each with a rose petal, if desired.

Let guests spritz their cocktails with a hint of rosewater.

MAKE-AHEAD/STORAGE
The gin, water, lemon juice, and rose syrup can be stirred together up to 4 hours in advance and stored in an airtight container in the refrigerator until ready to garnish and serve.

Beetlini

This lovely twist on a Bellini has an unexpected sweetness and a shocking color, and the addition of vanilla simple syrup gives the vegetable a pleasantly fruitlike taste.

YIELD: Serves 12
SPECIAL EQUIPMENT: atomizer

For the vanilla simple syrup:
1 cup (200 g) granulated sugar
1 cup (240 ml) water
2 vanilla beans

To assemble:
6 vanilla beans
¾ cup (180 ml) beet juice
6 cups (1.4 L) prosecco brut (about 2 standard 750-ml bottles)
12 mini radishes for garnish (optional)

Make the vanilla simple syrup: In a 2-quart (2-L) saucepan, combine the sugar and water and bring to a simmer over medium heat, stirring frequently until the sugar has dissolved. Split the vanilla beans lengthwise and scrape out the

seeds. Add the seeds and scraped pods to the pan with the sugar syrup, stir to combine, and remove from the heat. Cover and let sit for 30 minutes to allow the vanilla to infuse the syrup.

Strain the syrup through a fine-mesh sieve into a clean bowl, then transfer to an atomizer (use a funnel, if necessary). Discard the vanilla bean pods or let them dry and reserve them for another use.

Assemble the cocktail: Split the vanilla beans in half lengthwise and scrape out the seeds. Discard the pods or reserve them for another use. In a 3-quart (2.8-L) punch bowl or other serving vessel, whisk the vanilla bean seeds and the beet juice together. Add the prosecco and divide the mixture among twelve champagne flutes or coupes. Serve with a mini radish for garnish, if desired, and the vanilla simple syrup in an atomizer for spritzing.

MAKE-AHEAD/STORAGE
The vanilla simple syrup can be made up to 1 month in advance; strain into an airtight container and store in the refrigerator until ready to use.

We've said it before, and we'll say it again—thank God for silicone. Because of this clever material, we're able to find ice cube trays that make pretty much any shape under the sun, from simple spheres to stars to skulls-and-crossbones to long swizzle sticks. If you are feeling extra creative, go online to make your own food-grade silicone mold. You'll find convenient collections of mold-making products and kits, and step-by-step videos to help you pour liquid silicone and capture high-quality details every time. But no matter what shape your ice is destined to be, when you are making them follow this pro tip: Boil water, then allow it to cool slightly before pouring it into your specialty ice cube molds. Boiling removes impurities in tap water, making sure each cube pops out crystal clear instead of cloudy.

CUBE MELTS

Even if you're not dropping specialty-shaped ice cubes into your drink, a plain old plastic ice cube tray can be a crucial tool in making memorable cocktails. Instead of water, we often make ice cubes from juices and simple syrups in flavors like mint, coconut, raspberry, and more—as the cubes melt, they change the composition and flavor of the drink, so guests get two drinks in one! Try it at home with the following recipes or with your favorite fruit juices to mix and match your own cocktail combinations.

La Bourbonne

With distilleries popping up in almost every state, it is clear that bourbon is hotter than ever, and it's usually best served neat or with one giant cube. But how hard could it be to make this sipping drink a bit more party friendly? Turns out it's not that hard! With a little citrus and sweetness, this chest-hair-sprouting spirit is now palatable for any occasion. Although any large ice cube would do, we recommend a large sphere of ice for this drink. Not only does it look spectacular in a rocks glass, but it also melts more slowly than regular ice cubes, which keeps the drink from getting too watered down.

YIELD: Serves 12
SPECIAL EQUIPMENT: spherical ice mold or other specialty ice cube tray, bamboo skewer with side twist

3 cups (720 ml) bourbon or rye
¾ cup (180 ml) fresh lemon juice (from about 4 lemons)
6 tablespoons (90 ml) sweet vermouth
6 tablespoons (90 ml) simple syrup
12 thick twists lemon rind

In a 2-quart (2-L) punch bowl or serving vessel, stir together the bourbon, lemon juice, vermouth, and simple syrup.

Divide the bourbon mixture among twelve rocks glasses, with one giant spherical ice cube in each. Insert the lemon rinds into bamboo skewers and use them to garnish each drink.

MAKE-AHEAD/STORAGE
The bourbon, lemon juice, vermouth, and simple syrup can be stirred together up to 4 hours in advance and stored in an airtight container in the refrigerator until ready to garnish and serve.

Watermelon-Basil Splash

Whether in a scrumptious watermelon-and-feta salad or in this simple cocktail concoction, nothing screams summertime like the combination of watermelon and basil. This cocktail is always a standout recipe on a hot August day, preferably sipped outdoors.

YIELD: Serves 12

For the basil ice cubes:
½ cup (30 g) minced fresh basil leaves or whole micro basil sprigs

For the watermelon juice:
3 pounds (1.4 kg) seedless watermelon, rind removed and flesh roughly cubed

To assemble:
3 cups (720 ml) gin
¾ cup (180 ml) fresh lime juice (from about 6 limes)
¾ cup (180 ml) agave nectar
12 mini watermelon wedges

Make the basil ice cubes: Place 1 teaspoon minced basil or micro basil into each well of two standard twelve-well ice cube trays. Fill the tray with water. Freeze until the cubes are solid.

Make the watermelon juice: Puree the watermelon in a blender, then strain through a fine-mesh sieve into a bowl. Discard the solids. You should have approximately 3 cups (720 ml) watermelon juice.

Assemble the cocktail: In a 3-quart (2.8-L) punch bowl or serving vessel, stir together the watermelon juice, gin, lime juice, and agave.

Place 2 basil ice cubes in each of twelve highball glasses. Divide the cocktail among the glasses and garnish each with a mini watermelon wedge.

MAKE-AHEAD/STORAGE
The basil ice cubes can be made up to 2 days in advance and stored in the freezer until ready to use. The watermelon juice, gin, lime juice, and agave can be stirred together up to 4 hours in advance and stored in an airtight container in the refrigerator until ready to garnish and serve.

Smoked Pineapple Colada

Do you like piña coladas? Well, we must confess . . .
we do. But instead of the quintessential blended version,
we've deconstructed it slightly to create a progressive flavor
profile while enhancing the individual flavor "stars"—coconut
and pineapple. We spice up the pineapple with some smoky
mezcal and chipotle, then slowly cool the experience down
with a large melting sphere of coconut ice. It's like two drinks
in one!

YIELD: Serves 12
SPECIAL EQUIPMENT: spherical ice mold or other
specialty ice cube tray

For the coconut ice cubes:
Agave nectar or superfine sugar
1 (13.5-ounce/385-g) can regular or light coconut milk

To assemble:
4½ cups (1 L) silver mezcal
3 cups (720 ml) pineapple juice or fresh pineapple puree
1½ cups (360 ml) fresh lime juice (from about 12 limes)
1½ cups (360 ml) fresh orange juice (from 5 to 6 oranges)
1 bottle chipotle oil, or 12 fresh red chiles

Make the coconut ice cubes: Whisk agave or sugar into
the coconut milk, a few drops or spoonfuls at a time, until the
liquid is sweet enough for your taste.

Pour the coconut milk into an ice cube tray (standard or
specialty-shaped), and freeze until the cubes are solid.

Assemble the cocktail: In a 4-quart (3.8-L) pitcher or
serving vessel, stir together the mezcal, pineapple juice, lime
juice, and orange juice.

Place a coconut ice cube in each of twelve highball glasses.
Divide the cocktail among the glasses, and garnish the top of
each with a few dots of chipotle oil or a fresh red chile.

MAKE-AHEAD/STORAGE
The coconut ice cubes can be made up to 2 days in advance
and stored in the freezer until ready to use. The mezcal,
pineapple juice, lime juice, and orange juice can be stirred
together up to 4 hours in advance and stored in an airtight
container in the refrigerator until ready to garnish and serve.

{ NIBBLES, ELEVATED }

Norm Peterson of *Cheers* might be content with a bowl of beer nuts as an accompaniment to his endless supply of pints, but we like our bar snacks to be a little more exciting.

We've put a lot of thought into creating perfect snacks. Because bar snacks are one of the opening salvos against hunger at a cocktail party, they should always be plentiful and easy to grab. We stick to recipes that produce large quantities of tasty goods, and that stand up even when made well ahead of time.

And because the best bar snacks are addictive, we keep tweaking our recipes to create craveable flavors that strike the right balance between familiar and new. We punch up the salty, sour, and spicy elements in our chips, sticks, and handfuls to make each sip of a drink that much more refreshing.

Another important component in the success of our bar snacks is truly keeping it to a one-bite, one-step experience. We've removed the dip element and incorporated all the flavors you'd normally associate with hummus, for example, into the flavor profile of the snack itself via dry powders and spices. The added bonus is that the snacks leave little residue, so guests aren't wiping oil and salt off their hands after they scoop a handful or snag a stick.

But it's not just figuring out what can we throw into the dehydrator and transform into a powder; on top of all this, we make sure to amp up the crisp and crunch in many of the Pinch bar snacks to make the texture as captivating as the flavor. For example, not only are the angel hair breadsticks (see page 39) fun to look at and simple to make, but their addictive crunch keeps guests coming back for more.

One of the most visually impressive ways to serve these easy snacks to guests at home is to suspend them, hanging bowls from various hooks and stands or from chandeliers instead of simply setting them atop buffets, bars, and coffee tables.

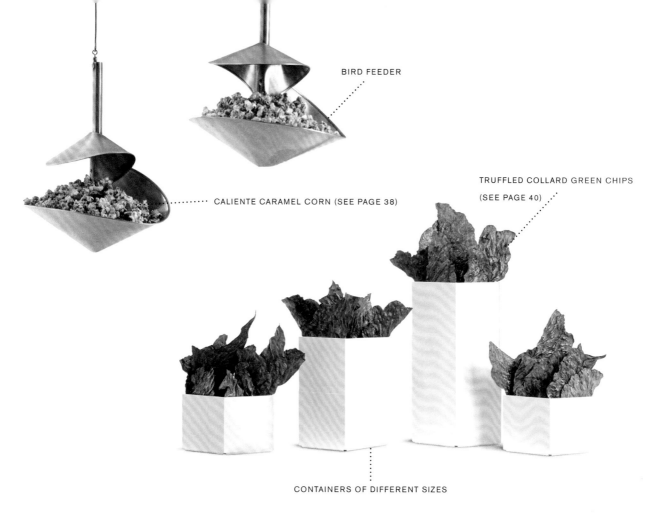

BIRD FEEDER

CALIENTE CARAMEL CORN (SEE PAGE 38)

TRUFFLED COLLARD GREEN CHIPS (SEE PAGE 40)

CONTAINERS OF DIFFERENT SIZES

DIY

YOU CAN SUSPEND SNACKS FROM ANY OBJECT THAT IS EASY TO HANG, AND THE PERFECT SERVING CONTAINER MAY BE SOMETHING YOU WOULDN'T USUALLY ASSOCIATE WITH HUMAN FOOD. FOR OUTDOOR PARTIES, CREATE "HUMAN FEEDERS" BY HANGING BIRD FEEDERS FROM LANTERN HOOKS THAT SPIKE INTO THE GROUND. OR USE HOOKS FOR HANGING PLANTERS AS IMPROMPTU HOLDERS FOR BASKETS AND PAILS. FLOAT A CLUSTER OF BASKETS AROUND THE BAR OR HANG A GROUP OF MODERN BIRD FEEDERS FROM A TREE. INDOORS, KITCHEN ACCESSORIES LIKE HANGING VEGETABLE BASKETS OR EVEN LIGHTING FIXTURES CAN DO DOUBLE DUTY. YOU CAN ALSO CREATE YOUR OWN HANGING CONTAINERS BY SIMPLY STAPLING RIBBONS TO EITHER DIXIE CUPS OR BAMBOO PAPER CONES AS SHOWN ON PAGES 36–37.

IF YOU'D RATHER KEEP YOUR BOWLS ON TERRA FIRMA, YOU CAN STILL SPRUCE UP YOUR SERVING PIECES AND CREATE VISUALLY EXCITING SNACK STATIONS. WRAP CLEAN, DRY ALUMINUM CANS (LEFT OVER FROM PEELED TOMATOES, BEANS, OR OTHER VEGETABLES), CARDBOARD TUBES, OR OTHER OPEN CYLINDERS WITH BANDS OF COLORFUL WASHI TAPE. YOU CAN ALSO PAINT CONTAINERS SUCH AS VASES, PENCIL HOLDERS, AND FLOWERPOTS ANY COLOR YOU LIKE. CLUSTER CONTAINERS OF DIFFERENT HEIGHTS TO PROVIDE A PLAYFUL HORIZON OF EDIBLE TREATS.

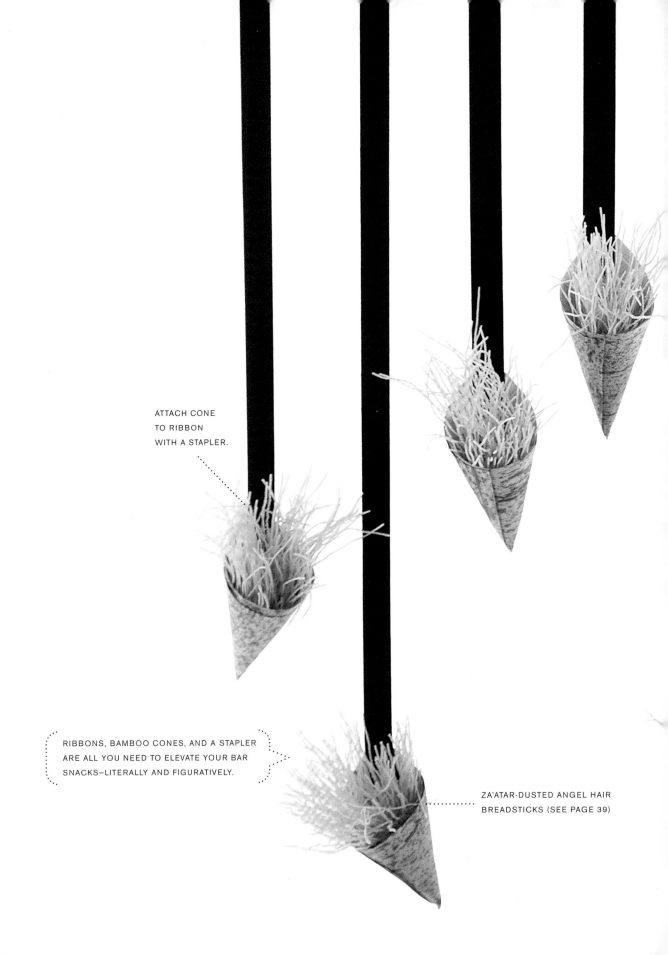

ATTACH CONE
TO RIBBON
WITH A STAPLER.

RIBBONS, BAMBOO CONES, AND A STAPLER
ARE ALL YOU NEED TO ELEVATE YOUR BAR
SNACKS—LITERALLY AND FIGURATIVELY.

ZA'ATAR-DUSTED ANGEL HAIR
BREADSTICKS (SEE PAGE 39)

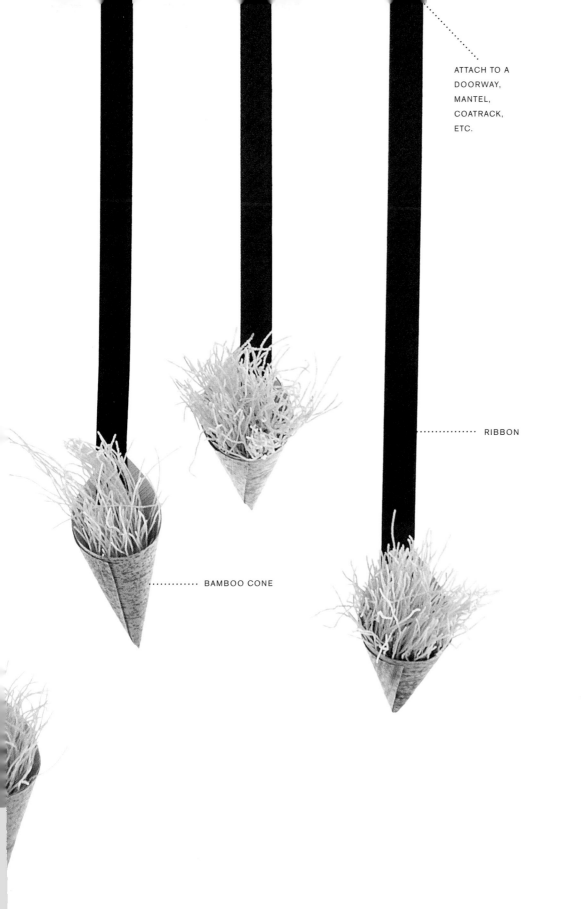

ATTACH TO A
DOORWAY,
MANTEL,
COATRACK,
ETC.

RIBBON

BAMBOO CONE

Caliente Caramel Corn

This bar snack was inspired by the classic ballpark treat Cracker Jack, which got its name in the 1800s from a colloquialism meaning "of excellent quality." As if it isn't addictive enough in its sweet-and-salty form, add a little cayenne and there will be no debates about this snack's quality. You will be eating it all night.

YIELD: Serves 12
SPECIAL EQUIPMENT: candy thermometer

1 teaspoon vegetable oil
5 cups (40 g) freshly air-popped plain popcorn
½ cup (110 g) packed light brown sugar
¼ cup (60 ml) light corn syrup
3 tablespoons unsalted butter
1 tablespoon water
¼ teaspoon kosher salt
2 teaspoons cayenne pepper
¼ teaspoon baking soda
1 teaspoon vanilla extract
1 cup (120 g) shelled pistachios

Preheat the oven to 200°F (90°C). Line a rimmed baking sheet with parchment paper.

Grease a large bowl with the vegetable oil. Add the popcorn and set aside.

In a 2-quart (2-L) saucepan, heat the brown sugar, corn syrup, butter, water, and salt over medium heat. Clip a candy thermometer to the pan. Stir the mixture occasionally until the butter melts, the brown sugar dissolves, and the mixture comes to a boil. Continue to cook for about 5 minutes more, until the caramel registers 250°F (120°C) on the candy thermometer.

Remove the pan from the heat and use a silicone spatula to stir in the cayenne, baking soda, and vanilla.

Carefully pour the caramel over the popcorn and gently stir to thoroughly coat the popcorn. Transfer the caramel corn to the prepared baking sheet and bake for 1 hour, stirring occasionally so that the popcorn does not clump.

While the caramel corn bakes, heat a wide skillet over medium heat. Toast the pistachios in the pan just until fragrant, then pour them onto a clean kitchen towel. Gently rub the pistachios in the towel to remove their papery husks. Transfer the nuts to a large bowl.

Break up any remaining clumps in the baked caramel corn, then transfer it to the bowl with the pistachios and toss to combine.

MAKE-AHEAD/STORAGE
The caramel corn can be made up to 5 days in advance and stored in an airtight container at room temperature.

Za'atar-Dusted Angel Hair Breadsticks

Frying pasta was something we had been experimenting with for years, and after trying nearly every noodle shape under the sun, we hit the jackpot with the fine and crispy texture of fried angel hair pasta. Tossed with za'atar, a cool Middle Eastern spice blend of dried herbs, sesame, and sumac, this simple snack is truly something unique.

YIELD: Serves 12

2 tablespoons olive oil
¼ pound (115 g) angel hair pasta
2 teaspoons za'atar
1 teaspoon sea salt

Line a large baking sheet with paper towels.

Heat the oil in a 12-inch (30.5-cm) sauté pan or skillet over low heat. Add the pasta and cook "popcorn-style" for about 5 minutes, shaking the pan constantly while keeping the pasta flat and in a single layer, until the strands are light brown.

Transfer the pasta to the lined baking sheet and sprinkle with the za'atar and sea salt while still warm.

MAKE-AHEAD/STORAGE
The breadsticks are best when made the same day you plan to serve them.

Truffled Collard Green Chips

No doubt you've tried kale chips—collards are very similar, but because they're flatter, you can stack them on top of each other like napkins. Beware, though: The first time we served these, a big gust of wind blew the chips all over the party the minute our waiter walked up to the bar. The moral of the story is: Don't serve these chips in windy places!

YIELD: Serves 12

1 tablespoon kosher salt
12 large collard green leaves
2 teaspoons white truffle oil
½ teaspoon shichimi togarashi spice mix (Japanese seven-spice)
½ teaspoon Maldon sea salt

Preheat the oven to 175°F (80°C). Line two large baking sheets with parchment paper or nonstick baking mats.

In a large stockpot, bring 4 quarts (3.8 L) water to a boil and add the kosher salt. Meanwhile, fill a large bowl with ice water.

Add the collard greens to the boiling water, a few leaves at a time, and cook for 3 minutes. Transfer to the ice bath to chill and repeat with the remaining leaves.

Pat each leaf dry with kitchen towels or paper towels.

Cut each leaf into 2 pieces by slicing along each side of the leaf's center rib; discard the rib. Place the leaves on the prepared baking sheets and bake for 30 minutes, or until dry and crispy.

Lightly brush each chip with truffle oil, then sprinkle with some of the togarashi and salt.

MAKE-AHEAD/STORAGE
The chips can be stored in an airtight container at room temperature for up to 2 days, depending on humidity levels.

Brussels Sprout Chips

Besides their world-famous *frites*, the Belgians are known for their endive and for this sneakily sweet vegetable. Sometimes we use Brussels sprout leaves as part of a potpourri that includes nuts, fried chickpeas, fried herb leaves, and fried pasta. But they're most certainly delicious as a stand-alone snack, too.

YIELD: Serves 12

1 cup (240 ml) extra-virgin olive oil
2 pounds (910 g) Brussels sprouts, trimmed and separated into individual leaves
½ teaspoon red pepper flakes
½ teaspoon Maldon sea salt

Line a large baking sheet with paper towels.

Heat the oil in a 3-quart (2.8-L) sauté pan over medium-high heat. Add half the Brussels sprouts leaves and fry, stirring frequently, just until the edges begin to brown. Remove the crispy leaves with a slotted spoon and transfer to the lined baking sheet.

Sprinkle the fried leaves with ¼ teaspoon of the red pepper flakes and ¼ teaspoon of the salt, then repeat with the remaining Brussels sprouts, red pepper flakes, and salt.

Let the Brussels sprout chips cool for 1 hour to fully crisp up.

MAKE-AHEAD/STORAGE
The chips can be made up to 6 hours in advance. Store in an airtight container at room temperature until ready to serve.

Hummus Chips

Pita and hummus: It's the most popular Middle Eastern dish ever—so popular, in fact, that many Californians think it's native to their state. While we were shopping for some all-natural seeds at Integral Yoga on 13th Street in Manhattan, we stumbled upon an instant hummus mix for Appalachian Trail hikers. Once the mix is in your mouth, it tastes just like hummus. No dipping required.

YIELD: Serves 12

6 (6-inch/15-cm) pita bread rounds, each cut into 12 wedges
¼ cup (60 ml) extra-virgin olive oil
½ cup (60 g) organic instant hummus mix
2 tablespoons roughly chopped fresh flat-leaf parsley
2 tablespoons thinly sliced pitted sun-dried black olives

Preheat the oven to 350°F (175°C). Line two large baking sheets with parchment paper or nonstick baking mats.

Spread the pita wedges in a single layer on the baking sheets, then brush each wedge with olive oil. Bake for 20 minutes, or until golden brown and crispy.

Transfer the chips to a large bowl and gently toss with the hummus mix to coat, then add the parsley and olives and gently toss to mix.

MAKE-AHEAD/STORAGE
The chips can be stored in an airtight container at room temperature for up to 2 days. Re-toss the chips in the hummus mix before serving.

Jamaican Curry Parsnip Crisps

Parsnips are so naturally sweet that they can be eaten raw, but because of their high sugar content, it's difficult to crisp them up—so don't try this on a humid or rainy day. The goal here was to conjure up the taste of a Jamaican beef patty—a curry-infused empanada-style island treat. It's pretty close, but a hundred times less messy. Because of the sugar in the parsnips, they'll be crispy but pliant immediately upon removal from the oven, so you can bend them into wavy shapes before they harden. It's fun.

YIELD: Serves 12
SPECIAL EQUIPMENT: mandoline or Japanese slicer

1 pound (455 g) parsnips
2 tablespoons vegetable oil
2 teaspoons Jamaican curry powder or Indian curry powder with allspice
½ teaspoon sea salt

Preheat the oven to 300°F (150 °C). Line two large baking sheets with parchment paper or nonstick baking mats.

Using a mandoline or Japanese slicer, thinly slice the parsnips lengthwise into translucent strips.

Toss the parsnip strips with the oil, curry powder, and salt to coat evenly. Transfer the parsnip strips to the prepared baking sheets and bake for 20 minutes, or until crispy and golden brown. Remove the strips from the oven and twist them into curls or spirals before they cool, if desired.

MAKE-AHEAD/STORAGE
The chips can be stored in an airtight container at room temperature for up to 2 days, depending on humidity levels.

Though we try to mix it up as much as possible, the plain truth is that a party just isn't a party without hors d'oeuvres. From bunches of grapes nibbled at Roman toga parties, to Marie Antoinette's petits fours, to the classic canapés prepared by 1950s hostesses, a one-bite teaser has been the staple of nearly every party since time immemorial.

And at Pinch, we take hors d'oeuvres very seriously, putting a lot of pressure on ourselves to deliver an entire plate's worth of taste and an entire party's worth of pleasure in that single bite. Yes, in our world, it's one bite—not one and a half, not two—and it's our first chance to wow our guests with the patented Pinch blend of vibrant, contrasting flavors and textures. And, of course, it has to look really good.

Think of how you assemble "perfect bites" on your own fork or spoon when eating a meal: stabbing just the right stack of blue cheese, avocado, bacon, and tomato in a Cobb salad, or finding the golden ratio of noodles, sauce, and beef in a spoonful of pot roast. That's what we want you to experience with our hors d'oeuvres. We go through a lot of trial and error when designing each bite to find the balance that feels exactly like that great forkful, giving each guest the perfect proportion of each ingredient.

And though many parties have shifted away from shrimp cocktail, tournedos Rossini, and caviar-topped blinis and headed toward mini quiches and pot stickers over the years, we can't resist the original cocktail party standards. As caterers and generally hungry people, we can't deny that they're all really good combinations—in fact, we'd call them downright legendary. But how can we reimagine them and make them current and relevant again?

We've shape-shifted our hors d'oeuvres—without deconstructing each bite too much—to provide a textural punch that gives each bite a little zip of surprise. So at Pinch, the classic blini becomes a buckwheat crêpe mille-feuille interspersed with layers of cream. It's a familiar taste wrapped in a whole new texture, and a far cry from what we've seen passed around for the past three decades.

Or we capitalize on the big effect created by the little act of cutting a familiar food into visually appealing shapes—a spiky Parmesan cracker as the base for a half-moon of eggplant in our eggplant Parmigiana, or a hollowed-out carrot as a vessel for rich pea-and-Pecorino puree in our reinvention of traditional peas and carrots.

Basil-Crusted Filet Mignon with Shallot Marmalade

Filet of beef on baguette is a quintessential cocktail party hors d'oeuvre. Here, the baguette crumbs become a garnish on the filet with vibrant green basil instead of a serving vehicle.

YIELD: Serves 12
SPECIAL EQUIPMENT: butcher's twine, electric deep-fryer or deep-fry thermometer

For the filet mignon:
1½ pounds (680 g) center-cut filet of beef, trimmed of fat
Extra-virgin olive oil
Kosher salt and freshly ground black pepper

For the basil crust:
2 cups (480 ml) vegetable oil
Leaves from 2 bunches fresh basil, patted completely dry
1 cup (100 g) panko bread crumbs
1 teaspoon kosher salt

For the shallot marmalade:
½ cup (80 g) finely diced shallots
1 cup (240 ml) red wine
3 tablespoons granulated sugar
2 whole cloves

For the pâte à choux toppers:
½ cup (120 ml) water
2 tablespoons unsalted butter, at room temperature
½ teaspoon kosher salt
⅔ cup (80 g) unbleached all-purpose flour
3 large eggs

To assemble:
1 egg white, beaten

Make the filet mignon: Cut the beef, with the grain, into strips about the size and shape of a thin hot dog. Wrap each piece with butcher's twine. Rub the beef on all sides with extra-virgin olive oil and season with salt and pepper.

Heat a cast-iron skillet or sauté pan over high heat until very hot, then sear the beef on all sides until very dark, about 1 minute per side. Transfer to a rimmed baking sheet and refrigerate until completely chilled.

Make the basil crust: In an electric deep-fryer or a heavy, high-sided stockpot or Dutch oven, heat the oil over medium-high heat until it registers 350°F (175°C) on a deep-fry thermometer. Line a baking sheet with paper towels.

Working in batches if necessary, gently add the basil leaves to the hot oil. Fry for about 20 seconds, until crisp but not brown, then use a slotted spoon to transfer the leaves to the baking sheet to drain and cool.

Place the cooled leaves in a food processor, add the panko and salt, and pulse to combine, making sure not to overmix—the crust should be crumbly and not too wet. Transfer to a clean bowl, cover, and refrigerate until needed. The crust will keep for 2 days without discoloring.

Make the shallot marmalade: Combine all the ingredients in a small saucepan and cook over medium heat, stirring, until the sugar has dissolved. Bring to a simmer and cook for 20 minutes, then strain through a fine-mesh sieve into a bowl.

Reserve the shallots in a small bowl and return the strained liquid to the saucepan. Bring back to a simmer and cook until the liquid becomes thick and syrupy.

Stir the syrup into the reserved shallots and refrigerate until needed.

Make the pâte à choux: Follow the recipe on page 162. Pipe the dough into ½-inch (12-mm) dots before baking.

Assemble the bites: Remove the butcher's twine from the beef. Dip the beef pieces in the beaten egg white, then roll them in the basil crust so it adheres evenly to all sides.

Cut each strip of beef into 1¼-inch (3-cm) pieces and plate them so the cylinder stands on one cut end.

Spoon shallot marmalade on each filet and top with the pâte à choux before serving.

MAKE-AHEAD/STORAGE

The basil crust can be made up to 2 days in advance and stored in an airtight container at room temperature. The shallot marmalade can be made up to 2 weeks in advance and refrigerated. The beef is best cooked the same day it is served. If all components are made and assembled the same day, the completed bite can be made up to 4 hours in advance. The pâte à choux can be made up to 1 week in advance and stored in an airtight container in the freezer. Thaw before serving.

Buffalo Chicken Wings with Celery and Cambozola Blue

Although their namesake is not a city known as a culinary mecca, Buffalo wings boast a combination of flavors best described as magical. Here, the essence of the wings is unchanged, but we've removed both the Buffalo sauce and the blue cheese dip by drying the peppers and using pure Cambozola blue cheese to make it less messy.

If you've never deboned a chicken wing before, don't worry—with just a yank and a twirl, you'll have a meaty piece of poultry that makes the spicy bite even more succulent (not to mention easier to eat). Grab a few extra wings for practice; you can always eat the evidence of less-than-perfect pieces.

Drying the peppers for the Buffalo spice mix could take as long as eight hours, but it's all hands-off time, and the intense flavor is worth the wait.

YIELD: Serves 12
SPECIAL EQUIPMENT: food dehydrator (optional), electric deep-fryer or deep-fry thermometer, needle-nose pliers (optional), unflavored dental floss (optional)

For the Buffalo spice mix:
1 red bell pepper, stemmed, seeded, and finely diced
2 teaspoons kosher salt
½ teaspoon cayenne
1½ teaspoons sweet Hungarian paprika

For the chicken wings:
2 cups (480 ml) vegetable oil
12 large chicken wings

To assemble:
3 celery stalks from the heart of the bunch
2 ounces (55 g) very cold Cambozola blue cheese

Make the Buffalo spice mix: If you are using a food dehydrator, place the bell pepper on food dehydrator trays. Gently and completely dry the pepper according to the manufacturer's instructions. (Timing will vary based on your equipment.) If you do not have a dehydrator, preheat the oven to its lowest temperature (170°F/77°C or 175°F/80°C is ideal). Spread the bell pepper in a single layer on a baking sheet lined with parchment paper or a nonstick baking mat. Let the pepper dry in the oven until completely dry, up to 8 hours.

Grind the cooled dehydrated peppers in a spice or coffee grinder, or in a high-speed blender such as a Vitamix, until reduced to a powder. Transfer to a bowl and whisk in the salt, cayenne, and paprika.

Make the chicken wings: In an electric deep-fryer or a heavy, high-sided stockpot or Dutch oven, heat the oil until it registers 375°F (190°C) on a deep-fry thermometer. Line a baking sheet with paper towels.

Fry the chicken wings until they begin to brown, 3 to 4 minutes, then transfer to the lined baking sheet until cool enough to handle. Keep the oil at temperature.

Cut both ends off the wings with kitchen shears, leaving the two unconnected bones in the middle section (like an archery bow that doesn't join at the ends). Reserve the drumette portion for eating later and the skinny winglet for soups or stock, and debone the middle section. Firmly grab one of the two bones with shears, needle-nose pliers, or small tongs, and shimmy the bone away from the wing meat, pulling it out completely. Repeat with the second bone.

Assemble the bites: Slice the celery into 2-inch (5-cm) matchstick pieces; you will need a total of 12 celery matchsticks.

Dice the blue cheese into ½-inch (12-mm) cubes (freeze your cheese for 30 minutes to make it easier to slice, if necessary, or use unflavored dental floss to cut it).

Refry the boneless chicken until golden, then return to the baking sheet just until the excess oil drains off. Sprinkle with the Buffalo spice mix.

Cut the edges off the wings and stand each up on one cut side. Skewer each wing with a celery stalk, top with a cube of diced cheese, and serve immediately.

MAKE-AHEAD/STORAGE
The Buffalo spice mix can be made up to 1 week in advance and will keep for up to 6 months. Store in an airtight container at room temperature until ready to use. The chicken wings should be fried just before you're planning to serve them. The cheese can be cut and refrigerated up to 6 hours prior to serving.

Buckwheat Blinis with Caviar

Blinis with caviar have been served at parties forever, but the only (time-consuming) way to serve them has been to freshly make the blinis to order. Our layered squares are filled in advance and microwave perfectly when you are ready to serve them. Then you just need to add the finishing touches: chives and caviar.

YIELD: Serves 12

For the buckwheat blini:
¼ cup (60 ml) warm (not hot) water
1½ teaspoons granulated sugar
1½ teaspoons fresh yeast, or ¾ teaspoon active dry yeast
1 cup (125 g) all-purpose flour
¾ cup (90 g) buckwheat flour
½ teaspoon kosher salt
1 large egg, beaten
1½ cups (360 ml) whole milk
4 tablespoons (55 g) melted unsalted butter, plus more for the pan

To assemble:
1 cup (250 g) crème fraîche
2 bunches fresh chives, chopped razor-thin
2 ounces (55 g) caviar, on ice

Make the buckwheat blini: In a small bowl, whisk the water, sugar, and yeast together and set aside in a warm place for 20 minutes to activate the yeast and begin fermentation. After 20 minutes, it should be cloudy and bubbly.

In a large bowl, sift or whisk the flours and salt together.

Whisk the egg and milk into the bubbly yeast, then whisk the wet ingredients into the flour, by hand or with an electric mixer on medium speed, until the batter is no longer lumpy.

Whisk the melted butter into the batter, then let it rest at room temperature for 30 minutes to fully hydrate the flour and develop gluten strands.

Heat a crêpe pan or 10-inch (25-cm) nonstick or cast-iron skillet over medium-low heat. Grease the pan with butter, and drop batter into the pan using a ½-cup measuring scoop to make blinis about 7 inches (17 cm) in diameter and no more than ⅛ inch (3 mm) thick. Add butter to the pan as necessary between blinis.

Stack the blinis on a plate and let cool to room temperature.

Assemble the bites: Whip the crème fraîche to loosen it to the consistency of whipped cream.

Create a blini stack: Place 1 blini crêpe on a cutting board and spread a thin, even layer of the crème fraîche over the blini with an offset spatula. Top with another crêpe and repeat this layering process until the stack is about ¾ inch (2 cm) high. Cut the stack into 1-inch (2.5-cm) squares.

To serve, place 10 to 15 blini pieces on a plate, cover with plastic wrap, and microwave for 20 seconds. Press one side of each warm blini in the chopped chives and stand them up on a serving plate so the chives face to one side. Spoon a liberal scoop of caviar on top of each blini and serve immediately.

MAKE-AHEAD/STORAGE
The blini stacks can be made up to 24 hours in advance and refrigerated. Once cut into cubes, they can be refrigerated, covered in plastic wrap, for up to 6 hours. The chives can be cut several hours before serving.

Fennel-Glazed Duck with Grappa Cherries and Polenta

In the United States, duck has been served overcooked for years, but now it's acceptable to serve it rare and it's so much tastier. Add crispy-creamy polenta and grappa-soaked cherries, and the sensation in your mouth will surely distract you from your casual cocktail conversation. But you don't have to tell anyone!

YIELD: Serves 12
SPECIAL EQUIPMENT: electric deep-fryer or deep-fry thermometer

For the grappa cherries:
½ cup (80 g) dried cherries
½ cup (120 ml) grappa
3 tablespoons honey

For the polenta:
4 cups (960 ml) water
1 tablespoon kosher salt
1 tablespoon extra-virgin olive oil
1 cup (160 g) stone-ground yellow cornmeal
1 tablespoon unsalted butter
3 tablespoons grated Parmigiano-Reggiano
   cheese
2 cups (480 ml) vegetable oil

For the fennel-glazed duck:
1 teaspoon freshly ground fennel seed
½ teaspoon kosher salt
¼ teaspoon freshly ground black pepper
¼ pound (115 g) Magret duck breast, skin on,
   trimmed of excess fat

To assemble:
Mini basil leaves
Maldon salt

Make the grappa cherries: In a small saucepan, combine the cherries and the grappa and set aside to soak for 1 hour. After soaking, add the honey, set the pan over low heat, and cook for 10 minutes. Transfer to a small bowl, cover, and chill overnight.

Make the polenta: In a 3- to 4-quart (2.8- to 3.8-L) stockpot, bring the water to a boil over medium heat. Add the salt and olive oil. Slowly sprinkle the cornmeal into the water, whisking constantly to make sure no lumps form. Reduce the heat to low halfway through to maintain a simmer so you don't get splashed; it hurts!

Cook the polenta for 45 minutes. (Ask any Italian: If you cook polenta for less than 45 minutes, it will taste raw!)

While the polenta cooks, grease a 9-by-13-inch (23-by-33-cm) baking dish with the butter.

Stir the cheese into the cooked polenta and pour it into the prepared baking dish. Cover and refrigerate until firm, at least 2 hours.

In an electric deep-fryer or a heavy, high-sided stockpot or Dutch oven, heat the oil over medium-high heat until it registers 350°F (175°C) on a deep-fry thermometer. Line a baking sheet with paper towels.

Cut the chilled polenta into ½-by-1½-inch (12-mm-by-4-cm) rectangles. Fry the polenta sticks until golden brown at the edges, 3 to 4 minutes, then use a slotted spoon to transfer them to the prepared baking sheet. Set aside at room temperature until needed.

Make the fennel-glazed duck: Heat a dry cast-iron or other heavy-bottomed skillet over medium-high heat until very hot.

While the pan heats, in a small bowl, stir the fennel seed, salt, and pepper together and rub the duck with the spice blend.

Carefully add the duck to the hot pan, skin side down, and sear on all sides, keeping the duck rare to medium-rare, or about 125°F/52°C to 130°F/55°C on a meat thermometer, for about 10 minutes. (If you desire more cooking, bake it in a 350°F/175°C oven to your preferred degree of doneness.) Let rest for 5 minutes to redistribute the juices, then cut into ½-inch (12-mm) strips.

Assemble the bites: Place the fried polenta on serving plates. Slice the duck strips into ½-inch-thick (12-mm-thick) rectangles, and place at the very edge of the polenta, cut side up. Spoon a couple of cherries on top, garnish with basil leaves and Maldon salt, and serve immediately.

MAKE-AHEAD/STORAGE
The basil-grappa cherries can be made up to 1 month in advance; store in an airtight container in the refrigerator until ready to use. The polenta can be chilled and cut 3 days in advance, then fried 1 hour before serving. The duck should be prepared just prior to assembling and serving.

Spaghetti and Meatballs

This Pinch classic has a secret. It's your nonna's spaghetti and meatballs: tomato sauce bubbled on the stove until the flavors are pure and concentrated, plus angel hair noodles and classic meatballs flecked with parsley and softened with bread crumbs. Sounds like familiar comfort food, right? But here's the catch: The spaghetti is rolled and chilled, bound by the sauce, then cut into pretty pedestals for each teeny meatball. The family-style dish gets the Pinch treatment, and suddenly it's dainty and drop-dead gorgeous.

YIELD: Serves 12

For the angel hair rolls:
1 (28-ounce/800-g) can peeled whole tomatoes
2 tablespoons extra-virgin olive oil
3 cloves garlic, thinly sliced
1½ (6-ounce/170-g) cans tomato paste
1 tablespoon kosher salt, plus more as needed
½ pound (225 g) angel hair pasta
Freshly ground black pepper

For the meatballs:
½ pound (225 g) ground beef
½ pound (225 g) ground pork
1 cup (240 ml) plus 2 tablespoons extra-virgin
    olive oil
2 cloves garlic, smashed
1 tablespoon roughly chopped fresh flat-leaf
    parsley
½ cup (50 g) toasted bread crumbs
1 large egg
¼ cup (25 g) freshly grated Parmigiano-
    Reggiano cheese
1 teaspoon kosher salt
½ teaspoon freshly ground black pepper

To assemble:
1 cup (100 g) freshly grated Parmigiano-
    Reggiano cheese
Freshly ground black pepper

Make the angel hair rolls: Pour the can of whole tomatoes and their juices into a blender or food processor and puree until smooth. Measure out 2 cups (480 ml) and reserve the remaining puree for another use.

Heat the oil in a large high-sided skillet or sauté pan over medium heat. Add the garlic and cook for 1 minute, or until lightly browned. Add the 2 cups (480 ml) tomato puree and simmer for 20 minutes.

Scoop out ¼ cup (60 ml) of the sauce and reserve for finishing the dish. Reduce the heat to low and add the tomato paste to the remaining sauce. Cook, stirring frequently, for about 45 minutes, until all the excess liquid has evaporated, then remove from the heat.

Fill a 4-quart (3.8-L) stockpot with water; bring to a boil and add the salt. Cook the pasta according to the package directions until al dente, then drain in a colander but do not rinse.

Toss the pasta with the reduced tomato sauce and season with salt and pepper to taste.

Pull a handful of the dressed pasta out of the sauce and arrange it on a sheet of plastic wrap so the pasta strands are facing in roughly the same direction. Use the plastic wrap to roll the pasta into a tube about 1 inch (2.5 cm) thick. Twist the ends of the plastic wrap like you were wrapping a piece of candy, then fold the twisted ends under the roll and place on a rimmed baking sheet. Repeat with the remaining pasta to make a total of 5 to 6 rolls.

Refrigerate the rolls for at least 2 hours or overnight.

Reserve any remaining sauce in the pan.

Make the meatballs: In a large bowl, combine the beef and pork. Add 1 cup (240 ml) of the oil, the garlic, parsley, bread crumbs, egg, cheese, salt, and pepper and mix well until the oil is completely absorbed.

Refrigerate the mixture for 30 minutes, then roll into dime-size balls.

Place the remaining 2 tablespoons oil in a large, wide skillet or sauté pan. Add the meatballs—in batches if necessary to avoid crowding the pan—and cook, turning with tongs, until browned on all sides and cooked through.

Assemble the bites: Add the cooked meatballs to the reserved tomato sauce and reheat, if necessary.

Unwrap the chilled pasta and slice each roll into ¾-inch-thick (2-cm-thick) rounds. Place on a microwave-safe plate and zap in the microwave for 15 seconds, in batches if necessary, to rewarm. (Alternatively, the pasta rolls can be placed on a rimmed baking sheet and warmed in a 250°F/120°C oven for 2 minutes.)

Place the grated cheese in a large, wide bowl and roll the spaghetti pieces in the cheese to coat the sides. Top each spaghetti round with a warm meatball, a spoonful of the reserved sauce, and some freshly ground pepper. Serve immediately.

MAKE-AHEAD/STORAGE

The pasta rolls can be made and frozen up to 2 weeks in advance; then you can cut them into rounds while still frozen. The meatballs can be cooked up to 1 day in advance; store, with the reserved tomato sauce, in an airtight container in the refrigerator, and reheat before assembling and serving.

Prosciutto and Melon Wraps

We've been working on a way to get the classic Italian *misto* into a handheld bite for many years, and we finally figured out this modern twist—er, roll—with a little homemade Fruit Roll-Up. Thin slices of honeydew are dried until sticky and pliable, then wrapped around the cured meat. Pinch chef Rideiby figured out how to dry this melon just right while keeping the integrity of the two ingredients. Just like the classic, this bite is a sweet-and-salty snack, but ours has an addictive crunch.

Note: It may take longer to prepare the melon in an oven or on humid days.

YIELD: Serves 12
SPECIAL EQUIPMENT: mandoline or Japanese slicer, food dehydrator (optional)

For the dried honeydew melon:
1 honeydew melon

To assemble:
4 ounces (115 g) thinly sliced Parma prosciutto
Black peppercorns in a grinder

Make the dried honeydew melon: Preheat the oven to 175°F (80°C) if you don't have a food dehydrator.

Cut the melon into 1½-by-3-inch (4-by-7.5-cm) rectangles, then slice each rectangle with a mandoline or Japanese slicer into thin pieces no more than ⅛ inch (3 mm) thick.

Arrange the melon slices in a single layer on a baking sheet lined with a nonstick baking mat or on a food dehydrator tray. Place in the oven or dehydrator and bake or dry for about 3 hours, until dry but still tacky.

Assemble the bites: Slice the prosciutto into matchsticks about 1½ inches (4 cm) long.

Place a ½-inch (12-mm) pinch of sliced prosciutto at the short edge of a dried melon piece. Grind pepper over the prosciutto and gently roll the melon and prosciutto into a tube. (If the melon is too brittle, rewarm it in the oven for a second or two.)

Repeat with the remaining melon and prosciutto and serve.

MAKE-AHEAD/STORAGE
The melon slices can be dehydrated up to 2 days in advance and stored in an airtight container at room temperature until ready to use. The rolls can be made up to 30 minutes before serving.

Truffled Quail Egg on Mini English Muffin

We all grew up with English muffins, but most cooks have never made them or tasted a fresh batch. We make ours a little larger than the yolk of a soft, sunny-side-up quail egg, so it looks like the original was attacked by a shrink ray. Whether you are having breakfast, after-work cocktails, or late-night snacks, it's always the perfect time for truffles, eggs, and English muffins. It is impossible not to eat one of these as you cook them.

YIELD: Serves 12
SPECIAL EQUIPMENT: 1-inch (2.5-cm) round cookie cutter, truffle slicer or mandoline (optional)

For the mini English muffins:
2 cups (250 g) all-purpose flour, plus a little extra
    for rolling
2 tablespoons granulated sugar
2¼ teaspoons (1 packet) active dry yeast
1 teaspoon kosher salt
¾ cup (180 ml) whole milk
¾ cup (180 ml) water
2 large egg whites
1 tablespoon unsalted butter, melted, plus 2 tablespoons
    unsalted butter
1 teaspoon vegetable oil or baking spray
3 tablespoons cornmeal

For the quail eggs:
2 tablespoons unsalted butter
24 quail eggs

To assemble:
2 tablespoons black truffle butter
Maldon sea salt
1 scallion, dark and light green parts, minced
1 (1- to 2-ounce/28- to-55-g) fresh black truffle, sliced
    paper-thin with a truffle slicer or mandoline (optional)

Make the mini English muffins: In a bowl, sift or whisk together the flour, sugar, yeast, and salt.

In a small saucepan, combine the milk and water and heat just until hot to the touch but not steaming or bubbling. Pour into the bowl of a stand mixer fitted with the paddle attachment.

With the mixer on medium speed, slowly add one-third of the flour mixture, then half of the egg whites. Repeat with another third of the flour, the remaining egg whites, then the remaining flour. Switch the mixer attachment to the dough hook, add the melted butter, and reduce the mixer speed to low. Knead on low speed until a soft dough forms. Pat the dough into a ball and transfer to a clean, oiled bowl.

Cover loosely with a towel or plastic wrap and let rise in a warm place for 45 minutes, or until the dough doubles in size. Punch down the dough, cover, and let rise for 30 minutes more.

Sprinkle the cornmeal and a healthy pinch of flour across a clean work surface. Roll the dough out until approximately ½ inch (12 mm) thick, then use a 1-inch (2.5-cm) round cookie cutter to cut out 24 circles. Place the dough rounds on a large baking sheet and let rise for 30 minutes more.

Line a baking sheet with paper towels.

Melt the remaining 2 tablespoons butter in a large nonstick skillet over very low heat and add the English muffins. Cook until golden brown, about 3 minutes per side. Transfer to the prepared baking sheet while you cook the quail eggs.

Make the quail eggs: Melt the butter in the pan in which you cooked the English muffins. Crack the quail eggs into the pan, in batches if necessary, and cook sunny-side-up, keeping the yolk soft.

Transfer the quail eggs to a cutting board and cut around each yolk with the same cookie cutter so the egg will fit cleanly on the English muffin.

Assemble the bites: Smear a little truffle butter on each English muffin, then top with a quail egg. Sprinkle Maldon sea salt and minced scallions over each egg and top with a slice of truffle, if desired.

MAKE-AHEAD/STORAGE
The English muffins can be cooked up to 1 day in advance; store in an airtight container at room temperature until ready to use. The quail eggs should be fried immediately before serving.

Steak Frites with Béarnaise

There is no better sauce than béarnaise, period. It's the savory version of ice cream—an eggy mixture that coats your taste buds in luxurious richness. Paired with frites and steak? C'mon, how good is that!

YIELD: Serves 12
SPECIAL EQUIPMENT: mandoline or Japanese slicer, takeout chopsticks, deep-fry thermometer

For the frites:

1 (1-pound/455-g) russet potato, roughly 2 inches (5 cm) in diameter, peeled
2 cups (480 ml) vegetable oil

For the béarnaise:

¼ cup (60 ml) tarragon vinegar
3 tablespoons white wine
4 fresh tarragon sprigs
1 teaspoon freshly cracked black pepper
2 tablespoons roughly chopped shallots
2 large egg yolks
5 tablespoons (70 g) unsalted butter, at room temperature
Kosher salt and freshly ground black pepper

To assemble:

6 ounces (170 g) hanger steak
1 teaspoon Maldon sea salt
½ teaspoon freshly ground black pepper
1 tablespoon chopped fresh tarragon

Make the frites: Line a baking sheet with paper towels.

Using a mandoline or Japanese slicer, cut the potato into wafer-thin slices, no more than ¹⁄₁₆ inch (2 mm) thick. Cut two parallel ½-inch (12-mm) slits into each slice, about ¾ inch (2 cm) apart from each other. "Thread" the potato onto the end of a chopstick by gently poking the pointed end of the stick through each cut to hold it open.

In a heavy-bottomed 2-quart (2-L) sauté pan, heat the oil until it registers 350°F (175°C) on a deep-fry thermometer. Fry the potato on both sides until golden and crispy, then transfer to the prepared baking sheet. Gently pull out the chopstick and repeat with the remaining potato slices.

Make the béarnaise: Put the tarragon vinegar, wine, tarragon sprigs, cracked pepper, and shallots in a small saucepan and bring to a simmer over medium-low heat. Cook until the liquid has reduced by one third.

Strain the liquid through a fine-mesh sieve into a blender. Discard the solids in the sieve.

With the blender running, immediately add the egg yolks, then whole tablespoons of butter, one at a time, while blending until incorporated. (By adding the eggs and butter slowly, the reduction and the friction from the machine will cook the eggs.) Season with salt and freshly ground pepper.

Assemble the bites: Slice the steak into 1½-inch (4-cm) rectangles. Season each piece with salt and pepper.

Heat a heavy-bottomed stainless-steel or cast-iron skillet over high heat. Add the steak and cook until medium-rare, about 3 minutes total. Slice the steak into small pieces the same diameter as the chopsticks and thread the steak through the chip "pockets," as shown below. Spoon a little béarnaise on top of each piece and garnish with tarragon. Serve immediately.

MAKE-AHEAD/STORAGE
The béarnaise can be made no more than 1 hour in advance, due to the partially cooked eggs in the sauce—it will separate if refrigerated. Hold the béarnaise, warmed, until ready to assemble the dish. The steak and potatoes should be prepared just prior to assembling and serving.

Banana Semifreddo with Cocoa-Rice Crunch

If you've ever made Rice Krispie treats, you're already halfway to making this Pinch favorite like a pro. The crunchy base is studded with pleasingly bitter cocoa nibs and topped with banana semifreddo and caramelized bananas for a grown-up version of the snack we all know and love. Chef Stacy came up with this concoction, and sure, it's indulgent, but the best part of making desserts in miniature is that you can have the whole thing, and maybe even seconds.

YIELD: Serves 12
SPECIAL EQUIPMENT: kitchen/crème brûlée torch

For the cocoa-rice crunch:
1 tablespoon unsalted butter
3 cups (150 g) mini marshmallows
1 tablespoon cocoa powder
2 cups (60 g) Rice Krispies cereal
1 tablespoon cocoa nibs

For the banana semifreddo:
3 overripe bananas
6 sheets leaf gelatin
1 cup (240 ml) honey
3 cups (720 ml) heavy cream
6 large egg yolks
2 tablespoons granulated sugar

To assemble:
1 firm banana
Granulated sugar

Make the cocoa-rice crunch: Line a rimmed baking sheet with parchment paper or a nonstick baking mat.

Using the well-known technique on the side of the cereal box: Melt the butter with the marshmallows in a 4-quart (3.8-L) stockpot or Dutch oven over medium heat, stirring constantly, until the marshmallows are fully melted.

Remove from the heat and stir in the cocoa powder, then the Rice Krispies and cocoa nibs. Mix until evenly coated and combined. Scrape the mixture onto the prepared baking sheet and, with oiled hands, gently press it into a ½-inch-thick (12-mm-thick) rectangle.

Let the crunch cool completely, then transfer to a cutting board and slice into 1¼-by-½-inch (3-cm-by-12-mm) rectangles.

Make the banana semifreddo: Peel the bananas and puree in a blender or food processor until smooth. Set aside.

Place the gelatin sheets in a bowl of cold water and set aside to soften for 5 minutes.

In a small saucepan, heat the honey over medium-low heat, stirring frequently, until it begins to caramelize, deepen in color, and develop a nutty aroma. Scrape into a medium bowl and set aside.

In a small saucepan, heat 1½ cups (360 ml) of the cream over medium-low heat just until bubbles form around the edges. Whisk the hot cream into the caramelized honey.

Squeeze the softened gelatin gently between your fingers to wring out excess water, then add the gelatin to the cream and honey. Whisk until the gelatin is fully dissolved.

In the bowl of a stand mixer fitted with the whisk attachment, beat the egg yolks and sugar together until thickened and pale yellow. Add the banana puree to the egg yolk mixture and mix on low speed until incorporated.

With the mixer still on low speed, pour the honey-cream mixture into the banana mixture in a slow, steady drizzle until fully incorporated.

Nest a stainless-steel bowl in a larger bowl filled with ice water to form an ice bath.

Strain the banana cream through a fine-mesh sieve into the stainless-steel bowl and stir frequently until the mixture is cool.

Using a hand mixer or in a stand mixer fitted with the whisk attachment, whip the remaining cream until stiff peaks form. Gently fold the whipped cream into the cooled banana cream.

Line a 9-by-13-inch (23-by-33-cm) baking pan with plastic wrap. Pour the banana cream into the prepared pan and freeze until set, at least 6 hours.

Assemble the bites: Slice the banana in half lengthwise, then slice crosswise into ⅛-inch-thick (3-mm-thick) half-moons.

Place the banana slices in a single layer on a baking sheet and sprinkle lightly and evenly with sugar. Caramelize the slices with a kitchen torch.

Slice the set banana semifreddo into 1¼-by-½-inch (3-cm-by-12-mm) rectangles. Place a semifreddo piece on top of each cocoa-rice crunch piece, then top with a caramelized banana slice. Serve immediately.

MAKE-AHEAD/STORAGE
The cocoa-rice crunch and the banana semifreddo can be made up to 2 days in advance; store the crunch in an airtight container at room temperature and the semifreddo in an airtight container in the freezer until ready to assemble.

{ U N O , D O S , T R A Y S }

The meeting of the minds that is Pinch Food Design actually started with the humble serving tray. We realized we had a knack for working together when we discovered our mutual respect for its existence and purpose. We believe that even something as "basic" as a tray deserves as much careful thought and specific consideration as the food it's serving, so we design the food and the tray at the same time.

It's so much more than lining up each hors d'oeuvre on the first tray you find. There's so much to consider: Does the color of the tray compete with or complement the food it's carrying? Is the food sticky? Does it slide? Does it have a flat or a round bottom? How should the guest pick up the bite? All these things need to be well thought out when choosing a tray, so when we design our trays, we think of what kind of hors d'oeuvre will be placed on its surface.

Because we're not constrained by serving food on a plate, we feel like we've got an easier job than a restaurant would. To serve potato chips standing on their sides, we designed a tray with grooves to hold each chip in place. We've served bites on pedestals, hanging from nails–any way that gets the food to our guests' fingertips in a visually striking (but also efficient) way.

A party is alive; it ebbs and flows based on timing, guest energy, entertainment, and environment. We love this about events; however, we don't want the same kind of wiggle room on our trays. We believe every bite deserves a home and that each tray is a canvas. Once placed by the chef, we do not want the hors d'oeuvre to move until the guest picks it up. As we mentioned, there are many different shapes and textures to consider when designing a tray. We've used everything from silicone mats to spikes to hollowed-out divots to make our food behave instead of crashing around like bumper cars the minute we step into the party. On our Pinch Fork trays and Wood Block (see page 212), for example, magnets keep everything in place, allowing the metal forks to stand on end and be plucked like flowers. Other cork and nail trays take the guesswork out of plating, indicating exactly where to place each piece on the tray.

DIVOTS

CUT OUTS

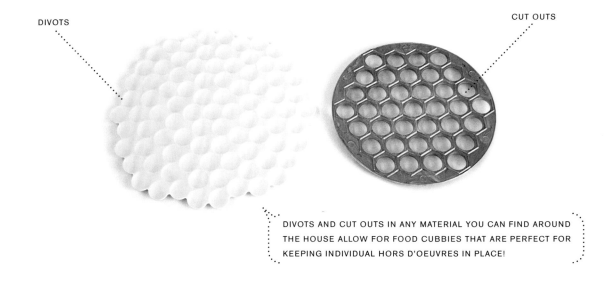

DIVOTS AND CUT OUTS IN ANY MATERIAL YOU CAN FIND AROUND THE HOUSE ALLOW FOR FOOD CUBBIES THAT ARE PERFECT FOR KEEPING INDIVIDUAL HORS D'OEUVRES IN PLACE!

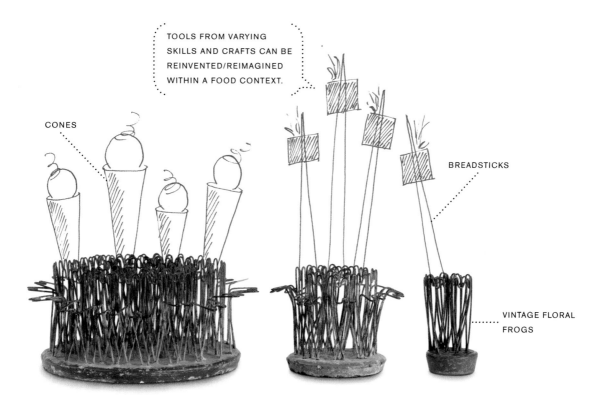

TOOLS FROM VARYING SKILLS AND CRAFTS CAN BE REINVENTED/REIMAGINED WITHIN A FOOD CONTEXT.

CONES

BREADSTICKS

VINTAGE FLORAL FROGS

DIY

DON'T FEEL HAMPERED BY THE IDEA THAT YOU DON'T HAVE THE RIGHT LARGE PLATTER OR SERVING PLATE TO DO THE JOB. ALMOST ANY SURFACE IN THE HOUSE OR GARAGE CAN BECOME A SERVING PIECE. FOR A MORE PERSONALIZED (AND, MIGHT WE SAY, MORE EXCITING) PRESENTATION:

- STACKS OF SUITCASES
- FLOWER FROGS
- PICTURE FRAMES
- PILLOWS

- ASTROTURF
- WINE CORKS WRAPPED INTO A BUNDLE WITH RUBBER BANDS
- TAPE WITH RIBBON ACCENTS

FOR DELICATE PIECES OR ITEMS YOU'D PREFER NOT TO PERMANENTLY STAIN WITH FOOD, USE PLASTIC WRAP OR CLEAR CELLOPHANE TO KEEP THE "TRAYS" PRISTINE. STRETCH IT TAUT AND TAPE IT WELL, THEN REMOVE IT AT THE END OF THE NIGHT. YOU CAN ALSO USE GLASS OR PLEXI ON TOP.

COLLECT, RINSE, AND DRY ABOUT 150 WINE CORKS TO MAKE A
ROUND TRAY 12 TO 16 INCHES (30.5 TO 40.5 CM) IN DIAMETER. (THE
TRAY SHOWN HERE IS SMALLER AND ONLY REQUIRED 20 CORKS.)

WHEN CONNECTED,
WINE CORKS FORM
A BEAUTIFUL NON-
SLIP SURFACE.

GROUP CORKS TOGETHER TO CREATE THE
DESIRED DIAMETER OR LENGTH OF THE
TRAY. USE GLUE, RUBBER BANDS, OR TAPE
TO ATTACH THE CORKS TOGETHER.

CREATE A MORE REFINED EDGE
BY WRAPPING A RIM OF WIDE
RIBBON AROUND THE TRAY.

WITH RIBBONS AND WASHI TAPE,
THE CUSTOMIZING OPTIONS FOR
TRAYS ARE ENDLESS!

A CIRCLE OF PLEXI (OR
YOU CAN USE A MIRROR)

RUBBER BANDS ARE A
GREAT NON-SLIP SURFACE.
SIMPLY WRAP THEM AROUND
ANYTHING RELATIVELY FLAT.

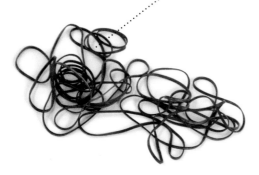

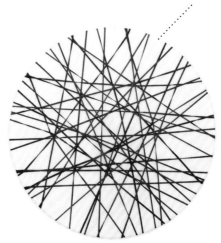

Eggplant Parmigiana

Though the presentation is unusual, the classic flavors of this bite will conjure up memories of hearty Italian-American meals of yesteryear.

To make the thin, crispy cheese crackers that support the eggplant and tomato in this bite, you'll need to make a simple stencil. Grab a deli container lid on your next trip to the olive bar or a thin sheet of acetate from the crafts store—both are easy to cut and washable for reuse.

YIELD: Serves 12
SPECIAL EQUIPMENT: triangle stencil (see next page), kitchen/crème brûlée torch

For the Parmigiano-Reggiano cracker:
3 tablespoons unsalted butter, softened
3 tablespoons all-purpose flour
1 large egg white
2 tablespoons finely grated Parmigiano-Reggiano cheese

For the fried eggplant:
1 Japanese eggplant
¼ cup (30 g) all-purpose flour
1 large egg, lightly beaten
½ cup (50 g) panko bread crumbs
3 tablespoons vegetable oil

For the roasted tomatoes:
6 cherry tomatoes, halved lengthwise
Extra-virgin olive oil
Maldon sea salt

To assemble:
Micro shiso

Make the Parmigiano-Reggiano cracker: Photocopy the triangle shape (see page 66) and trace it onto a piece of acetate or the clean lid of a deli container. Cut the triangles out of the acetate or plastic to make a triangle stencil.

Preheat the oven to 325°F (165°C). Line two large baking sheets with nonstick baking mats or parchment paper.

In the bowl of a stand mixer fitted with the paddle attachment, combine the butter, flour, egg white, and cheese and mix gently on low speed until the butter is fully incorporated, taking care not to whip air into the batter.

(RECIPE CONTINUES)

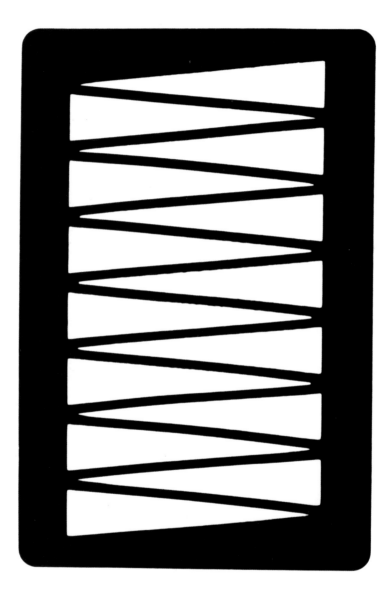

PHOTOCOPY STENCIL AT 200%

SO DIMENSIONS EQUAL 7½ BY 11¼ INCHES (19 BY 28.5 CM)

Using the triangle stencil and an offset spatula, spread the batter into fourteen triangles on the prepared baking sheets. Place the stencil on the sheet, spread with batter, lift the stencil carefully, and repeat. (Do a few extra in case of breakage.)

Bake the triangles for 8 minutes, or until the edges of each triangle are just starting to turn golden. Remove from the oven and carefully transfer the baking mats or parchment paper to a wire rack and let the crackers cool completely.

Make the fried eggplant: Slice the eggplant in half lengthwise, then crosswise into ¼-inch-thick (6-mm-thick) half-moons.

Place the flour, egg, and bread crumbs in individual bowls or shallow dishes. Bread the eggplant rounds by dredging them in the flour, then dipping in the egg, then in the bread crumbs until evenly coated. Set the breaded eggplant rounds on a baking sheet.

Heat the oil in a large skillet over medium heat. Pan-fry the breaded eggplant, in batches if necessary, until golden brown on both sides. Reserve at room temperature until needed.

Make the roasted tomatoes: Line a rimmed baking sheet with foil or parchment paper. Place the tomatoes in a single layer. Brush the tomatoes lightly with oil and sprinkle with salt.

Caramelize the tomatoes with a kitchen torch until gently shriveled and starting to brown at the edges. Or broil them in the oven at high heat for no more than 2 minutes. (Broiling them too long will make them saucy.)

Assemble the bites: Gently spear a piece of fried eggplant onto each cracker, then top with a tomato and a spring of micro shiso and serve.

MAKE-AHEAD/STORAGE

The crackers can be made up to 3 days in advance; store in an airtight container at room temperature until ready to assemble and serve. The eggplant rounds can be fried up to 4 hours in advance. The roasted tomatoes can be broiled or caramelized up to 10 hours in advance and either refrigerated or stored at room temperature. Bring to room temperature before serving.

DIY

WE SERVE THESE BITES ON A SLOT TRAY, WHICH MAKES THE EDGES OF THE CRACKER EASIER TO GRAB. TO CREATE THE TRAY SHOWN HERE, USE A ROUTER OR CIRCULAR SAW. CUT EVENLY SPACED GROOVES (1½ INCH LONG BY ¼ INCH DEEP BY ⅛ INCH THICK/4 BY 0.6 BY 0.3 CM) INTO A FLAT PIECE OF MATERIAL (WOOD, PLEXI, SALT BLOCK, ETC.). OR IF YOU DON'T WANT TO BREAK OUT THE SAW, THE IDEA OF THE SLOT TRAY CAN BE EASILY ADAPTED. THE CRACKERS CAN BE SECURED WITH OLD-TIMEY CLOTHESPINS THAT HAVE BEEN GLUED TO A DOWEL ROD, OR STUCK BETWEEN THE TINES OF A FORK PLACED ON A TRAY.

The Pinch Lobster Roll

For those of us who grew up within driving distance of New England, this bite conjures up memories of meals eaten at seaside shacks, where the briny smell of the ocean mingled with the hot butter and sweet meat of a lobster roll. This lobster roll is a simple hors d'oeuvre, in essence—hot brioche bun, cold lobster salad—but its tweezerlike design gives it a modern playfulness.

YIELD: Serves 12

For the lobster salad:
1 (1¼-pound/570-g) cooked lobster
1 tablespoon mayonnaise
1 tablespoon chopped scallion, green parts only
1 tablespoon chopped fresh chervil
½ teaspoon kosher salt
½ teaspoon freshly ground black pepper
¼ teaspoon cayenne

For the buttered rolls:
½ cup (120 ml) warm water
¼ cup (60 ml) whole milk
1 tablespoon granulated sugar
1 tablespoon active dry yeast
3 cups (420 g) bread flour or 3 cups (375 g) all-purpose flour
1 teaspoon sea salt or kosher salt
1 tablespoon unsalted butter, at room temperature, plus 2 tablespoons unsalted butter, melted
1 large egg, at room temperature

To assemble:
2 tablespoons unsalted butter

Make the lobster salad: Remove the lobster meat from the shell and finely chop it. Transfer the lobster meat to a large bowl and stir in the mayonnaise, scallion, chervil, salt, pepper, and cayenne until combined.

Cover and refrigerate for at least 6 hours or overnight, until well chilled.

Make the buttered rolls: In a large bowl, whisk together the water, milk, sugar, and yeast and cover loosely with a piece of plastic wrap or a damp towel. Let rest in a warm place for 20 minutes to activate the yeast.

Stir in half of the flour and all of the salt, and cover. Let rest in a warm place for 20 minutes more; a loose, bubbly dough will form.

Knead in the room-temperature butter and egg, cover, and let rest for 20 minutes more.

Transfer the dough to the bowl of a stand mixer fitted with the dough hook and add the remaining flour. Knead on low speed for 10 minutes, then cover and let rest for 40 minutes, or until the dough doubles in volume.

Preheat the oven to 375°F (190°C). Line a large rimmed baking sheet with parchment paper.

Roll the dough into a rectangle about ½ inch (12 mm) thick. Transfer the dough to the prepared baking sheet and brush with the melted butter.

Use a pizza or pastry cutter to slice the dough into rectangles approximately ½ inch (12 mm) wide and 2 inches (5 cm) long, but don't pull them apart—leave them stuck together until after they bake.

Bake for about 12 minutes, until the bread is turning golden brown, then remove from the baking sheet and cool on a wire rack.

Assemble the bites: Slice the cooled rolls along the lines that you scored before baking.

Melt the butter in a large skillet over medium-low heat. Fry the rolls in batches until crispy and golden brown on both sides, like a grilled cheese sandwich.

Slice each roll three-quarters of the way open down the length of the roll, like a hot-dog bun, and fill with some of the lobster meat. Serve immediately.

MAKE-AHEAD/STORAGE

The lobster salad should be prepared at least 2 hours and up to 12 hours in advance; store in an airtight container in the refrigerator until ready to use. The rolls can be baked and cut 2 weeks in advance and frozen until you're ready to fry them and serve.

DIY

MAKE YOUR OWN NAIL TRAY: CUT A PIECE OF WOOD TO 20 BY 6 BY ¾ INCHES (51 BY 15 BY 2 CM). OR YOU CAN USE AN EXISTING WOOD PLATTER OR A DRAWER FACE. USING COPPER FLAT-HEAD FINISHING NAILS, HAMMER FOUR ROWS ½ INCH (12 MM) APART DOWN THE CENTER OF THE WOOD. EVERY OTHER NAIL IN THE TWO ROWS IN THE MIDDLE SHOULD BE LOWER THAN THE OUTSIDE ROWS TO CREATE NOOKS FOR FOOD TO LEAN ON.

Miso Branzino with Pineapple on Crisp Tortilla

This is our version of the "fish stick," inspired by Nobu's classic miso cod. We are big fans of sweet Italian sea bass, but you can always substitute your favorite local fish. The fish is only cooked with a kitchen torch: The flame caramelizes the miso paste and sears the fish just enough while keeping it moist. This great technique can also be quite the show in an open kitchen!

YIELD: Serves 12
SPECIAL EQUIPMENT: kitchen/crème brûlée torch

For the sweet-and-sour pineapple:
1 cup (165 g) roughly diced ripe pineapple
½ cup (120 ml) unseasoned rice vinegar
1 teaspoon kosher salt

For the miso paste:
2 tablespoons yellow miso paste
1 tablespoon honey
1 tablespoon sambal paste

For the tortilla chips:
2 corn tortillas
2 teaspoons vegetable oil

To assemble:
12 ounces (340 g) branzino, skin removed
1 teaspoon chiffonade of fresh mint leaves

Make the sweet-and-sour pineapple: In a 1- or 2-quart (960-ml or 2-L) saucepan, combine the pineapple, vinegar, and salt and bring to a simmer over medium-low heat. Cook for about 5 minutes, until most of the liquid has evaporated.

Transfer the pineapple to a blender or food processor and puree until smooth. Reserve in a bowl at room temperature or in a covered container in the refrigerator until needed.

Make the miso paste: In a small bowl, whisk together the miso, honey, and sambal until fully combined. Reserve at room temperature or in a covered container in the refrigerator until needed.

Make the tortillas: Slice the tortillas into 2-by-½-inch (5-cm-by-12-mm) strips.

Heat a heavy-bottomed stainless-steel or cast-iron skillet over high heat. Line a baking sheet with paper towels.

Lightly brush each tortilla strip with oil and carefully place in the hot skillet. Cook on both sides until crispy, pressing with a spatula to keep the tortilla as flat as possible.

Transfer to the lined baking sheet to cool.

Assemble the bites: Slice the branzino into 1½-by-⅜-inch (4-by-1-cm) rectangles and place on a rimmed baking sheet.

Rub a thin layer of miso paste across the top of each fish rectangle with your fingers, then caramelize each piece of fish with a kitchen torch until the miso is golden and lacquered.

Place a piece of branzino on each tortilla strip, placing it off-center to leave a chip "handle" for guests to grab. Spoon a dollop of sweet-and-sour pineapple on the branzino, sprinkle with mint, and serve.

MAKE-AHEAD/STORAGE
The sweet-and-sour pineapple and miso paste can be prepared up to 1 week in advance; store each component separately in an airtight container in the refrigerator until ready to use, then bring to room temperature before assembling. The tortillas can be fried up to 3 days in advance and stored in an airtight container at room temperature. The branzino can be caramelized up to 6 hours before serving and refrigerated; remove it from the refrigerator ½ hour before serving.

DIY

SOMETIMES A FLAT TRAY JUST WON'T WORK.
TO HELP GUESTS GRAB THE FLAT CHIPS, IT'S
FUN TO TILT THE BITES AT AN ANGLE. LEAN
THEM AGAINST A SLICED PIECE OF PINEAPPLE
OR LEMONGRASS. TO CREATE A MORE
PERMANENT SERVING TRAY, GLUE TOGETHER
CROWN MOLDING TO CREATE PEAKS AND
VALLEYS THAT MAKE THIS FLAT TORTILLA CRISP
EASIER FOR GUESTS TO PICK UP. SEE THE
NEW WAVE ON PAGE 168 FOR HOW PIECES
OF CROWN MOLDING CAN FIT TOGETHER AND
FORM A TRAY.

Pea Pudding and Carrots

If you haven't been holding on to the rinds of your Parmigiano-Reggiano and Pecorino Romano cheeses, start now! Toss the rinds into a plastic bag once they've been scraped of cheese and keep them in your refrigerator. Use them to flavor soups and stews, as well as to make flavorful broths like the simple version below. For this recipe, if you don't have a bunch of rinds on hand, just ask your local cheesemonger—they're swimming in 'em.

YIELD: Serves 12
SPECIAL EQUIPMENT: apple corer, pastry bag fitted with an extra-large round piping tip

For the Parmigiano-Reggiano carrots:
4 ounces (115 g) Parmigiano-Reggiano or Pecorino Romano rinds, chopped into chunks
1 pound (455 g) large carrots (at least ¾ inch/2 cm in diameter), cut crosswise into 1¼-inch (3-cm) pieces

For the pea pudding:
½ cup (100 g) freshly shucked English peas, plus 2 tablespoons roughly chopped freshly shucked English peas
¼ cup (60 ml) heavy cream
1 tablespoon roughly chopped fresh flat-leaf parsley
2 cloves garlic, roughly chopped
½ teaspoon kosher salt, plus more as needed

To assemble:
¼ cup (25 g) freshly grated Parmigiano-Reggiano or Pecorino Romano (preferably grated with a Microplane)
1 tablespoon chiffonade of fresh mint leaves

Make the Parmigiano-Reggiano carrots: Place the cheese rinds and 4 cups (960 ml) water in a 3-quart (2.8-L) saucepan and bring to a simmer over medium-low heat. Cook for 15 minutes.

Add the carrots to the cheese broth. Cook for 10 to 15 minutes, until they are al dente—tender but still crunchy.

Remove the carrots from the broth and, while they're still warm, hollow out their centers with an apple corer or sharp paring knife. Each carrot piece should resemble a tube.

Make the pea pudding: In a small saucepan, combine the whole peas, cream, parsley, garlic, and salt and bring to a simmer over medium-low heat. Cook for 10 to 15 minutes, until the cream begins to turn green.

Scrape the pea mixture into a blender or food processor and puree until smooth. Don't be alarmed; the mixture should be thick, similar in consistency to mashed potatoes, because of the starchiness of the peas.

Stir the 2 tablespoons chopped peas into the puree. Taste and season with salt, if needed.

Scrape the puree into a pastry bag fitted with an extra-large round piping tip.

Assemble the bites: Pipe the pea pudding into each hollowed-out carrot. Stand each carrot on end and top with grated cheese and mint.

MAKE-AHEAD/STORAGE
The pea pudding can be made up to 3 days in advance; store it in an airtight container in the refrigerator and bring to room temperature before serving. The carrots can be made up to 1 day in advance. Reserve the carrots at room temperature or refrigerate overnight in a covered container. Bring to room temperature before serving.
The bites can be prepped 2 hours in advance.

THOUGH WE USUALLY AREN'T FANS OF TRAY GARNISH, ESPECIALLY IN FLOWER FORM, HERE THE DRIED PEAS IN THE NOOK FORESHADOW THE DELICIOUS PEA PUREE INSIDE THE STEAMED CARROT CYLINDER AND ADD AN EXTRA TOUCH OF COLOR. YOU CAN SIMPLY ARRANGE A BED OF GARNISH ON ANY TRAY THAT YOU OWN. OR TO CREATE A GARNISH NOOK TRAY, GRAB FIVE PIECES OF MATERIAL: A BASE, LIKE THE WOOD BOTTOM LAYER PICTURED HERE, TWO SMALLER PIECES (ONE SHOULD BE HALF THE WIDTH AND THE OTHER ONE-FOURTH THE WIDTH OF THE BASE), AND TWO END CAPS (WE USED 1-INCH BRASS PLATE). GLUE, SCREW, OR RUBBERBAND THE PIECES TOGETHER BEFORE SCREWING ON THE END CAPS. THEN FILL THE VOID WITH YOUR GARNISH OF CHOICE.

Watermelon Ice Pop

Find the reddest, ripest watermelon possible for these simple treats—with an ingredient list as short as this, the ruddy color of the fruit is paramount for a presentation that pops (pun intended). We like to use cone-shaped silicone candy molds to make our ice pops into a stylized "bomb pop" shape, but feel free to use any small, fun mold that strikes your fancy. (See page 30 for more details on silicone molds.)

YIELD: Serves 12
SPECIAL EQUIPMENT: 1-ounce (28-g) silicone molds or ice cube trays, bamboo toothpicks or bamboo skewers with side twist

¼ **cup (60 ml) water**
¼ **cup (50 g) granulated sugar**
2½ **cups (450 g) seeded and diced ripe watermelon**
2 teaspoons fresh lemon juice
Pinch of kosher salt

In a small saucepan, combine the water and sugar. Bring to a simmer over medium heat, stirring frequently until the sugar has dissolved.

Place the sugar syrup, watermelon, lemon juice, and salt in a blender or food processor and puree until smooth.

Place 1-ounce (28-g) silicone molds or other small molds (such as novelty ice cube trays) on a baking sheet to stabilize them. Pour the watermelon puree into the molds.

Cover the molds with a sheet of plastic wrap and poke toothpicks through the plastic to keep them upright while the liquid freezes around them. Freeze for at least 6 hours or overnight.

Unmold the ice pops and serve immediately.

MAKE-AHEAD/STORAGE
The pops can be made up to 1 week in advance if stored in the molds, or 1 day in the freezer if they are popped out of the molds.

> **DIY**
>
> IF YOU ARE LOOKING FOR FUN WAYS TO SERVE FOOD ON STICKS, FEED YOUR BAMBOO SKEWERS ONTO A BRANCH SO THAT YOUR BITES CAN DANGLE. EVEN A CLEAR DOWEL CAN BE MADE INTO A SERVING TRAY, WHICH ALLOWS FOOD TO LOOK LIKE IT IS ALMOST FLOATING THROUGH A CROWD. ANOTHER GOOD OPTION FOR PRESENTING THIS PARTICULAR DESSERT IS TO DRILL ICE POP–SIZE HOLES IN A TWO-BY-FOUR AND LINE THE ICE POPS UP ON THE BOARD. OR JUST SERVE THEM UPSIDE-DOWN IN YOUR FAVORITE COCKTAIL GLASSES.

Salted Chocolate–Rosemary Ice Cream Sandwich

When you're designing a one-bite ice cream sandwich combination, it has to have impact. You are only working with two components—cookie and ice cream—so making each one memorable is key. We add a tasty salt and a strong herb to help accentuate the flavors, then we play with the structure by balancing the free-form cookie shape on top of the clean-cut lines of the ice cream cylinder to create an original take on this dessert classic.

YIELD: Makes about 18 sandwich cookies
SPECIAL EQUIPMENT: candy thermometer, ice cream maker, ¾-inch (2-cm) round cookie cutter

For the rosemary ice cream:
1 vanilla bean, split and scraped
3 cups (720 ml) heavy cream
1 cup (200 g) granulated sugar
1 tablespoon finely chopped fresh
   rosemary leaves

For the salted chocolate sandwich cookie:
8 tablespoons (230 g) unsalted butter
¼ cup (50 g) granulated sugar
1 cup (140 g) roughly chopped semisweet
   or bittersweet chocolate
¼ cup (60 ml) corn syrup
1 large egg
1 cup (125 g) all-purpose flour
1⅓ cups (115 g) cocoa powder
½ teaspoon baking soda
1 tablespoon finely chopped fresh rosemary
1 tablespoon Maldon sea salt

Make the rosemary ice cream: Split the vanilla bean lengthwise and scrape out the seeds. Place the seeds and pods in a 2-quart (2-L) high-sided saucepan and add the cream, sugar, and rosemary. Clip a candy thermometer to the pan and place over medium heat. Cook, stirring occasionally, until the mixture registers 170°F (77°C) on the thermometer.

Remove from the heat and allow to cool to room temperature. Remove the vanilla bean pods and pour the custard base into a container with a lid. Refrigerate for at least 4 hours or overnight.

Pour the chilled custard base into an ice cream maker and freeze according to the manufacturer's instructions.

Transfer to a clean container and freeze until ready to use.

Make the salted chocolate sandwich cookie:
Preheat the oven to 350°F (175°C). Line a baking sheet with parchment paper or a nonstick baking mat.

In the top of a double boiler, melt the butter and sugar, stirring until the sugar is no longer grainy. Add the chocolate and corn syrup and stir until the chocolate is fully melted.

Remove from the heat and scrape into the bowl of a stand mixer fitted with the paddle attachment. With the mixer on low speed, add the egg and stir until fully incorporated.

In a medium bowl, whisk or sift together the flour, cocoa powder, and baking soda. Add the flour mixture to the chocolate mixture in increments, mixing on low speed until just combined after each addition.

Place parchment paper or a nonstick baking mat on a clean work surface and roll the dough out on the paper or liner until ⅛ inch (3 mm) thick.

Sprinkle the dough evenly with the rosemary and salt.

Bake for 5 to 7 minutes, until crispy, then transfer the paper or liner to a wire rack to cool the cookie completely. Break the cooled cookie into irregular pieces of roughly 1 inch (2.5 cm).

(RECIPE CONTINUES)

Assemble the bites: Line a rimmed baking sheet with waxed paper or parchment paper.

Scrape a knife around the inside of the ice cream storage container to loosen the ice cream, then shake or scrape the ice cream onto a cutting board in a single block.

Slice the block of ice cream into ½-inch-thick (12-mm-thick) slices, then cut circles out of each slice with a ¾-inch (2-cm) round cookie cutter.

Place each ice cream round on the prepared baking sheet, then return the baking sheet to the freezer for about 1 hour, until the ice cream is

hard. Sandwich each ice cream round between two cookie shards and freeze again until ready to serve.

MAKE-AHEAD/STORAGE
The cookies and ice cream can be made up to 2 days in advance; store the cookies in an airtight container at room temperature and the ice cream in an airtight container in the freezer until ready to assemble. Once assembled, the cookies can be served immediately as long as the ice cream remains cold and unmelted, or the assembled cookies can be frozen overnight until ready to serve.

DIY

TO KEEP YOUR ICE CREAM SANDWICHES FROM SLIDING AROUND ON THE TRAY, DRILL 2-INCH (5-CM) DIAMETER HOLES INTO A 5-BY-22-BY-¼-INCH-THICK (13-BY-56-BY-0.6-CM-THICK) PIECE OF PLEXI AND INSERT THE CORKS, WHICH NOT ONLY OFFER TRACTION BUT ALSO PROVIDE PEDESTALS TO DISPLAY THE BITES AND LET YOU KNOW EXACTLY WHERE TO PLATE THEM.

{ PINCH FORKS AND SPINS }

Skewers and toothpicks have reigned supreme at cocktail parties since the 1950s and '60s, serving an all-important function by keeping your fingers clean while getting that one-biter in your mouth. But we're always working to make every aspect of the party enjoyable and easy for our guests, and we just don't think that making our friends hold on to dirty toothpicks or skewers, or tuck them into a balled-up cocktail napkin, feels comfortable at all! (*Curb Your Enthusiasm* even made an episode about the skewer!)

So we went to the drawing board and asked ourselves, "How can we make these useful catering utensils more sophisticated?" We not only needed to create something gorgeous and functional, but we also needed to find a way to dispose of the used piece without feeling intrusive. (Believe us, we're not huge fans of the cut lemon stabbed with used toothpicks that sits on the tray right next to the fresh hors d'oeuvres. Staring at garbage while you are eating takes a special kind of denial.) Though edible skewers are fun and playful, not to mention delicious, we wanted to do something a little cooler, so we made our own set of utensils, adapting traditional forks and spoons to suit our needs. While you don't need to craft your own utensils at home, the lessons we learned from designing them and creating the appetizers to be served on them can help you craft creatively presented dishes that perfectly showcase your inventive ingredient combinations.

In the following recipes, you'll find suggestions for dishes to serve on both forks and spoons, but as always, feel free to experiment with various ways of presenting your favorite recipes.

THE PINCH FORK

We designed special aerodynamic Pinch Forks, but at home, you can use small cocktail or salad forks to assemble your bites. Serving food on a fork evokes the ultimate satisfaction of building that "perfect forkful," along with nostalgic memories of playing "airplane" with your food as a child. Coming in for a landing: one tasty bite!

The key to serving an hors d'oeuvre on a fork is to make it look like you would if you were stabbing the ideal bite out of what's on your plate. Don't make it too precise or organized—let things hang off, and don't bother cutting things into perfect squares here. Just be careful not to let things drip too much!

THE SPIN

Clearly, we're punny folks. The Spin is equal parts spoon and pin—plus, you spin it when you eat off it. Playing off the idea of a spork, it combines the stabby functionality of a skewer and the depth of a bowl to serve both crispy-crunchy and creamy-smooth at the same time.

The Spin makes partygoers an essential part of "plating" the dish: They get to choose which half of the bite they eat first, then spin it around to finish the dish in their mouth. It's completely up to each guest how to attack the bite. Do you start with the warm shrimp or the cool horseradish? Do you crave a snappy bite or a smooth finish? It's a personal preference, and you can change your mind; we do all the time.

This strategy of separating elements of each bite by texture also solves a longtime problem of party hosts everywhere: How do you prepare your hors d'oeuvres in advance without having them sink into a soggy mess? By keeping the textural pieces separate until the absolute last minute, the bite stays intact and tastes exactly as it was intended. While it's totally possible to whittle your own wooden Spins from your grandma's wooden spoons or reusable bamboo spoons, JBPrince has thankfully taken the work out of the equation with tapered wooden spoons inspired by our signature Spin utensils. If you don't want to invest in new wooden spoons, we've offered suggestions for plating on the spoons you already own in the Spin recipes that follow.

DIY

THERE ARE MANY FUN WAYS TO PRESENT FOOD THAT IS SERVED ON FORKS AND SPOONS. YOU CAN SHOWCASE FORKS AND SPOONS LYING DIRECTLY ON DIFFERENT SURFACES, AT DIFFERENT LEVELS, AS WITH THE SUITCASES SHOWN HERE, OR SIMPLY ARRANGED ON CLASSIC SERVING TRAYS. WE ALSO LIKE TO GO VERTICAL. DISPLAY FORKS STANDING UP BY PLACING A 2-INCH (5-CM) THICK PIECE OF FOAM COVERED WITH YOUR MATERIAL OF CHOICE (FABRIC, PAPER, MOSS) INSIDE A SUITCASE OR OTHER CONTAINER AND CUT SLITS FOR THE FORKS TO POKE THROUGH. USED FORKS AND SPOONS SLIDE INTO AN INTERIOR DRAWER ON OUR TRAYS, KEEPING THEM OUT OF SIGHT AND OUT OF MIND. BUT AT HOME, A CLASSIC JULEP CUP, A CHAMPAGNE BUCKET, OR ANY OTHER TALL, OPAQUE VESSEL CAN EASILY BE DOCTORED WITH A SLOTTED LID TO KEEP THE DISCARDED UTENSILS AWAY FROM YOUR BITES.

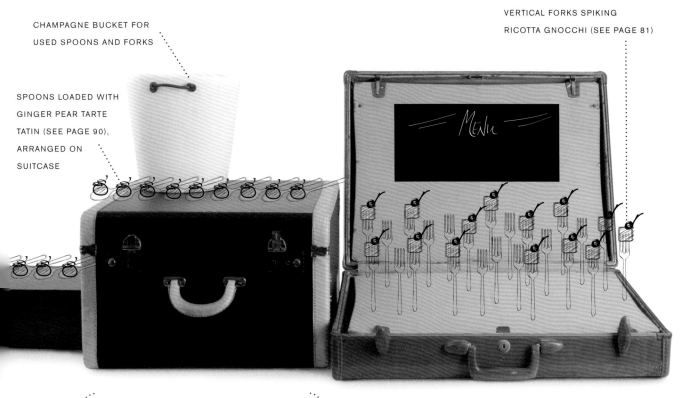

CHAMPAGNE BUCKET FOR USED SPOONS AND FORKS

VERTICAL FORKS SPIKING RICOTTA GNOCCHI (SEE PAGE 81)

SPOONS LOADED WITH GINGER PEAR TARTE TATIN (SEE PAGE 90), ARRANGED ON SUITCASE

VINTAGE SUITCASES CREATE RISERS OF VARYING HEIGHTS TO DISPLAY FORKS AND SPOONS

Endive, Gorgonzola, and Marinated Fig

Endive has been an hors d'oeuvre vessel for years. Naturally shaped like a spoon, it encourages you to take a wonderful bite, but then awkwardly leaves you with the remainder of the leaf, which overpowers the bite you just ate. Cutting the tip off the endive leaves you with a better proportion. As for the discarded bits, they make a great "family-meal" salad for you before guests arrive!

YIELD: Serves 12

4 heads of Belgian endive
3 fresh or dried black Mission figs
1 tablespoon sherry vinegar
2 ounces (55 g) Gorgonzola dolce, cut into
 1½-by-1-by-¼-inch (4-by-2.5-by-0.6-cm) slices
Maldon sea salt
Freshly ground black pepper

Slice the root end off each endive, and halve or quarter (depending on the size of each head) the head into 1½-inch (4-cm) pieces.

Cut the figs into ⅛-inch-thick (3-mm-thick) slices. Sprinkle the fig slices with the vinegar.

Stab the curved side of an endive piece with a fork and place a piece of Gorgonzola on the flat side of the endive that's facing up. Stack a slice of fig on top of the cheese, then sprinkle with salt and a grind of fresh pepper. Repeat with the remaining endive pieces, cheese, and figs.

MAKE-AHEAD/STORAGE
This bite can be assembled on the fork up to 1 hour before serving. Reserve at room temperature.

Ricotta Gnocchi with Escarole and Roasted Tomatoes

The key to good gnocchi is keeping it light, not dense. You don't want too much resistance in the bite. Here, the flour serves as a binder, accentuating the flavor and texture of the potato and ricotta.

YIELD: Serves 12

For the ricotta gnocchi:
½ pound (225 g) russet potatoes
1 large egg
½ cup (125 g) fresh ricotta
½ cup (65 g) all-purpose flour
2 tablespoons finely grated Parmigiano-Reggiano cheese
1 teaspoon plus 1 tablespoon kosher salt
½ teaspoon freshly ground black pepper
⅛ teaspoon freshly grated nutmeg
1 tablespoon unsalted butter

For the escarole:
5 tender escarole leaves, from the inside of the head
1 tablespoon extra-virgin olive oil
1 clove garlic, thinly sliced
⅛ teaspoon red pepper flakes
Pinch of kosher salt
Pinch of freshly ground black pepper

For the roasted tomatoes:
4 ripe plum tomatoes
1 clove garlic, crushed
2 tablespoons extra-virgin olive oil
½ teaspoon kosher salt
Freshly ground black pepper

To assemble:
Maldon sea salt

Make the ricotta gnocchi: Preheat the oven to 400°F (205°C).

Bake the potatoes until tender, 30 to 45 minutes, then set aside until cool enough to handle. Reduce the oven temperature to 350°F (175°C).

Peel the potatoes, then grate them on the small holes of a box grater into a medium bowl.

In a small bowl, mix together the egg and ricotta, then stir the mixture into the grated potato.

In a large bowl, whisk together the flour, cheese, 1 teaspoon of the salt, the pepper, and the nutmeg. Make a well in the center of the flour mixture and fill with the potato mixture. Stir slowly until a soft dough forms.

Transfer the dough to a clean, floured work surface. Roll pieces of the dough into logs about 1 inch (2.5 cm) in diameter, then cut each log into ½-inch (12-mm) gnocchi.

In a large stockpot, bring 4 quarts (3.8 L) water to a boil, then add the remaining 1 tablespoon salt. Add the gnocchi in batches and cook until they float, about 2 minutes.

In a large skillet, melt the butter over medium-low heat.

Using a spider or a flat metal strainer, skim the gnocchi out of the boiling water and transfer to the skillet. Brown the gnocchi on one side, then use the spider or strainer to transfer the gnocchi to a bowl. Set aside at room temperature until ready to serve. Keep the water at a boil to use for the escarole.

Make the escarole: Slice the escarole leaves into 1-inch (2.5-cm) pieces, then boil for 5 minutes in the same water you used to cook the gnocchi. Drain and reserve.

Heat the oil in a 10-inch (25-cm) skillet over medium heat, then add the garlic. Cook until the garlic is just starting to brown at the edges, then add the red pepper flakes and the escarole. Season with salt and black pepper. Set aside at room temperature until ready to serve.

Make the roasted tomatoes: Slice the tomatoes in half lengthwise and de-seed each half. Cut each half into 3 short pieces.

In a small bowl, toss the tomatoes with the garlic, oil, salt, and pepper. Place the slices, flat side down, on a baking sheet or in a small baking pan. Transfer to the oven and roast for 25 minutes. Set aside at room temperature until ready to serve.

(RECIPE CONTINUES)

Assemble the bites: Stab the gnocchi with the fork, and top with a piece of escarole, then a piece of the roasted tomato. Season with salt. Serve at room temperature.

MAKE-AHEAD/STORAGE
The gnocchi can be prepared (but not cooked) up to 1 week in advance and frozen; they can be boiled while still frozen. The escarole and tomatoes can be made up to 8 hours in advance; store the components in separate mixing bowls or on baking sheets at room temperature until ready to assemble.

Spicy Truffle Fries with Tuscan Herbs

It is rare for the French and Italians to eat with their hands—even fries are eaten with a fork! In the United States, we might see this as a waste of time. But it is quite nice not to have greasy fingers when you're meeting new people and shaking hands at a party. So stab a few fries on a fork for your guests; they will surely appreciate it.

YIELD: Serves 12
SPECIAL EQUIPMENT: electric deep-fryer or deep-fry thermometer

1 quart (960 ml) vegetable oil
1 pound (455 g) russet potatoes
2 teaspoons minced fresh flat-leaf parsley
1 teaspoon minced fresh oregano
2 teaspoons truffle oil or melted truffle butter
½ teaspoon red pepper flakes
¾ teaspoon Maldon sea salt

In an electric deep-fryer or a heavy, high-sided stockpot or Dutch oven, heat the vegetable oil over medium-high heat until it registers 375°F (190°C) on a deep-fry thermometer. Line one baking sheet with paper towels and another rimmed baking sheet with waxed paper.

Slice the unpeeled potatoes into matchsticks ⅜ inch (1 cm) wide and 1 inch (2.5 cm) long.

Fry the potatoes for 2 to 3 minutes. Make them tender but not brown or crisp. Use a spider or flat metal strainer to transfer them to the paper towel–lined baking sheet to drain, then place the fries on the waxed paper–lined baking sheet, making sure they don't touch one another. Freeze for at least 1 hour, until frozen through.

In a medium bowl, whisk the herbs, truffle oil, red pepper flakes, and salt together.

Reheat the vegetable oil and fry the frozen potatoes again until they're crisp and golden.

Add the warm potatoes to the bowl with the herb mixture and toss to coat.

Stack the fries on the tines of a fork to serve.

MAKE-AHEAD/STORAGE
The potatoes can be initially fried and frozen up to 2 days in advance; freeze on a waxed paper-lined baking sheet for about 1 hour until completely frozen, then transfer to an airtight container and store in the freezer until ready to refry for serving.

Peanut Butter Funnel Cake with Concord Grape Flan

Pinch pastry chef Stacy designed this Spin concoction, which marries two American kiddie classics—crunchy carnival funnel cakes with everyone's favorite sandwich combination—in an elegant presentation.

YIELD: Serves 12

SPECIAL EQUIPMENT: pastry bag fitted with small round piping tip, electric deep-fryer or deep-fry thermometer, Spin (optional)

For the Concord grape flan:
1½ cups (225 g) Concord or black grapes, washed and de-seeded
3 sheets leaf gelatin
½ cup (120 ml) whole milk
½ cup (120 ml) heavy cream
2 tablespoons granulated sugar

For the peanut butter funnel cake:
2 tablespoons creamy peanut butter
1½ teaspoons granulated sugar
¼ teaspoon kosher salt
½ cup (65 g) all-purpose flour
3 large eggs
2 quarts (2 L) vegetable oil

To assemble:
1 tablespoon confectioners' sugar
4 Concord or black grapes, washed, de-seeded, and thinly sliced

Make the Concord grape flan: In a blender, puree the grapes on low speed until smooth—resist the temptation to blend on high speed; this will incorporate too much air into the puree, which makes it frothy. Strain the puree through a fine-mesh sieve.

Place the gelatin sheets in a bowl of cold water and set aside to soften for 5 minutes.

In a small saucepan, heat the milk, cream, and sugar over medium-low heat just until bubbles form around the edges.

Squeeze the softened gelatin gently between your fingers to wring out excess water, then add the gelatin to the hot milk and whisk until the gelatin is fully dissolved.

Let the custard cool for 15 minutes, then whisk in the grape puree.

Pour the custard into a clean square or oblong container about 1 inch (2.5 cm) deep and refrigerate until set, about 3 hours.

Make the peanut butter funnel cake: Line a large baking sheet with parchment paper.

In a 1-quart (960-ml) high-sided saucepan, combine ½ cup (120 ml) water, the peanut butter, sugar, and salt and cook over medium heat until the peanut butter has melted into the water and the liquid starts to bubble around the edges of the pan.

Using a silicone spatula or a wooden spoon, stir in the flour and cook, stirring constantly, until a ball of dough forms and pulls away from the sides of the pan.

Scrape the dough into the bowl of a stand mixer fitted with the paddle attachment and, with the mixer on low speed, add the eggs to the dough, one at a time, allowing each to incorporate before adding the next.

Scrape the dough into a pastry bag fitted with a small round piping tip and pipe randomly squiggled "webs" of dough, each about 1½ inches (4 cm) in diameter, onto the parchment paper. Leave about 1 inch (2.5 cm) of space between webs.

In an electric deep-fryer or large, high-sided pot, heat the oil until it registers 375°F (190°C) on a deep-fry thermometer. Line a baking sheet with paper towels.

Gently place each web of dough, along with the parchment paper, in the hot oil. The dough will separate from the paper and slide into the oil; remove the paper carefully with tongs and discard.

Fry the dough until golden brown; timing will vary based on your equipment, but it should take no longer than 4 minutes.

Use tongs to remove the funnel cake and place on the paper towel–lined sheet to drain. Repeat with the remaining dough.

Assemble the bites: Slice the flan into 1-by-½-by-½-inch (2.5-cm-by-12-mm-by-12-mm) pieces. Place 1 piece of flan on the spoon end

of a Spin and garnish with 3 or 4 grape slices. Stab the funnel cake with the pin end and sprinkle with confectioners' sugar. Or place the flan on a large spoon, garnish with grape slices, and lay the funnel cake directly on top of the flan. Serve immediately.

MAKE-AHEAD/STORAGE

The flan can be prepared up to 3 weeks in advance and stored in an airtight container in the freezer. Thaw the flan in the refrigerator before slicing and serving. The funnel cake dough can be piped up to 6 hours in advance; carefully cover the baking sheet with foil, making sure it does not touch the dough webs, and refrigerate until ready to fry.

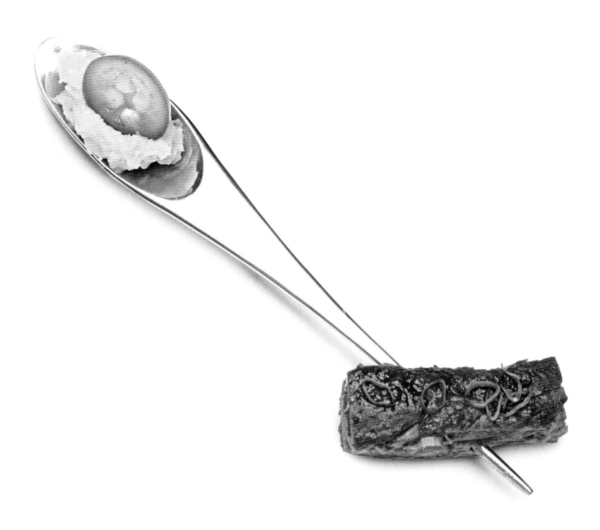

Baby Back Ribs with Creamed Corn and Jalapeño

This Spin lets you experience all the comfort of a backyard barbecue without the mess. The natural sweetness of the corn puree and the jolt from the jalapeño partner perfectly with the tangy, boneless rib meat.

YIELD: Serves 12
SPECIAL EQUIPMENT: mandoline or Japanese slicer, Spins (optional)

For the baby back ribs:
2 tablespoons brown sugar
2½ teaspoons kosher salt
½ teaspoon chili powder
½ teaspoon sweet paprika
¼ teaspoon garlic powder
¼ teaspoon onion powder
¼ teaspoon freshly ground black pepper
⅛ teaspoon dry mustard
⅛ teaspoon ground cumin
⅛ teaspoon cayenne
1 rack baby back ribs (about 8 ribs)

For the creamed corn:
1 ear yellow corn
1 cup (240 ml) whole milk
½ teaspoon kosher salt

To assemble:
1 jalapeño pepper
1 scallion, green part only, finely sliced
Maldon sea salt

Make the baby back ribs: In a small bowl, whisk together all the ingredients except the ribs.

Rub the ribs with the spice mixture. Place the ribs on a rimmed baking sheet, cover with plastic wrap, and refrigerate overnight.

Preheat the oven to 250°F (120°C). Bring the ribs to room temperature. Remove the plastic wrap.

Bake the ribs for 2 hours, then transfer to a clean baking sheet. Cover and refrigerate until cool.

Once cooled, cut the meat from between the bones and slice the meat into 1-by-½-inch (2.5-cm-by-12-mm) rectangles. Bring the meat to room temperature before serving.

Make the creamed corn: Slice the corn kernels off the cob and place them in a small saucepan. Add the milk and salt and cook over low heat for 3 to 4 minutes, until the kernels are very soft. Transfer the corn mixture to a blender or food processor and puree until smooth.

Assemble the bites: Using a mandoline or Japanese slicer, slice the jalapeño wafer-thin.

Stab a piece of rib meat on the pin end of a Spin. Sprinkle it with sliced scallion. Place a dollop of warm creamed corn on the spoon end, top the corn with a slice of jalapeño, and sprinkle with salt. Or place the ribs on a large spoon, sprinkle with sliced scallion, place a dollop of creamed corn on top, and garnish with a jalapeño slice and salt.

MAKE-AHEAD/STORAGE
Once baked, the ribs can be stored up to 1 day in advance; cool in the refrigerator, loosely covered with plastic wrap, as a rack, or slice after cooling and store the sliced meat in an airtight container in the refrigerator until ready to assemble. Bring the meat to room temperature before serving. The creamed corn can be made up to 1 day in advance; store in an airtight container in the refrigerator until ready to use.

Shrimp Cocktail with Horseradish Whipped Cream

This is a contemporary, deconstructed twist on the classic shrimp cocktail. As the horseradish, hot sauce, and tomato marry with the saline taste of shrimp, you will be taken back to that wedding at the Plaza for just a few seconds.

YIELD: Serves 12
SPECIAL EQUIPMENT: Spins (optional)

For the horseradish whipped cream:
½ cup (120 ml) heavy cream
2 tablespoons grated fresh horseradish
½ teaspoon kosher salt

For the spicy tomatoes:
1 ripe plum tomato, peeled and seeded
6 drops hot sauce such as Tabasco
Pinch of kosher salt

For the poached shrimp:
1 lemon
1 cup (240 ml) white wine
6 fresh thyme sprigs
8 medium (21–25 count) shrimp, peeled
   and deveined

To assemble:
1 6-inch flour tortilla, sliced into 1½-inch
   (4-cm) julienne strips

Make the horseradish whipped cream:
In a small saucepan, stir together the cream, horseradish, and salt and bring to a boil over medium heat. Reduce the heat to medium-low and simmer for 5 minutes. Remove from the heat, cover, and let steep for 30 minutes.

Strain the cream through a fine-mesh sieve into a small bowl. Cover and refrigerate until cold, about 1 hour.

Using a hand mixer or in a stand mixer fitted with the whisk attachment, whip the cream until stiff peaks form.

Make the spicy tomatoes: Finely dice the tomato, then place it in a small bowl and add the hot sauce and salt. Stir to combine, then set aside until ready to use.

Make the poached shrimp: Line a baking sheet or plate with paper towels.

Using a paring knife or peeler, slice the peel off the lemon, taking as little white pith off with the peel as you can.

In a 2-quart (2-L) saucepan, combine 3 cups (720 ml) water, wine, lemon peel, and thyme sprigs and bring to a boil over medium heat.

Slice the shrimp in half lengthwise. Poach for 1 minute in the boiling liquid, then use a spider or flat metal strainer to transfer the shrimp to the prepared baking sheet to drain.

Make the tortilla chips: Toast the strips in a 350°F (175°C) oven until crispy, 4 to 5 minutes.

Assemble the bites: Stab a warm shrimp with the pin end of a Spin, place some spicy tomatoes on the spoon end, and top with a dollop of horseradish cream and a tortilla strip. Or place a warm shrimp on a large spoon, top with a dollop of horseradish cream, and garnish with a tiny portion of the tomatoes and a tortilla strip. Serve immediately.

MAKE-AHEAD/STORAGE
The horseradish whipped cream can be made up to 8 hours in advance; store in an airtight container in the refrigerator until ready to use. The tomatoes and the shrimp can be made up to 1 hour in advance; store at room temperature until ready to use.

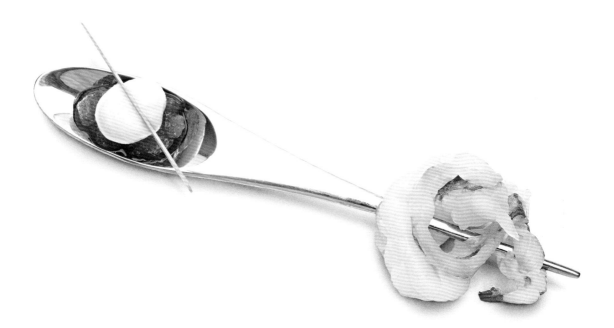

Pear Tarte Tatin with Ginger Whipped Cream

This exquisite combination of rich caramel, butter, and cooked pears is mind-blowing; it's the French version of apple pie, but so much better.

YIELD: Serves 12
SPECIAL EQUIPMENT: 1-inch (2.5-cm) round cookie cutter, Spins (optional)

For the pear tarte tatin:
2 Bartlett or other firm pears, peeled, quartered, and cored
1 cup (200 g) granulated sugar
½ cup (120 ml) water
3 tablespoons unsalted butter

For the ginger pastry:
3 tablespoons raw, turbinado, or demerara sugar
1 teaspoon ground ginger
1 (4-inch/10-cm) square puff pastry

For the ginger whipped cream:
3 tablespoons heavy cream
2 or 3 pieces crystallized ginger, grated with a Microplane

To assemble:
12 paper-thin slices of pear (optional)

Make the pear tarte tatin: Preheat the oven to 350°F (175°C).

Slice each pear quarter into ¼-inch-thick (6-mm-thick) slices.

Place the sugar and water in a 2-quart (2-L) sauté pan. Bring to a simmer over medium-low heat, stirring just until the sugar has dissolved. Cook, without stirring, until caramelized, then remove from the heat and carefully whisk in the butter. Immediately pour the caramel into an 8-inch (20-cm) square baking pan. Stir the pear slices into the caramel.

Bake for 35 minutes. Remove from the oven and let cool for 5 minutes, then scrape into a loaf pan and pack the fruit down with a spoon. Refrigerate for at least 3 hours, until cold and firm.

Cut the tarte tatin into 1-by-½-inch (2.5-cm-by-12-mm) rectangles. Refrigerate in a covered container until needed.

Make the ginger pastry: Preheat the oven to 375°F (190°C).

In a small bowl, whisk together the sugar and ginger. Lay the puff pastry out on a clean work surface and sprinkle the sugar-ginger mixture evenly over it. Using a rolling pin, gently roll the sugar and ginger into the pastry.

Cut out pastry circles with a 1-inch (2.5-cm) round cookie cutter. Place the circles on a baking sheet and bake for 10 minutes, or until golden brown. Cool completely and reserve at room temperature until ready to serve.

Make the ginger whipped cream: Whip the cream and fold in the grated ginger.

Assemble the bites: Place a piece of room-temperature tarte tatin on the spoon end of a Spin and top with a dollop of the whipped cream and a slice of pear, if desired. Stab the ginger pastry with the pin end. Or place a piece of tarte tatin on a large spoon and top with a ginger pastry, ginger whipped cream, and a slice of pear, if desired. Serve immediately.

MAKE-AHEAD/STORAGE
The tarte tatin can be made and sliced up to 2 days in advance; store in an airtight container in the refrigerator until ready to use. The ginger pastry can be made up to 1 day in advance; store in an airtight container at room temperature until ready to use. The whipped cream can be made up to 8 hours in advance; store in an airtight container in the refrigerator until ready to use.

THE CHEF'S TABLE

AN INTIMATE, INTERACTIVE PERFORMANCE IN YOUR KITCHEN

Let's face it: Guests gravitate to the kitchen when you're having a party, and everyone likes to feel like they're getting a sneak peek, a little extra piece of the action. Who doesn't love the intimacy of leaning on the counter, taking a spoon from a chef as he or she preps a meal, and having the cook say, "Taste this—I just made it. What do you think?"

The Chef's Table is both a workspace and a performance space. The chef preparing the food gets to exercise an element of drama; the dish is assembled in real time in front of the guests, to be eaten directly off the table: a little surprising, a little messy, a little rebellious. Everyone's fixated as the chef layers flavors one by one. Nobody knows what the next step is going to be.

In this chapter, we'll talk about the elements we devised and developed for our Chef's Table, and show you how you can apply these principles to small gatherings in your own home. Whether you're ready to spread out some silicone place mats on your counter or just use the butcher block cutting boards you already own, it's easy and fun to make an interactive Chef's Table spread.

Don't worry: Any complicated prep is done before guests arrive. We've streamlined the process so that home cooks can impress their guests—and enjoy the party!—with simple assembly of each recipe. All of the steps under the "Assemble and Serve" portion of the recipe are meant to be completed in front of your guests.

WARM MOZZARELLA CAPRESE (SEE PAGE 105) BEING PREPARED AT THE CHEF'S TABLE.

{ THE TOOLS OF THE TABLE }

The first time we tried the Chef's Table in our kitchen, we used a sharp mandoline. We thought it would be cool for guests to see an apple being sliced so precisely, and that we were just good enough that we didn't have to look at our fingers as we sliced, but instead could watch where the apples fell on the table. Bob sliced his finger. So Rideiby tried it, and he cut *his* finger. Ouch. The pain of learning. We now cut the apples prior to events.

After that defining moment, we had to refine and pare down. Now, though we still love to play with brushes, spatulas, Microplanes, and squeeze bottles—because it's always fun to squeeze something with a rebellious flourish—we could abandon all of our formal chef training and do the whole thing with two hands and one spoon.

The edible components of each Chef's Table bite, originally displayed in vessels scattered artfully on a silicone-covered table, got a similar simplification. Instead of the visually hectic piles of produce and ingredients, the elements are held in a custom vacu-formed tray with multiple wells, inspired by the idea of an artist's palette: compartmentalized, efficient, and finger-friendly. The guests get to muse over the chemistry kit of ingredients on display, anticipating how they're going to be used, waiting to see how things will (literally) stack up.

Perhaps the most important (and highly anticipated) part of the show is cleaning the silicone table for the next batch of bites. Bob's one-o'clock-in-the-morning flash of inspiration—a squeegee—solved the dilemma of how to wipe the table back to its blank-slate state in appropriately dramatic fashion. Cool vintage atomizers, filled with a mix of vodka and water, are used to spritz the table as a lubricant and sanitizer for the squeegee.

DIY

HERE'S HOW TO CREATE YOUR OWN CUSTOM CHEF'S TABLE TABLEAU FOR YOUR NEXT GATHERING, USING EASY-TO-FIND EQUIPMENT FROM YOUR FAVORITE HOME GOODS AND HARDWARE STORES. THOUGH THE CHEF'S TABLE LOOKS MINIMAL, ITS FEW COMPONENTS DO A LOT OF HEAVY LIFTING. CREATING AN INTERACTIVE SPACE FOR SERVING GUESTS CHEF'S TABLE–STYLE AT HOME CAN BE AS SIMPLE AS CLEARING SPACE FROM YOUR KITCHEN COUNTER AND GRABBING A PAINTBRUSH.

THE MOST CRUCIAL ELEMENT IS A CLEAN, APPEALING SURFACE ON WHICH TO DISPLAY AND PRESENT THE FOOD—THIS ISN'T A TIME FOR BEAT-UP CUTTING BOARDS OR BAKING SHEETS TARNISHED FROM YEARS OF ABUSE. IF YOU HAVE A MARBLE OR GRANITE KITCHEN COUNTER, NOW'S THE TIME TO LET IT SHINE. COUNTERS NOT SO CHIC? PICK UP A MARBLE PASTRY BOARD, A SET OF SILICONE PLACE MATS, OR AN OILCLOTH TABLECLOTH THAT CAN BE WIPED CLEAN. JUST REMEMBER TO CHOOSE A NEUTRAL COLOR; RED FOODS SERVED ON A RED BOARD WON'T HAVE THE SAME IMPACT AS THEY WOULD IF SERVED ON A WHITE BACKGROUND.

FOR A MORE DISPOSABLE SOLUTION, A ROLL OF WAXED BUTCHER PAPER GIVES YOU THE OPTION TO ADD DRAMA BY TEARING AND CRUMPLING EACH SECTION AFTER IT'S BEEN USED, AND STARTING FRESH WITH ANOTHER PIECE OF PAPER "CANVAS."

INSTEAD OF HUNTING DOWN AN INDUSTRIAL COMPANY TO MAKE A VACU-FORMED TRAY OF YOUR OWN LIKE WE DID, PICK UP A RETRO-STYLE TV DINNER TRAY OR EVEN A KITCHEN UTENSIL TRAY—YOU KNOW, THE KIND YOU PLACE IN A DRAWER TO DIVIDE YOUR FORKS, KNIVES, AND SPOONS.

CHANCES ARE YOU DON'T HAVE AN ARSENAL OF VINTAGE ATOMIZERS AT YOUR DISPOSAL, BUT UNTIL THE PERFECT RETRO FIND POPS UP ON ETSY OR EBAY, HEAD TO YOUR LOCAL PLANT STORE. SPECIALTY FLORISTS AND UPSCALE GARDEN CENTERS OFTEN CARRY PLANT ATOMIZERS IN GLASS, CERAMIC, OR BRASS; IN A PINCH, A COOL SPRAY BOTTLE IN COLORFUL PLASTIC OR STAINLESS STEEL WORKS EQUALLY WELL. FILL IT WITH A 50/50 MIX OF VODKA AND WATER, AND SPRAY THIS ACROSS YOUR WORK SURFACE. PURCHASE A SQUEEGEE TO WIPE CLEAN.

FIND YOUR OWN CHEF TRAYS
FOR COMPARTMENTALIZING
INGREDIENTS.

UTENSIL ORGANIZER

CERAMIC PLATE

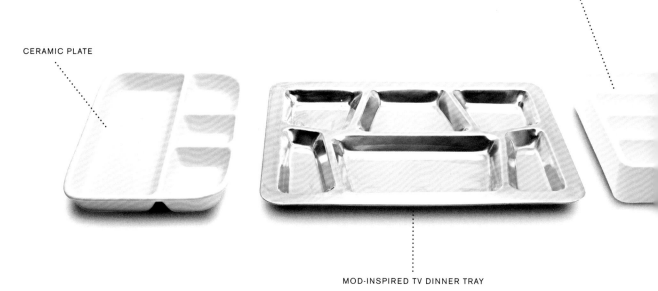

MOD-INSPIRED TV DINNER TRAY

YOU CAN USE MANY DIFFERENT
MATERIALS AS SURFACES FOR
THE CHEF'S TABLE.

WAXED BUTCHER PAPER

CUTTING BOARD

MARBLE SLAB

{THE CRUCIAL TOOTHPICK}

The toothpick has always been a functional presence at cocktail parties, but we think the standard version is far from ideal. We use double-pronged bamboo picks, which are sold by many kitchen supply stores, because they make it difficult for the finished bite to slide off—a bite that's sometimes slippery and hard to stab. The two prongs pull apart but act like a fork, squeezing and skewering the food.

Sticking the bamboo pick into a stack of ingredients is a precise move. It needs to go straight through to the silicone and catch each ingredient cleanly, so the chef needs to stab the finished bite with purpose and dead aim. Because the guests don't know when the bite is done, they get itchy trigger fingers and can't wait to grab the whole thing off the table. We tell them: *Wait for the toothpick. That's the signal.*

The idea of disposing of the toothpick doesn't feel like an afterthought, either. We place elegant rubber vases on the table that don't detract from the experience. Guests can toss their picks easily and cleanly into the unobtrusive receptacle and wait with clean hands and eager eyes for the next round.

{BUILDING A CHEF'S TABLE BITE}

A Chef's Table dish needs to look simple but its flavors need to surprise. It's a one-bite magic trick that makes the guest say, "Wow, I didn't think it was going to taste like that!"

It took us a little bit of tweaking to work out the kinks and make these dishes seem so effortless. The silicone "cloth" soaks up certain colors and textures, as we learned when early efforts with beets and balsamic syrup left us with stains and stickiness. So we steer away from certain ingredients. We also realized that the composition of the bite is a delicate balancing act. Each layer has a structural purpose beyond its place in the flavor profile, and after a few tries, we've got it down to a science.

The first layer of food is the all-important foundation, anchoring the entire stack as it travels from table to mouth, but it can't look like an obvious base. Each piece needs to feel organic. Maybe it's an apple slice, a celery spear, or a meltingly tender piece of gnocchi; whatever it is, it needs to be firm enough to stay in place, but not too heavy to slide off the toothpick as the guest grabs the bite.

The compositions are free from the concerns of serving traditional canapés, where trays need to be prepped and portions need to be clean enough that guests can grab them with their fingers. It's a beautiful moment: Each individual guest gets a single bite curated by the chef especially for them. Every piece is slightly different but perfectly seasoned, giving the guest the feeling of personalized attention.

{ FLAVOR ANATOMY DIAGRAM }

Both the food and the design of the Chef's Table are exercises in high contrast: crunchy paired with smooth, salty with sweet, glossy against matte, scattered ingredients on a streamlined surface. It's a dance for the eyes and the palate.

The recipes in this chapter exemplify the Chef's Table philosophy of bringing together contrasting tastes and textures. The sheep's-milk ricotta recipe, as diagrammed here, is a prime example of how we build our bites for maximum impact. Use this template as a springboard for your own surprising and tasty combinations.

CREAMY | RICOTTA

BITTER | OREGANO & THYME

SWEET | ORANGE

AROMATIC | HONEY

CRUNCHY | CELERY

Whipped Ricotta with Orange Slices and Truffle Honey

As shown opposite, this bite brings together a bunch of contrasting—but pleasing—flavors and textures. It's a great, simple way to try out the Chef's Table.

YIELD: Serves 12
SPECIAL EQUIPMENT: pastry bag with large round piping tip, silicone tabletop or mat, bamboo toothpicks

For the whipped ricotta:
1 cup (250 g) sheep's-milk ricotta or fresh ricotta
3 tablespoons whole or reduced-fat milk

For the orange slices:
2 oranges

To assemble:
3 celery ribs, sliced on the bias about ⅛ inch (3 mm) thick
¼ cup (60 ml) truffle honey
Leaves from 12 sprigs fresh thyme, roughly chopped
Leaves from 12 sprigs fresh oregano, roughly chopped
Maldon sea salt
Black peppercorns in a pepper mill

Make the whipped ricotta: In a stand mixer fitted with the paddle attachment, whip the ricotta and milk together until frothy. Scrape the ricotta into a pastry bag fitted with a large round piping tip and set aside at room temperature.

Make the orange slices: Before guests arrive, cut the peels off each orange with a sharp paring knife, then slice each orange into ⅛-inch-thick (3-mm-thick) rounds, removing any seeds. Cut each slice into irregularly shaped pieces about the size of a quarter.

Assemble and serve: Randomly lay pieces of celery on the silicone table or mat, place the orange slices on top, then pipe bite-size portions of ricotta onto the orange slices. Drizzle with truffle honey, sprinkle with the thyme and oregano, and sprinkle with salt and pepper. Stab with bamboo picks to serve.

MAKE-AHEAD/STORAGE

The orange slices can be made up to 1 day in advance; store in an airtight container in the refrigerator until ready to use. The whipped ricotta can be made up to 1 hour in advance; store in the piping bag at room temperature until ready to use. The celery can be cut and the herbs can be chopped up to 2 hours in advance.

Diver Scallop Cruda with Kimchi and Apple

The key to this dish is the ginger puree, unexpectedly neutral in flavor but creamy in texture. It picks up the aromas from the lime and shiso, and salt from the scallop.

YIELD: Serves 12
SPECIAL EQUIPMENT: 2-inch (5-cm) paintbrush or silicone basting brush, silicone tabletop or mat, bamboo toothpicks

For the kimchi gastrique:
1 cup (150 g) cabbage kimchi (we like Mother-in-Law's kimchi)
½ cup (120 ml) light corn syrup

For the ginger puree:
1 cup (240 ml) vegetable oil
2½ tablespoons grated peeled fresh ginger, plus 1 (1-inch/2.5-cm) piece fresh ginger, peeled and sliced ⅛ inch (3 mm) thick
½ teaspoon coriander seeds
½ teaspoon coarsely crushed star anise

To assemble:
1 Fuji apple, cored, sliced ¼ inch (6 mm) thick, and sprinkled with lemon juice
3 shiso leaves
3 large fresh diver scallops, at least 2 inches (5 cm) thick, each sliced crosswise into 4 thin rounds
1 lime
Maldon sea salt
Black peppercorns in a pepper mill

Make the kimchi gastrique: In a blender or a food processor, puree the kimchi and corn syrup until smooth, then pour the liquid into a small heavy-bottomed saucepan. Bring to a boil and cook until thickened to the consistency of ketchup. Let cool to room temperature before serving.

Make the ginger puree: In a small heavy-bottomed saucepan, combine the oil, grated ginger, coriander, and star anise and heat over medium-low heat until the spices start to release their aromas. Be careful not to overheat the oil.

Remove from the heat, cover, and let steep for 30 minutes.

In a small saucepan, bring 1 cup (240 ml) water to a boil. Add the sliced ginger and cook for 5 minutes, then drain the ginger and discard the water. Repeat six times with fresh water. Drain the ginger.

Strain the steeped oil through a fine-mesh sieve into a blender. Add the blanched ginger and puree until smooth. Let cool to room temperature.

Assemble and serve: Paint a 6-inch (15-cm) line of gastrique on the silicone table with the paintbrush. Place the apple slices on the gastrique, then rip small pieces of shiso from the leaves and place them on top of the apples. Layer a raw scallop slice onto each piece of apple.

Generously spoon ginger puree over the scallop, then use a Microplane to zest lime over the puree.

Sprinkle with salt and pepper, then stab the scallop bites with bamboo picks to serve.

MAKE-AHEAD/STORAGE
The ginger puree and the kimchi gastrique can be made up to 2 weeks in advance and stored in airtight containers in the refrigerator. Bring to room temperature before serving.

Beet Gnocchi with Butternut Squash and Chestnut Honey

We stumbled upon this Chef's Table dish by accident when a vegetarian guest was added to one of our tastings at the last minute. Bob ran into the walk-in refrigerator and grabbed some gnocchi on its way to another party, along with some roasted butternut squash, and this addictive combination was born. We added chestnut honey, which we'd discovered thanks to our friend, chef Cesare Casella, and the only question we heard that night was, "Is honey vegetarian?"

YIELD: Serves 12
SPECIAL EQUIPMENT: ricer or food mill, silicone tabletop or mat, bamboo toothpicks

For the beet gnocchi:
1 medium beet
2 pounds (910 g) Yukon Gold potatoes, scrubbed
1 large egg
Heaping ½ cup (about 60 g) finely grated Parmigiano-Reggiano cheese
2½ cups (375 g) all-purpose flour, plus more as needed
Kosher salt

For the butternut squash sauce:
1 cup (140 g) cubed butternut squash
1 small carrot, peeled and roughly chopped (about ½ cup/115 g)
1 (2-inch/5-cm) piece Parmigiano-Reggiano rind
3 cups (720 ml) water
Kosher salt

To assemble:
¾ cup (180 ml) chestnut honey
¼ cup (2.5 g) freeze-dried green peas, ground to a powder in a food processor
Extra-virgin olive oil in a squeeze bottle
Maldon sea salt
Black peppercorns in a pepper mill

Make the beet gnocchi: Preheat the oven to 400°F (205°C).

Wrap the beet in foil and roast for 45 minutes to 1 hour, until the beet is tender and cooked through. Carefully remove the foil (watch out for escaping hot steam) and let cool slightly. When cool enough to handle, rub the beet with a paper towel to remove the skin.

Coarsely chop the beet and puree in a blender or food processor until smooth. Reserve in a large bowl.

While the beet is roasting, place the potatoes in a large stockpot with enough water to cover the potatoes by 1 inch (2.5 cm). Bring to a boil and cook until the potatoes are tender, about 10 minutes.

Drain the potatoes and peel as soon as they're cool enough to handle. While they are still warm, run the peeled potatoes through a ricer or a food mill fitted with the fine disc into the bowl with the beets.

Add the egg to the beets and potatoes and mix with a wooden spoon.

Add the cheese, flour, and a pinch of salt and mix with your hands until the dough is semi-dry, like cookie dough. Roll a small piece into a ball to test whether or not it will keep its shape; you may need to add more flour if the consistency is too moist.

On a lightly floured work surface, divide the dough into 6 or 7 pieces. Use the palms of your hands to roll each piece into ¾-inch (2-cm) logs. Cut the logs into 1-inch (2.5-cm) pieces and set aside on a rimmed baking sheet until ready to serve.

Make the butternut squash sauce: Place the butternut squash, carrot, cheese rind, and water in a 2- or 3-quart (2- or 2.8-L) stockpot. Bring to a simmer over medium heat and cook for about 30 minutes, until the vegetables are tender.

Remove the cheese rind and pour the vegetables and broth into a blender. Puree until smooth, and season with salt to taste.

Assemble and serve: Bring a large pot of water to a boil. Immediately before serving, add the beet gnocchi, working in batches if necessary, and cook until they float, about 2 minutes. Drain the gnocchi.

Using a spoon, spread a generous scoop of butternut squash sauce across the silicone table or mat. Place the beet gnocchi on top of the sauce, and generously drizzle honey over the gnocchi.

Liberally sprinkle the gnocchi with the green pea powder, then squirt oil on top. Season with salt and pepper.

Stab the gnocchi with bamboo picks to serve.

MAKE-AHEAD/STORAGE
The beet gnocchi can be formed up to 2 days in advance; store on a baking sheet, loosely covered with a towel, at room temperature if cooking the same day they're formed, or freeze on a waxed paper–lined baking sheet for about 1 hour until completely frozen, then transfer to an airtight container and store in the freezer until ready to boil. The butternut squash sauce can be made up to 1 day in advance; store in an airtight container in the refrigerator until ready to use and reheat before serving.

Warm Mozzarella Caprese

Mozzarella and tomato: It's the peanut butter and jelly of Italy. But this bite turns a familiar cold combo into something unexpected by warming things up. Just barely heated mozzarella still containing its whey is paired with butter-smooth tomato fondue for a seductive surprise.

YIELD: Serves 12
SPECIAL EQUIPMENT: silicone tabletop or mat, bamboo toothpicks

For the tomato fondue:
5 tablespoons (75 g) unsalted butter
2 cloves garlic, smashed
1 cup (240 g) canned whole peeled tomatoes, crushed by hand
Kosher salt and freshly ground black pepper

For the fried capers:
Vegetable oil
20 capers, drained and patted dry

To assemble:
1 ball fresh mozzarella, roughly cut into 1-inch (2.5-cm) cubes
1 lemon
Extra-virgin olive oil in a squeeze bottle
Maldon sea salt
Black peppercorns in a pepper mill
6 fresh basil leaves

Make the tomato fondue: Melt 1 tablespoon of the butter in a small heavy-bottomed skillet over low heat. Add the garlic and slowly cook until the cloves are almost brown and someone in the house says, "What smells so good?"

Stir in the tomatoes and continue to cook slowly over low heat for 5 to 10 minutes more.

Scrape the tomatoes and garlic into a blender and add the remaining 4 tablespoons (60 g) butter. Puree until smooth and season with salt and pepper.

Make the fried capers: Line a plate with paper towels.

Add enough oil to a high-sided, heavy-bottomed saucepan to reach ½ inch (12 mm) up the sides of the pan. Heat over medium heat until a caper dropped into the oil sizzles. Add the remaining capers and fry until crispy.

Remove from the oil with a metal skimmer or strainer and drain on the paper towel–lined plate.

Assemble and serve: Heat the oven to 350°F (175°C).

Using a spoon, spread a generous scoop of tomato fondue across the silicone table or mat.

Place the mozzarella in a baking dish and warm it in the oven just until it starts to glisten—remove it from the oven before it melts. It should retain all of its delicious water. Place the warmed cubes of mozzarella on top of the fondue.

Crush the fried capers with your fingers and sprinkle over the mozzarella. Use a Microplane to zest lemon over the mozzarella, then squirt oil on top. Season with salt and pepper.

Rip the basil leaves in half and place a piece of basil on each piece of mozzarella. Stab with bamboo picks to serve.

MAKE-AHEAD/STORAGE
The tomato fondue can be made up to 1 week in advance; store in an airtight container in the refrigerator until ready to use and reheat before serving. The fried capers can be made up to 2 days in advance and stored in an airtight container at room temperature.

New York Strip Steak with Triple-Poached Garlic Cream

Because we're human, we love the taste of garlic. And because we're in the catering business, we're always coming up with ways to include garlic flavor without it being overwhelming for the guest. In this recipe, we poach the garlic three times, changing the water each time. The garlic taste is so smooth and rich that you will have no issues being a "close talker."

YIELD: Serves 12

SPECIAL EQUIPMENT: meat thermometer, silicone tabletop or mat, bamboo toothpicks

For the triple-poached garlic cream:
6 large cloves garlic
1 cup (240 ml) heavy cream
1 bunch fresh spinach, stem ends trimmed
Kosher salt

For the parsnip pickles:
¼ cup (60 ml) unseasoned rice vinegar
2 tablespoons granulated sugar
1 teaspoon kosher salt
Pinch of red pepper flakes
2 parsnips, sliced crosswise ¼ inch (6 mm) thick

For the New York strip steak:
1 pound (455 g) New York strip steak
Kosher salt and freshly ground black pepper
Red pepper flakes

To assemble:
Maldon sea salt
Black peppercorns in a pepper mill
Microgreens (optional)
Balsamic syrup (optional)

Make the triple-poached garlic cream: In a small saucepan, bring 2 cups (480 ml) water to a boil and add the garlic cloves. Cook for 5 minutes, then drain the garlic in a fine-mesh sieve, discarding the water. Repeat two more times with fresh water. Drain the garlic.

In a separate saucepan, bring the cream to a boil, then stir in the poached garlic and the spinach and cook for about 2 minutes, until the spinach wilts and absorbs the cream.

Transfer the creamed spinach and garlic to a blender and puree to a deep green. Season with salt. Transfer to a covered container and refrigerate if not serving immediately.

Make the parsnip pickles: In a medium bowl, whisk together the vinegar, sugar, salt, and red pepper flakes until the sugar and salt have dissolved.

Add the sliced parsnips and marinate for at least 1 hour at room temperature or up to 3 days in the refrigerator.

Make the New York strip steak: Season both sides of the steak liberally with salt, pepper, and red pepper flakes.

Heat a cast-iron or other heavy-bottomed skillet over high heat. Add the steak and sear on both sides, flipping as needed, until the steak is cooked to medium-rare and a thermometer inserted into the steak registers an internal temperature of 140°F (60°C).

Let the steak rest for 5 minutes before slicing it into twelve 1½-inch (4-cm) cubes. Assemble the dish immediately while the steak is still warm.

Assemble and serve: Reheat the garlic cream, if necessary. Drain the parsnip pickles, discarding the pickling liquid.

Spoon the garlic cream onto the silicone table or mat. Drop a piece of steak on the garlic cream. Sprinkle salt and grind pepper over the steak, top with a parsnip pickle and microgreens, and drizzle with balsamic syrup, if desired.

Stab the steak bites with bamboo picks to serve.

MAKE-AHEAD/STORAGE
The garlic cream and parsnip pickles can be made up to 3 days in advance; store each component separately in an airtight container in the refrigerator until ready to use. Reheat the cream before serving and bring the pickles to room temperature.

Shrimp and Grits

Though you might think you know your friends well, it's sometimes hard to remember who's keeping kosher, who's a pescatarian, who's dairy-free, and so on. Pork and seafood are two often-dicey menu items at parties, given varying tastes and dietary restrictions. Here, we're obvious about what we're serving, so the guests can identify the sausage or the shrimp and see exactly what they are getting before grabbing the bite.

YIELD: Serves 12
SPECIAL EQUIPMENT: silicone tabletop or mat, bamboo toothpicks

For the roasted onion:
½ small onion

For the seared cotecchino:
12 (½-inch-thick/12-mm-thick) slices
    cotecchino sausage

For the stone-ground grits
2 cups (480 ml) water
Kosher salt
3 tablespoons stone-ground grits (preferably
    Anson Mills)
Freshly ground black pepper

To assemble:
12 large (31–40 count) tiger shrimp, peeled
    and deveined
1 tablespoon smoked paprika
1 tablespoon vegetable oil
Maldon sea salt
Black peppercorns in a pepper mill
1 tablespoon finely sliced chives

Make the roasted onion: Heat a grill or griddle over medium-low heat. Place the onion, cut side down, on the grill or griddle and let it cook for about 20 minutes; the cut side will burn, but the onion will slowly steam through to cook completely.

Remove the onion from the grill and rub off the black char with a paper towel or kitchen towel. Separate the layers of the onion and cut them into roughly 1-inch (2.5-cm) pieces. Transfer to a bowl and refrigerate if not serving immediately.

Make the seared cotecchino: Line a plate with paper towels.

In a small saucepan, bring 3 cups (720 ml) water to a boil and add the cotecchino slices. Cook for 5 minutes, or until the sausage is just cooked through.

Drain the cotecchino and set aside on the paper towel–lined plate, at room temperature or refrigerated if not serving immediately.

In a sauté pan over high heat, sear the cotecchino until crispy on both sides, about 2 minutes total. Transfer to paper towels and reserve.

Make the stone-ground grits: In a 1-quart (960-ml) saucepan, bring the water and a large pinch of salt to a boil over medium heat.

Whisk in the grits and reduce the heat to maintain a very low simmer. Cook for about 10 minutes, until the grits have absorbed most of the water and have the consistency of a cream soup. The grits should still pour like a sauce, since they will continue to thicken once removed from the heat. Season with salt and pepper and reserve at room temperature in the saucepan.

Assemble and serve: In a small bowl, toss the shrimp and paprika together—don't worry if the shrimp look overly coated in the spice.

Line a plate with paper towels.

In a large skillet or sauté pan, heat the oil over high heat and add the shrimp. Make sure not to crowd the pan, so the shrimp will take on caramelized color instead of steaming. Cook for 1 minute, then flip the shrimp and cook for 1 minute more. Remove the shrimp from the pan and place on the paper towel–lined plate.

Place the shrimp randomly across the silicone table or mat and spoon some of the grits over each piece of shrimp.

Lay a piece of onion over the grits, season with salt and pepper, sprinkle with the chives, and top with a slice of the cotecchino. Stab with bamboo picks to serve.

MAKE-AHEAD/STORAGE

The roasted onion can be made and the cotecchino can be poached up to 1 day in advance; store each component separately in an airtight container in the refrigerator until ready to use. Bring to room temperature before assembling and serving.

Carrot Cake with Cream Cheese Frosting

We are big fans of vegetables used in dessert, like eggplant tatin or parsnip puree sweetening a cake. Carrot cake is so mainstream that it's not even considered to be in the vegetable realm, but by spooning bright-orange carrots on top of each bite, we dramatically (and deliciously) remind diners what they are eating.

YIELD: Serves 12
SPECIAL EQUIPMENT: pastry bag with large round piping tip, silicone tabletop or mat, bamboo toothpicks

For the carrot cake:

1 tablespoon unsalted butter
2 tablespoons plus 1½ heaping cups (about 325 g) granulated sugar
1⅝ cups (185 g) all-purpose flour
1 teaspoon ground cinnamon
½ teaspoon baking powder
½ teaspoon baking soda
½ teaspoon salt
3 large eggs
½ cup (120 ml) vegetable oil
1 vanilla bean
1 pound (455 g) carrots, grated

For the cream cheese frosting:

⅔ cup (5 ounces/150 g) cream cheese, softened
2 tablespoons unsalted butter, softened
½ teaspoon vanilla extract
1 cup (100 g) confectioners' sugar

For the carrots in syrup:

2 medium carrots, cut into ¼-inch (6-mm) cubes
½ cup (100 g) granulated sugar
½ cup (120 ml) water

For the crystallized walnuts:

½ cup (50 g) raw walnut halves
¼ cup (55 g) packed light brown sugar

Make the carrot cake: Preheat the oven to 350°F (175°C). Butter the bottom and sides of a 9-inch (23-cm) square baking pan, then dust with the 2 tablespoons granulated sugar.

In a medium bowl, whisk together the flour, cinnamon, baking powder, baking soda, and salt. Set aside.

In the bowl of a stand mixer fitted with the paddle attachment, combine the eggs, oil, and remaining 1½ heaping cups (325 g) sugar and beat together for about 3 minutes, until the batter is pale and thickened and forms a ribbon when the paddle is lifted from the bowl.

Halve the vanilla bean lengthwise and scrape out the seeds. Add the seeds to the batter and beat for 15 seconds more.

Reduce the mixer speed to low and add the dry ingredients in two or three batches. Using a silicone spatula, gently fold in the grated carrots.

Pour the batter into the prepared baking pan and bake for 25 to 30 minutes, until a toothpick inserted into the center of the cake comes out clean.

Let cool in the pan on a wire rack for 10 minutes, then turn the cake out of the pan onto the rack and let cool to room temperature. Cut into 1-inch (2.5-cm) cubes and set aside.

Make the cream cheese frosting: In the bowl of a stand mixer fitted with the paddle attachment, beat the cream cheese and butter together for about 3 minutes, until light and fluffy.

Add the vanilla extract and beat for 15 seconds more to combine.

Reduce the mixer speed to low and add the confectioners' sugar in two or three batches, beating until smooth after each addition.

Spoon the frosting into a large pastry bag fitted with a large round piping tip. Refrigerate if not serving immediately.

Make the carrots in syrup: Combine all the ingredients in a 2-quart (2-L) sauté pan or skillet. Cook over medium-low heat, stirring, until the sugar has dissolved, then continue to cook slowly until the carrots are very tender. Remove half of the carrots and syrup and puree in a blender. Refrigerate if not serving immediately.

Make the crystallized walnuts: Line a rimmed baking sheet with parchment paper or waxed paper.

In a medium high-sided saucepan, stir the walnuts and brown sugar together. Heat over medium heat for 5 to 7 minutes, until the sugar melts and coats the nuts evenly. Watch closely to make sure the sugar doesn't burn—it can happen quickly.

Pour the nuts out onto the prepared baking sheet and let cool to room temperature before breaking into individual pieces.

Assemble and serve: Bring the cream cheese frosting and carrots in syrup to room temperature. Spoon the carrot puree onto a silicone table and drag the back of the spoon through the sauce. Place the carrot cake cubes in the carrot puree. Pipe dots of cream cheese frosting onto each cube and spoon carrots in syrup over the frosting.

Garnish each cube with a crystallized walnut piece or two, and stab with bamboo picks to serve.

MAKE-AHEAD/STORAGE

The carrot cake, frosting, carrot puree, carrots in syrup, and crystallized walnuts all can be made up to 2 days in advance; store the cake and walnuts in separate airtight containers at room temperature, and store the frosting and carrots in separate airtight containers in the refrigerator until ready to use. Bring the chilled ingredients to room temperature before serving.

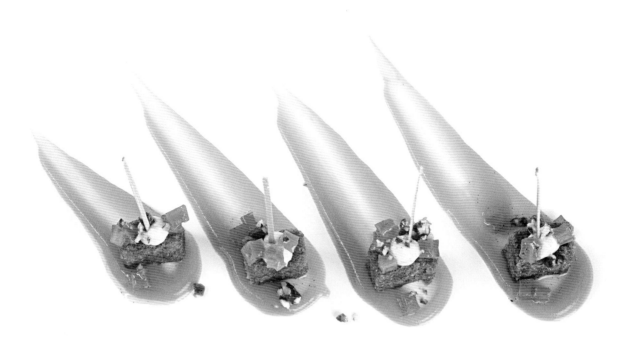

S'mores

Making s'mores is a perennially popular campfire activity, but the ingredients really do make a good threesome no matter where you're eating them. This bite will remind your guests of pleasant memories of camp and family outings, but with a smaller stick and no smoke in their eyes.

YIELD: Serves 12
SPECIAL EQUIPMENT: candy thermometer, silicone tabletop or mat, kitchen/crème brûlée torch, bamboo picks

For the marshmallows:
Vegetable shortening, for the pan
Cornstarch, for dusting
1 sheet leaf gelatin
2 tablespoons granulated sugar
1 tablespoon light corn syrup
2 tablespoons water
2 large egg whites

For the chocolate sauce:
½ cup (100 g) plus 5 teaspoons granulated sugar
½ cup (120 ml) water
⅓ cup (30 g) unsweetened cocoa powder
3 tablespoons finely chopped dark chocolate (64 percent)

To assemble:
6 graham crackers, crumbled coarsely by hand

Make the marshmallows: Grease the sides and bottom of an 8-inch (20-cm) square baking pan with shortening and dust with cornstarch. Tap out the excess cornstarch.

Place the gelatin sheet in a small, wide bowl and add enough cold water to cover. Set aside to soften.

In a small, deep saucepan, combine the sugar, corn syrup, and water and heat over medium heat until the sugar has dissolved. Clip a candy thermometer to the side of the pan. Bring the mixture to a boil, without stirring, and continue to cook, watching carefully, until it registers 285°F (140°C) on the thermometer. Do not allow the mixture to burn. Remove from the heat.

Using a hand mixer or stand mixer fitted with the whisk attachment, beat the egg whites until medium peaks form.

When the gelatin has softened, remove it from the water, wring it out, and add it to the egg whites. Whisk on low speed until the gelatin is incorporated, then, with the mixer running, carefully drizzle the sugar syrup into the bowl.

Raise the mixer speed to medium-high and beat for 3 to 5 minutes more, until the mixture expands and becomes opaque, white, and shiny.

Pour the marshmallow mixture into the prepared baking pan and smooth it with a silicone spatula to form an even layer. Dust the top of the marshmallow lightly with cornstarch and set aside at room temperature for 8 hours to set.

Make the chocolate sauce: In a small, heavy-bottomed saucepan, combine the sugar and water and heat over medium heat until the sugar has dissolved and the mixture comes to a boil.

Stir in the cocoa powder until incorporated, then add the chocolate and boil for 3 minutes. If not serving immediately, transfer to a covered container and refrigerate.

Assemble and serve: Reheat the chocolate sauce in a small saucepan, if necessary.

Cut the marshmallows into 1-inch (2.5-cm) cubes and char them lightly with a crème brûlée torch.

Spoon warm chocolate sauce across the silicone table or mat, then dot with the marshmallows. Sprinkle each marshmallow with graham cracker crumbs.

Stab the marshmallows with bamboo picks to serve.

MAKE-AHEAD/STORAGE
The marshmallows and chocolate sauce can be made up to 2 days in advance. Store the marshmallows in an airtight container at room temperature until ready to use, and store the chocolate sauce in an airtight container in the refrigerator until ready to use. Reheat the chocolate sauce before assembling and serving.

SMALL PLATES

....

PASSED, SHARED, AND PAIRED

When you imagine the food options at a typical cocktail party, no doubt you're thinking of a few hors d'oeuvres. You're usually not imagining miniaturized versions of full meals brought your way.

Serving small plates avoids the formality, effort, and cost of an all-out buffet or sit-down dinner, but still gives partygoers a little more substance and belly-filling satisfaction than one-bite appetizers. It's a pleasant surprise for those who've spent many a cocktail hour trying to make a meal out of a bunch of little bites, and it's a great way for hosts to plan a food budget in advance. You don't have to worry about second helpings, sneaky guests who hover around appetizer trays, or constant buffet replenishment—if you're hosting a shindig for twenty-five people, you know exactly how many plates you'll need to make.

This is also a place to let your creativity shine. Almost any of your favorite dishes can become a small plate at your next cocktail party, instantly transforming a go-to recipe into a stellar addition to your party repertoire.

You really can make almost any of your favorite dishes into a small plate, as long as you remember one simple rule: It needs to be fork-friendly. (And salad-fork-friendly at that; we use smaller forks with short handles for these plates so they don't extend too far off the plate.)

Most of our small plates contain no more than four components per dish—a spoonful of a starchy base or vegetables, like risotto or sautéed cucumbers, then slices of protein in bite-size pieces, then a sauce, and maybe a garnish on top. Everything can be easily stabbed or scooped with a fork, and there's nothing that's going to fall or drip off the utensil onto the floor.

So feel free to play around with your tried-and-true recipes, and think outside the box. Substitute spaghetti noodles with fork-friendly gnocchi and serve with pesto; replace peas with one-inch lengths of green beans in a deconstructed casserole.

In the pages that follow, we'll serve up tips and tricks for shrinking down a whole meal into an appetizer-ready plate in three slightly different forms: passed plates, shared plates, and paired plates.

SMALL PLATES SUCH AS THESE RICH SLICES OF SASHIMI OVER FLAVORFUL GRAINS (SEE PAGE 178) KEEP PARTY GUESTS FULL WITHOUT A SIT-DOWN DINNER.

{PASSED PLATES}

At our parties, passed plates are a foolproof way to make sure everyone has something substantial to eat. We use them as a defensive buffer during the transition from one-bite hors d'oeuvres into more filling stationary food, sending waiters with passed plates to intercept guests making beelines toward the buffets. It helps them relax when they realize they are being taken care of—and that there is plenty of food. We also use passed plates to put a "period" on hors-d'oeuvres passing, signaling the end of one-biters and the beginning of the next phase of the party.

Like the succession of plates that are whisked onto your table at a tapas bar, passed plates seem to arrive on the fly. The key to passing plates is to sweep the room, completely canvassing it to be sure everyone who wants a plate gets one. If you're not ready to balance plates on your arms like a circus act, it's fun to find a vintage bar cart and serve your guests airplane-style.

We usually serve two or three passed plates over the course of an evening, starting with vegetarian fare and moving to more carnivorous dishes. This is a matter of food expense: For the first round, nearly everyone grabs a plate, but by the third round, only half as many people accept. Because of this it's better to serve these plates as flights, one after the next, instead of all at once, so guests will feel there's an abundance of food and like they have a choice, even though you're carefully controlling the portions and food expense.

Though guests at our cocktail parties hungrily embraced the idea of passed small plates when we first introduced the idea, we had to grapple with the issue that the guests needed an extra hand to eat them. Since everyone at cocktail parties is standing, not seated at a table with a full complement of silverware, the larger serving of food that needed to be forked up meant that many of our early passed-plate guinea pigs were getting rid of their drinks to manage the food, or abandoning the plate entirely.

Either we'd need to invent a third hand for all our guests or we'd have to come up with another solution. Of course we went forth and designed a plate with a custom ridge on the underside that fits snugly on top of our glassware— no balancing act necessary. This little adaptation opened up a whole new world of passed plates at Pinch and made our guests giddy. They got to keep their drinks and avoided all the awkwardness of a potential mess.

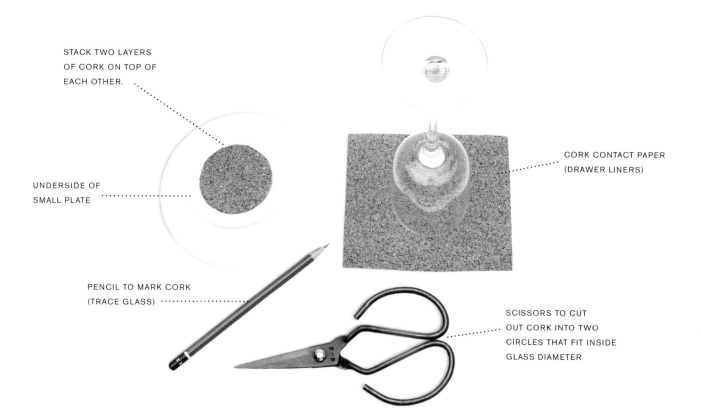

STACK TWO LAYERS
OF CORK ON TOP OF
EACH OTHER.

UNDERSIDE OF
SMALL PLATE

CORK CONTACT PAPER
(DRAWER LINERS)

PENCIL TO MARK CORK
(TRACE GLASS)

SCISSORS TO CUT
OUT CORK INTO TWO
CIRCLES THAT FIT INSIDE
GLASS DIAMETER

DIY

TO MAKE YOUR OWN VERSION OF THE PINCH PASSED
PLATE, GRAB A SHEET OR ROLL OF ADHESIVE CORK
CONTACT PAPER, A SMALL PLATE, A WINEGLASS
(REAL OR DISPOSABLE–YOUR CHOICE!), A PAIR OF
SCISSORS, AND A PENCIL. TRACE THE OUTLINE OF
THE GLASS TWO TIMES ONTO THE CORK PAPER. CUT
ALONG THE INSIDE OF THE TRACED LINE TO MAKE TWO
CIRCLES, THEN TRIM THEM AS NEEDED SO EACH CORK
CIRCLE FITS SNUGLY INSIDE THE RIM OF THE WINE
GLASS. USING THE SELF-ADHESIVE SIDE OF THE CORK
PAPER, PLACE THE TWO CIRCLES, ONE ON TOP OF THE
OTHER, CENTERED ON THE UNDERSIDE OF THE PLATE.
THE PLATE CAN THEN BALANCE SAFELY ON TOP OF THE
WINE GLASS.

TOO MUCH? IT'S NOT A COP-OUT IF YOU WANT TO
BUY A PREMADE VERSION; THERE ARE A NUMBER OF
DISHWARE DESIGNERS OUT THERE WITH SIMILAR
CONCEPTS LIKE HOOK CLAMPS AND ARTIST'S
PALETTES THAT ALLOW YOUR GLASSWARE TO "HOOK"
ONTO THE SIDE OF THE PLATE.

WITH JUST A FEW SUPPLIES,
YOU CAN CREATE A DIY
PINCH PASSED PLATE THAT
ALLOWS YOUR GUESTS TO
HOLD ON TO THEIR WINE
GLASSES WHILE EATING
WITH A FORK.

Skate Schnitzel with Spaetzle and Lemon-Caper Butter Sauce

In this recipe, we take the unique texture of skate wings and use them in a classic comfort food preparation usually reserved for veal. Topped with decadent lemon-caper butter sauce and paired with homemade noodles, just a little bit of this dish will fill your guests up and make them smile.

To form the spaetzle, you can use a spaetzle press or board specifically designed for the job, or use a large-holed colander that can rest over the stockpot without touching the water. The key to the sauce is to keep the lemon juice tasting raw, not cooked. And once the sauce cools, it will separate, so it's best to make the sauce last, just before you're ready to serve the dish. It should be warm, but not hot.

YIELD: Serves 12
SPECIAL EQUIPMENT: spaetzle press/board

For the spaetzle:
2 cups (250 g) all-purpose flour
2 teaspoons kosher salt
1 teaspoon freshly ground black pepper
½ teaspoon freshly grated nutmeg
3 large eggs
3 large egg yolks
2 tablespoons unsalted butter, melted,
    plus 2 tablespoons unsalted butter,
    at room temperature
3 tablespoons whole milk

For the skate schnitzel:
½ cup (65 g) all-purpose flour
4 large eggs, lightly beaten
1 cup (100 g) panko bread crumbs
8 (2- to 3-ounce/55- to 85-g) pieces of skate
1 teaspoon kosher salt
½ teaspoon freshly ground black pepper
3 tablespoons canola oil
3 tablespoons unsalted butter

For the lemon-caper butter sauce:
Zest and juice of 2 lemons
1 cup (230 g) chilled unsalted butter, cut into ½-inch
    (12-mm) cubes
½ cup (90 g) caper berries, thinly sliced
2 tablespoons minced fresh chives
½ teaspoon Maldon sea salt

Make the spaetzle: In the bowl of a stand mixer fitted with the paddle attachment, combine the flour, 1 teaspoon salt, the pepper, and nutmeg. Add the eggs and egg yolks and mix on low speed until a shaggy dough starts to form, then add the melted butter and milk and mix until a soft batter forms.

Lightly cover the bowl with a towel or plastic wrap. Let the batter rest for 30 minutes.

Bring a large stockpot of water to a boil.

In batches, scoop the batter into the spaetzle press or board, or into the bottom of a colander, and press through, cupping your hand below the press or colander to hold the strands together, so they are long once they hit the water. Gently stir the spaetzle with a spider or mesh strainer so they don't stick together as they cook; once they float, they are done.

Scoop the spaetzle into a large bowl and repeat until all the batter is used. Toss with the remaining butter and salt and reserve at room temperature.

Make the skate schnitzel: Set up a breading station by placing the flour, eggs, and panko in three separate wide, shallow bowls.

Season each side of each piece of skate lightly with salt and pepper.

Dredge the skate in the flour until the surface is completely dry, shaking lightly to tap off the excess, then coat the skate in the beaten egg. Toss the skate in the panko, but don't press the bread crumbs into the skate.

Heat the oil and butter in a large, high-sided saucepan over medium-high heat. Carefully add the fish to the hot pan in batches and cook until crisp on both sides.

Reserve at room temperature while you make the sauce.

Make the lemon-caper butter sauce: In a small saucepan, warm the lemon juice over very low heat, and add the butter a few cubes at a time, whisking constantly to keep the butter emulsified. Turn the flame off right before all of the butter is melted.

Stir in the lemon zest, caper berries, chives, and salt.

Keep the sauce in a warm spot if not serving immediately.

Assemble the dish: Place the buttered spaetzle in a small mound on each plate, then place the fish atop the spaetzle. Spoon the sauce over the fish and serve immediately.

MAKE-AHEAD/STORAGE

The fish can be prepared up to 1 day in advance: Place the breaded pieces on a waxed paper–lined rimmed baking sheet. Freeze on the baking sheet overnight, then defrost in the refrigerator for an hour until the skate pieces are pliable before cooking. Do not refrigerate overnight; refrigerating the pieces for more than 2 hours will make them sticky. The spaetzle can be prepared up to 3 hours in advance; keep warm in a covered dish and reheat before serving.

Fried Polenta with Wild Mushrooms, Brussels Sprouts, and Pesto

In this dish, we treat mushrooms like a protein, roasting them to seal in moisture so that they still taste earthy, then mixing their juices with olive oil and seasoning. You know you've got a good vegetarian dish when it's devoured by the most ardent carnivore who doesn't even realize the meat is missing.

YIELD: Serves 12

For the polenta:
4 cups (960 ml) water
1 tablespoon kosher salt
1 tablespoon extra-virgin olive oil
1 cup (160 g) stone-ground yellow cornmeal
1 tablespoon unsalted butter
3 tablespoons grated Parmigiano-Reggiano cheese

For the pesto:
2 cups (80 g) fresh basil leaves
¼ cup (25 g) toasted walnuts
2 tablespoons capers, rinsed and squeezed dry
1 large clove garlic
1 teaspoon kosher salt
½ cup (120 ml) extra-virgin olive oil, plus more as needed
¼ cup (25 g) grated Parmigiano-Reggiano cheese

For the wild mushrooms and Brussels sprouts:
1 pound (455 g) cremini mushrooms
½ pound (225 g) chanterelle mushrooms or other
  seasonal mushrooms
6 Brussels sprouts, trimmed and quartered
4 scallions, minced
¼ cup (60 ml) extra-virgin olive oil
2 teaspoons Maldon sea salt
1 teaspoon freshly ground black pepper

To assemble:
2 tablespoons olive oil

Make the polenta: In a 3- to 4-quart (2.8- to 3.8-L) stockpot, bring the water to a boil over medium heat. Add the salt and oil. Slowly sprinkle the cornmeal into the water, whisking constantly to make sure no lumps form. Reduce the heat to low halfway through to maintain a simmer so you don't get splashed; it hurts!

Cook the polenta for 45 minutes over low heat. (Ask any Italian: If you cook polenta for less than 45 minutes, it will taste raw!)

While the polenta cooks, grease a 9-by-13-inch (23-by-33-cm) baking dish with the butter.

Stir the cheese into the cooked polenta and pour it into the prepared dish. Cover and refrigerate for 2 hours, or until firm.

Make the pesto: In a blender or food processor, puree all the ingredients, adding more oil if needed and pulsing until combined.

Make the wild mushrooms and Brussels sprouts: Preheat the oven to 300°F (150°C).

Stem and halve the cremini mushrooms, and break, rip, or leave whole the other mushrooms so that they will be bite-size when cooked. In a large baking dish, toss the mushrooms, Brussels sprouts, and scallions with the oil, salt, and pepper.

Bake for about 15 minutes, stirring every 5 minutes or so, until the mushrooms and sprouts start to caramelize. Keep warm while you fry the polenta.

Assemble the dish: Cut the chilled polenta into 2-inch (5-cm) squares.

In a large skillet, heat the oil over medium heat until shimmering and add the polenta squares, in batches if necessary. Fry the polenta until golden brown, 2 to 3 minutes per side.

Place the polenta squares on plates. Scoop mushrooms and juice drippings on top of each square, then drizzle with pesto.

MAKE-AHEAD/STORAGE
The polenta can made and chilled up to 2 days in advance, then fried 1 hour before serving. The pesto can be made up to 3 days in advance and refrigerated. (To prevent the pesto from drastically darkening, pour a thin film of oil over the top to seal out air and slow oxidation.)

Magret Duck Breast with Chestnut Fried Rice and Demi-Glace Grapes

The duck and rice take the lead in this dish, but there's no mistaking the chestnut's flavor and texture. Cooking the grapes with the wine, which pairs raw and fermented tastes, creates a deep, well-rounded sauce.

YIELD: Serves 12

For the chestnut fried rice:
2 tablespoons vegetable oil

2 medium yellow onions, finely chopped

2 tablespoons finely chopped peeled fresh ginger

1 large clove garlic, minced

4 cups (600 g) cooked long-grain white rice

1 cup (140 g) peeled roasted chestnuts, roughly chopped

¼ cup (30 g) fresh or frozen fava beans, thawed if frozen and peeled if fresh

2 scallions, white and green parts, thinly sliced

Soy sauce

For the demi-glace grapes:
1 bunch red seedless grapes, stemmed

2 cups (480 ml) Zinfandel wine

1 cup (240 ml) duck or veal demi-glace

Kosher salt and freshly ground black pepper

For the Magret duck breast:
1 whole Magret duck breast

2 tablespoons kosher salt

1 tablespoon garam masala

1 teaspoon five-spice powder

Make the chestnut fried rice: In a wok or wide, high-sided sauté pan, heat the oil over high heat for a few seconds, then add the onions, ginger, and garlic. Cook for 1 minute to release the aromatics, then add the rice and cook, stirring frequently, until you hear popping sounds.

Stir in the chestnuts, fava beans, and scallions, then add soy sauce to taste. Remove from the heat but keep warm or reheat when ready to serve.

Make the demi-glace grapes: Heat a wide sauté pan over high heat for 2 minutes, then add the grapes in a single layer. Cook, stirring occasionally, until the grapes caramelize and almost split open.

Add the wine and reduce the heat to medium. Bring to a simmer and cook for about 20 minutes, until the wine and juice have reduced to a syrup.

Stir in the demi-glace until dissolved and season with salt and pepper. Keep warm or reheat when ready to serve.

Make the Magret duck breast: Trim excess fat from the duck breast, but retain the layer of fat on the top of the breast. Using a sharp paring knife, score this fat layer in a crisscross pattern.

In a small bowl, mix together the salt, garam masala, and five-spice powder, then liberally season the duck on both sides with the spice blend.

Heat a heavy skillet or sauté pan over high heat for 2 minutes, then reduce the heat to medium and add the duck, fat side down. Cook until the fat is crispy and golden brown, 8 to 10 minutes. Turn the breast over and brown again for 3 to 5 minutes. The duck should be served rare to medium-rare, or about 125°F (52°C) to 130°F (54°C) on a meat thermometer (if you desire more cooking, bake in a 350°F/175°C oven to your preferred degree of doneness). Remove from the pan and assemble the dish immediately.

Assemble the dish: Reheat the chestnut fried rice and the grapes, if necessary. Place a spoonful of fried rice on each dish, then slice the duck into forkable pieces and divide equally among the dishes. Spoon the grapes and sauce over the duck. Serve immediately.

MAKE-AHEAD/STORAGE
The fried rice and the grapes can be made up to 1 day in advance; store each component in an airtight container in the refrigerator until ready to use and reheat before assembling and serving. Because you'll want to serve the duck warm, it should be seared immediately before serving.

Double-Cut Rib Eye with Butternut "Risotto" and Pan Juice Bread

A true sign of a delicious sauce is when people want to soak up every last drop on the plate with some bread—even though this is a faux pas as far as table etiquette goes! That's the inspiration for this dish—but never fear, Emily Post; we toss bite-size pieces of bread into the meat juices to soak up the sauce for you. Another fun trick with this dish is that the risotto is not really risotto: It's flash-cooked finely grated butternut squash.

YIELD: Serves 8

For the butternut "risotto":
2 pounds (910 g) butternut squash, peeled and seeded
3 tablespoons unsalted butter
3 shallots, minced
4 cloves garlic, sliced
¼ cup (25 g) grated Parmigiano-Reggiano cheese
Kosher salt and freshly ground black pepper

For the rib eye and pan juice bread:
2 rib eye steaks, each 2 inches (5 cm) thick
Kosher salt and freshly ground black pepper
1 tablespoon unsalted butter
1 (8-inch/20-cm) piece of crusty baguette
¼ cup (15 g) roughly chopped fresh flat-leaf parsley
¼ cup (15 g) minced fresh chives

Make the butternut "risotto": Grate the butternut squash using the large holes of a box grater. Reserve 2 tablespoons of grated squash for assembly.

In a large sauté pan, melt the butter over medium-low heat, then add the shallots and garlic and cook for 3 to 5 minutes, until softened but not browned.

Add the squash and cook, stirring frequently, for 8 to 10 minutes, until the squash is tender and its texture resembles cooked rice.

Stir in the cheese and season with salt and pepper. Keep warm over very low heat until the steak is ready to serve.

Make the rib eye and pan juice bread: Preheat the oven to 400°F (205°C).

While the risotto cooks, generously season both sides of the rib eye steaks with salt and pepper.

Heat a large, ovenproof sauté pan or cast-iron skillet over high heat for 5 minutes, then add the steaks and butter. Sear on both sides until golden brown, 2 to 3 minutes per side, then carefully transfer the skillet to the oven and cook the steaks to your preferred degree of doneness (115°F/46°C for rare, 135°F/57°C for medium-rare).

Carefully remove the steaks from the oven and let rest in the pan for 5 minutes to allow the juices to redistribute and accumulate.

Set the oven to broil. Halve the baguette lengthwise and toast in the oven until very crispy, watching carefully to make sure it doesn't burn.

Pull, rip, and tear the bread into irregular bite-size pieces. Transfer the steaks to a cutting board and toss the bread in the pan juices, adding the parsley, chives, and salt and pepper to taste. Start assembling the dish immediately.

Assemble the dish: Slice the steak, against the grain, into 1½-inch (4-cm) rectangles, then thinly slice those rectangles into ⅛-inch-thick (3-mm-thick) pieces.

Scoop a spoonful of "risotto" onto each plate, then layer 4 to 6 slices of steak in a shingle effect over the risotto. Top with a spoonful of the bread and pan juices and a pinch of the reserved grated squash. Serve immediately.

MAKE-AHEAD/STORAGE
All components should be made and assembled just before you're planning to serve them.

Grilled Chicken with Orange Fregola, Truffle Honey, and Raw Herbs

This dish requires a perfectly cooked chicken breast: The minute the chicken turns from raw to cooked, it's done and shouldn't be cooked any longer, otherwise all the juices begin to escape. Fregola sarda, a round, toasted semolina pasta native to Sardinia, Italy, is a perfect textural accompaniment for the chicken. The raw herbs, honey, and oranges accent these mild but crowd-pleasing ingredients.

YIELD: Serves 12

For the grilled chicken:
¼ cup (60 g) plus 1 teaspoon kosher salt
2 boneless split chicken breasts, trimmed of excess fat (about 1¾ pounds/800 g total)
2 teaspoons extra-virgin olive oil
½ teaspoon freshly ground black pepper

For the fregola:
1 tablespoon kosher salt
1 pound (455 g) fregola sarda
2 oranges, peeled
1 tablespoon unsalted butter
1 teaspoon red pepper flakes
1½ teaspoons Maldon sea salt
1 teaspoon freshly ground black pepper

To assemble:
2 tablespoons roughly chopped fresh thyme leaves
2 tablespoons roughly chopped fresh oregano leaves
2 tablespoons truffle honey
Maldon sea salt

Make the grilled chicken: Heat 1 quart (960 ml) water in a 2-quart (2-L) saucepan over medium heat and add the ¼ cup (60 g) salt, stirring until dissolved to make a brine.

Transfer the brine to a large zip-top bag and refrigerate until cold (you may want to set it in a large bowl just in case of leaks!). Add the chicken to the brine and refrigerate for up to 6 hours.

Rinse the brined chicken and pat dry.

If grilling indoors, preheat the oven to 375°F (190°C) and heat a grill pan or cast-iron skillet over high heat for 4 to 5 minutes. If grilling outdoors, preheat a gas or electric grill for indirect heat.

Cut each chicken breast in half as if it were a cake you were cutting into two layers, and trim as needed to make two 1-inch-thick (2.5-cm-thick) rectangles out of each breast.

Rub the chicken pieces with oil and season with the remaining 1 teaspoon salt and the pepper. Grill the chicken on low heat until browned on all sides, and finish in the oven if necessary. The chicken is done when a meat thermometer inserted into the breast registers 165°F (74°C); rest the chicken on a cutting board for 5 minutes before serving.

Make the fregola: In a large stockpot, bring 2 quarts (2 L) water to a boil over medium-high heat, then add the salt. When it has dissolved, add the fregola. Cook for 12 minutes, or until al dente, then drain and reserve in the stockpot.

While the fregola cooks, use a serrated knife to slice the oranges into roughly ½-inch (12-mm) pieces. Include the pith so the orange pieces will stay whole.

Stir the oranges, butter, red pepper flakes, Maldon salt, and black pepper into the fregola.

Assemble the dish: Slice the chicken into forkable pieces. Spoon 3 to 4 tablespoons of fregola onto each plate, then top with 4 slices of chicken, a liberal sprinkling of herbs, a drizzle of truffle honey, and a sprinkling of salt. Serve immediately.

MAKE-AHEAD/STORAGE
The fregola can be cooked up to 1 day in advance, stored in an airtight container in the refrigerator, then warmed before adding the other ingredients and serving.

Pistachio Fallen Soufflé with Vanilla Bean Crème Anglaise

With late arrivals, gift-opening, and other delays sucking up precious minutes on a party timeline, it's virtually impossible to cater a hot soufflé to more than twenty people—or even to six guests. If your soufflé doesn't fall, you might pass out from a stress attack. Enter the fallen soufflé: perfect for any occasion. Light and airy, it's served at room temperature and couldn't care less if the bride takes forever to exclaim over her new towels.

YIELD: Serves 12

For the pistachio praline:
¼ cup (50 g) granulated sugar
1 tablespoon water
¼ cup (30 g) shelled pistachios

For the pistachio soufflé:
Nonstick baking spray
1 tablespoon plus ¼ cup (50 g) granulated sugar
3 large egg whites

For the vanilla bean crème anglaise:
½ vanilla bean
1 cup (240 ml) heavy cream
½ cup (120 ml) whole milk
4 large egg yolks
¼ cup (50 g) granulated sugar

Make the pistachio praline: Line a baking sheet with parchment paper or a nonstick baking mat.

In a small, heavy-bottomed saucepan, heat the sugar and water over medium heat, stirring until the sugar has dissolved. Bring the liquid to a boil and cook without stirring for about 5 minutes, until it starts to turn golden.

Remove the caramel from the heat and stir in the pistachios. Pour the mixture onto the prepared baking sheet to cool.

Let rest for 30 minutes to cool completely, then break the praline into pieces and pulse them in a food processor until the praline is crumbly. Measure out ¼ cup (about 25 g) to use in the soufflé and set the remainder aside.

Make the pistachio soufflé: Preheat the oven to 375°F (190°C). Lightly spritz the wells of a 12-cup muffin pan with nonstick baking spray, then use the 1 tablepoon sugar to coat the sides and bottom of the wells, tapping out any excess.

Using a hand mixer or a stand mixer fitted with the whisk attachment, beat the egg whites on medium-high speed until stiff peaks form. When the egg whites start to foam, start adding ¼ cup (50 g) sugar little by little.

Gently fold the ¼ cup (25 g) praline pieces into the beaten egg whites. Divide the batter evenly among the wells of the prepared muffin pan, making sure to fill them all the way. Sprinkle the tops with some of the remaining pistachio praline.

Bake for 10 minutes, or until the soufflés are puffed and just starting to brown.

Remove from the oven and cool completely in the pan on a wire rack. Set aside at room temperature until ready to assemble.

Make the vanilla bean crème anglaise: Place a stainless-steel bowl in a larger bowl filled with ice water to make an ice bath.

Halve the vanilla bean lengthwise and scrape out the seeds. Discard the pod or reserve it for another use.

In a saucepan, combine the cream, milk, and vanilla bean seeds and bring to a bare simmer over medium-low heat, just until bubbles start to form around the edges of the pan.

While the cream and milk heat, in a bowl, whisk the egg yolks and sugar together until the yolks are thickened and pale.

Add the hot cream to the thickened egg yolks in a slow, steady stream, whisking constantly to make a custard base. Return the custard to the saucepan and place over medium-low heat. Cook, stirring constantly with a silicone spatula or wooden spoon, for 7 to 10 minutes, until the custard starts to thicken and become opaque. When your spatula starts to "skid" across the slippery, thin layer of custard on the bottom of the pan, you'll know you're about 1 minute away from doneness.

Strain the crème anglaise through a fine-mesh sieve into the prepared stainless-steel bowl. Stir gently, making sure not to slosh water into the custard or vice versa, until the crème anglaise is cool. Cover and refrigerate if not using immediately.

Assemble the dish: Spoon a dollop of crème anglaise on each plate, then unmold a room-temperature soufflé on top. Sprinkle with some of the remaining pistachio praline, if desired, and serve immediately.

MAKE-AHEAD/STORAGE

The pistachio praline and crème anglaise can be made up to 2 days in advance; store the praline in an airtight container at room temperature and the crème anglaise in an airtight container in the refrigerator until ready to use. The soufflé can be made up to 8 hours in advance; store at room temperature until ready to serve.

{ SHARED PLATES }

If you thought party games went out of style with
piñatas and pin-the-tail-on-the-donkey, think again:
In the world of Pinch, we style our ice breakers with
an edible twist, encouraging party guests to mix
and mingle as they munch.

The game of sharing goes like this: One person
is handed an elegant dish of hummus, garnished
lavishly with olives and parsley but with no spoon,
crackers, crudités, or other obvious way to eat the
fragrant dip. The person next to them is handed a
stack of warm pitas brushed with olive oil. Aha! Initial
confusion leads to amused recognition and lots of
chatty conversation as everyone searches for other
guests with whom to share their delicious dips,
creamy spreads, crunchy crackers, and other nibbles.

We try not to be too obscure with the food and dip
combinations we use for sharing. Items that are
naturally compatible, like guacamole and chips, or
mini potato skins with sour cream and bacon, make
the best tools for this "mingling aid."

As the party host, you might need to prod your
guests a little bit to get them started with this
course. It's easiest in a home environment
where it's likely your party attendees know one
another already, but it's also fun at weddings
and engagement parties, to get the bride's side
mingling with the groom's side. (Plus, what says
"marriage" better than the pairing of two foods that
are clearly meant for each other?)

Warm Pita with Hummus and Olives

Hummus—creamy, comforting, nourishing—is a nearly perfect sharing food. It's easy to make at home, and the taste of a homemade bowl of hummus is far fresher and more vibrant than what you'll find in a premade tub. Serve it to your friends and watch them break into big smiles. Store-bought pita needs to be revitalized, so don't skip the warming step before serving.

YIELD: Serves 12

For the hummus:
1 (15-ounce/430-g) can chickpeas
⅓ cup (75 g) tahini
1 large clove garlic
2 tablespoons fresh lemon juice
3 tablespoons extra-virgin olive oil
3 tablespoons non-virgin olive oil
1 teaspoon kosher salt

To assemble:
6 packaged pita rounds (we like Toufayan)
1½ tablespoons extra-virgin olive oil,
    plus more as needed
20 leaves fresh flat-leaf parsley
36 chickpeas, deep fried
Sun-dried tomato skins, pulp and seeds removed
10 Alfonso olives (or other smooth-skinned black olive),
    pitted and roughly chopped
Maldon sea salt and freshly ground black pepper

Make the hummus: Drain the chickpeas in a mesh sieve or colander and rinse for 2 minutes under cold running water.

Place the chickpeas, tahini, garlic, and lemon juice in a food processor and process until smooth. While the food processor is running, drizzle in the oils. Season with salt.

Assemble the dish: Line a plate with paper towels.

Heat a skillet over low heat and add the pita, one at a time, crisping each side in a teaspoon of the oil until they're just a little more brown than they were originally. Transfer the pita to the paper towel–lined plate and stack as you go. Cut each pita into 8 wedges.

Stack 4 pieces of pita on each of six small plates. Spread the hummus on each of six additional small plates, then sprinkle with oil and divide the parsley, chickpeas, tomato skins, and olives evenly among the plates. Season with salt and pepper.

Serve the pita to half of your guests and the hummus to the other half, and watch the sharing happen.

MAKE-AHEAD/STORAGE
The hummus can be made up to 2 days in advance; store in an airtight container in the refrigerator until ready to serve.

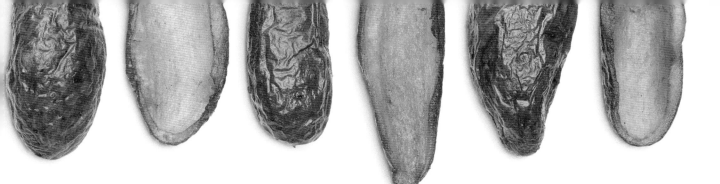

Potato Skins with Sour Cream, Bacon, and Chives

Quintessential bar food is hard to execute for events because it usually requires a deep-fryer, which means the food must be served immediately to achieve optimum crispiness and enjoyment. But if you bake these potatoes, they hold up better over the course of an evening and serve the same purpose: a vehicle for the decadence of the bacon and sour cream.

YIELD: Serves 12

For the potato skins:
1 tablespoon kosher salt
10 (3-inch/7.5-cm) fingerling potatoes
1 tablespoon unsalted butter, melted

To assemble:
¼ pound (115 g) slab bacon, skin removed,
    cut into ½-inch (12-mm) cubes
¼ cup (60 g) sour cream
4 teaspoons minced chives
Finely grated zest of 1 lemon

Make the potato skins: In a large stockpot, combine 2 quarts (2 L) water, the salt, and potatoes and bring to a simmer over medium heat. (Boiling the potatoes will loosen the skin and make them look ugly, so keep the water at a simmer.) Cook the potatoes until a knife pierces the potatoes with no resistance.

Drain the potatoes in a colander and spread them in a single layer on a rimmed baking sheet. Refrigerate the potatoes until cool.

Preheat the oven to 400°F (205°C).

Cut the cooled potatoes lengthwise, and scoop the insides of each potato out with a small spoon (a grapefruit spoon is great if you have one). Leave a ⅛-inch (3-mm) border of potato next to the skin. Reserve the scooped-out potato for another use.

Return the potatoes to the baking sheet, placing them skin side up, and brush the skins with the melted butter. Bake for 20 minutes, or until the skins are crispy and golden brown.

Assemble the dish: Line a plate with paper towels.

In a heavy-bottomed skillet, cook the bacon over medium heat until golden brown. Drain the crisped bacon cubes on the paper towel–lined plate.

Divide the potato halves among six plates, placing four or five potatoes on each plate.

Drop a shallow scoop of sour cream onto each of six additional small plates, and top with bacon, chives, and lemon zest.

Serve the potatoes to half of your guests and the sour cream to the other half, and watch the sharing happen.

MAKE-AHEAD/STORAGE
The potatoes can be boiled and scooped out up to 1 week in advance. Store in an airtight container in the freezer; the potatoes can be baked from frozen. The bacon can be cooked up to 2 hours in advance; store uncovered at room temperature until ready to use.

{ PAIRED PLATES }

Once we designed the Pinch passed plate, we had another revelation. Restaurants often offer tasting menus where wine pairings are chosen for each course; with our plate and glass already paired perfectly, we had the chance to do the same thing with our food and drink.

While it's completely possible to simply pre-pour wine, beer, or cocktails and serve them with plated dishes, you can also set up a pairing station on the kitchen counter or a buffet console where guests pick up a plate and a drink. (This works especially well if you don't have a snug-fitting glass-and-plate setup as described on page 117.)

Take your guests on a flavor trip around the world, pairing wines from Argentina, Australia, France, or your favorite vino region with dishes from the same country—grilled steak, a big paella, or whole roasted fish.

By taking your guests on a tapas-style tour, you're bringing them excitement and variety they don't get from a seated meal—not to mention the fact that they get to talk to more people than they would sitting in the same chair all night. Their curiosity and sense of exploration will be sated along with their taste buds, and you'll look like the party planner extraordinaire.

Oh, and don't be paralyzed by the idea of finding the perfect wine or beverage to pair with your food; there's no need to make yourself an instant wine expert if you don't know your Sauvignon from your Syrah! The folks at your local wine store are happy to answer questions like "Is there a wine with fruity undertones that will match the apricot sauce with my lamb?"

DIY

SET THE MOOD WITH COOL WOODEN WINE CRATES OR CARDBOARD BOXES WRAPPED WITH MAPS OF THE COUNTRY YOU'RE REPRESENTING, TURNED UPSIDE-DOWN AS RISERS FOR PRE-POURED GLASSES OF WINE OR PLATED DISHES. DISPLAY A FEW DIFFERENT FOOD AND DRINK PAIRINGS TOGETHER ON RISERS AT VARYING LEVELS FOR A MORE DRAMATIC EFFECT.

RED WINE + HANGER STEAK (SEE PAGE 136)

WHITE WINE + CURED SCALLOPS (SEE PAGE 137)

BEER + BRATWURST (SEE PAGE 139)

DESSERT WINE + BISCOTTI
(SEE PAGE 141)

Chimichurri Hanger Steak, Paired with Malbec

Hanger steak is a great steak for events because its marbling helps it stay juicy well after you have seared it. We like to pair this charred, umami-rich steak and pungent herb sauce with a medium-bodied, rich, and smoky Argentine Malbec. See page 135 for an image of how we present this dish.

YIELD: Serves 12
SPECIAL EQUIPMENT: grill pan or outdoor grill, meat thermometer

For the chimichurri:
¼ cup (60 ml) water
1 tablespoon Maldon sea salt
2 large cloves garlic
3 tablespoons fresh flat-leaf parsley leaves
2 tablespoons fresh oregano leaves
2 tablespoons fresh thyme leaves
2 tablespoons red wine vinegar
2 tablespoons red pepper flakes
2 teaspoons freshly ground black pepper

For the salsa verde rice:
1 cup (200 g) white rice
1 cup (250 g) tomatillo salsa (page 170)

For the hanger steak:
1 pound (455 g) hanger steak
2 teaspoons extra-virgin olive oil
Maldon sea salt

To assemble:
3 (750-ml) bottles Malbec wine

Make the chimichurri: In a small saucepan, bring the water and salt to a simmer over medium-high heat, stirring just until the salt has dissolved. Let cool to room temperature.

Transfer the salted water to a food processor and add the remaining ingredients. Process until a chunky puree forms, then transfer to a clean, lidded container and refrigerate for at least 8 hours.

Make the salsa verde rice: Bring 2 cups (480 ml) water to a boil in a lidded 1- to 2-quart (1- to 2-L) saucepan over medium-high heat. Add the rice, re-cover, and lower the heat to a simmer. Cook for about 20 minutes, until the rice is tender and fluffy and has absorbed all the water. Stir in the salsa.

Make the hanger steak: If grilling indoors, heat a grill pan or cast-iron skillet over high heat for 4 to 5 minutes. If grilling outdoors, preheat a gas or electric grill for direct heat.

Rub the steak all over with the olive oil and season with salt.

Grill the steak until charred and browned on both sides and cooked to your preferred degree of doneness. Let the steak rest for 5 minutes to redistribute the juices, then assemble the plate immediately.

Assemble the dish: Slice the warm steak into forkable slices. Divide the rice and steak among twelve serving plates and generously spoon chimichurri over the pieces. Serve with the Argentine red wine of your choice. We recommend a Malbec from the Mendoza region.

MAKE-AHEAD/STORAGE
The chimichurri can be made up to 1 week in advance; store in an airtight container in the refrigerator until ready to use. Bring to room temperature before serving. The rice can be made up to 2 days in advance; store in an airtight container in the refrigerator and reheat gently in saucepan before serving.

Cured Scallops, Paired with Sancerre

Yes, cucumbers are good cooked—the French have been cooking them for years! In this recipe, they are treated like pasta and really do have a noodlelike texture. But be careful not to overcook them, or they will get mushy. The floral, spicy flavors in this dish would be overwhelmed by a jammy, fruity red wine; go for an aromatic, dry Loire Valley Sancerre instead.

YIELD: Serves 12

For the cured scallops:
¼ cup (60 g) kosher salt
⅓ cup (65 g) granulated sugar
1 teaspoon grated unpeeled fresh ginger
1 serrano chile, chopped
¼ cup (15 g) chopped fresh tarragon leaves and stems
½ teaspoon freshly cracked black pepper
2 pounds (910 g) diver scallops

For the sautéed cucumbers:
2 English cucumbers
2 tablespoons extra-virgin olive oil
3 large cloves garlic
4 whole anchovy fillets
1 teaspoon red pepper flakes
1 teaspoon Maldon sea salt
½ teaspoon freshly ground black pepper

For the tomato cruda:
½ pound (225 g) baby tomatoes, sliced
1 teaspoon finely chopped peeled fresh ginger
1 teaspoon Maldon sea salt
Extra-virgin olive oil

To assemble:
3 (750-ml) bottles of Sancerre, chilled

Make the cured scallops: In a large bowl, whisk together the salt, sugar, ginger, chile, tarragon, and black pepper.

Toss the scallops in the spice blend, cover, and refrigerate for 3 to 5 hours. Remove the scallops from the spice blend and rinse well in a bowl of cold water. Pat dry.

Slice the scallops crosswise into ¼-inch-thick (6-mm-thick) rounds before serving.

Make the sautéed cucumbers: Cut the cucumbers into thirds. Using a peeler, peel strips lengthwise as you turn, creating multiple tones of green. Toss the seeds when you get close to the middle.

In a small skillet, heat the oil over medium heat until shimmering. Add the garlic and cook until browned, then remove the cloves.

Add the anchovies and cook until nearly "melted" into the oil, then stir in the red pepper flakes and cucumber peels. Cook for 1 minute.

Remove from the heat and season with salt and black pepper. Before serving, drain the cucumbers of any excess water that might have leached out.

Make the tomato cruda: In a bowl, toss the tomatoes, ginger, and salt and let sit for 10 minutes as the tomatoes leach out some of their water.

Toss with olive oil to lightly coat.

Assemble the dish: Divide the cucumbers among twelve serving plates, then shingle with slices of the scallops. Top with spoonfuls of tomato cruda. Serve with a glass of Sancerre.

MAKE-AHEAD/STORAGE
The scallops should be made 3 to 5 hours in advance; refrigerate in a lidded container and rinse before serving.

Bratwurst and Lentils, Paired with Weiss Beer

This dish is very forgiving because there is a large zone between undercooked and overcooked lentils, and the bratwurst can handle a less rigid cooking time as well. The combo goes down well with a German hefeweizen, or push the envelope further with a smoked beer like rauchbier or smoked porter.

YIELD: Serves 12

1 pound (455 g) black beluga lentils
4 bratwurst links, casing removed
2 teaspoons vegetable oil
1 large onion, diced
1 small carrot, roughly chopped
1 small fennel bulb, cored and roughly chopped
2 large cloves garlic, minced
2 tablespoons roughly chopped fresh thyme leaves
2 teaspoons kosher salt
1 teaspoon ground cumin
1 quart (960 ml) water
3 tablespoons roughly chopped fresh flat-leaf parsley
1 tablespoon sherry vinegar
12 (12-ounce/360-ml) bottles weiss beer, chilled

Place the lentils in a large bowl and add enough cold water to cover them by 1 inch (2.5 cm). Soak for an hour or two.

Thinly slice the skinned bratwurst links crosswise.

Heat the oil in a 3- to 4-quart (2.8- to 3.8-L) saucepan over medium heat. Add the bratwurst rounds and cook until browned on both sides.

Add the onion, carrot, fennel, garlic, thyme, salt, and cumin and cook for 5 minutes more, until the vegetables are crisp-tender.

Add the lentils and water and bring to a boil, then reduce the heat to maintain a simmer. Cover and cook for about 40 minutes, until the lentils are tender.

Stir the parsley and vinegar into the lentils just before serving. Serve with a chilled glass of beer.

MAKE-AHEAD/STORAGE
The lentils actually get better with time and can be made up to 3 days in advance; store in an airtight container in the refrigerator until ready to use. Reheat before serving.

Almond Biscotti, Paired with Vin Santo

Vin santo, the classic Tuscan dessert wine, is often served with almond cookies at the end of a lengthy, conversation-filled Italian meal. These crunchy cookies are deliberately made long and thin so they can handle a lengthy dip and swirl in the wine.

YIELD: Serves 12

4 cups (500 g) all-purpose flour,
    plus more as needed
2 cups (400 g) granulated sugar
2 tablespoons baking powder
2 teaspoons kosher salt
½ teaspoon ground cinnamon
½ teaspoon ground ginger
Zest of ½ lemon
Zest of ½ orange
14 tablespoons (200 g) chilled unsalted butter,
    cut into ½-inch (12-mm) cubes
3 large eggs
2 tablespoons amaretto liqueur
1 teaspoon vanilla extract
1½ cups (135 g) sliced almonds, toasted
1 large egg, mixed with 1 tablespoon water
    to make an egg wash
1 (750-ml) bottle vin santo, chilled

Preheat the oven to 350°F (175°C). Line two baking sheets with parchment paper or nonstick baking mats.

In the bowl of a stand mixer fitted with the paddle attachment, combine the flour, sugar, baking powder, salt, cinnamon, ginger, lemon zest, and orange zest and mix together on low speed.

Raise the speed to medium-low and add the butter. Mix until the butter breaks down and coats the dry ingredients and the texture of the mixture is like damp sand.

Add the eggs, one at a time, making sure each is fully incorporated before adding the next. Add the amaretto and vanilla extract.

Reduce the mixer speed to low once more and stir in the almonds, just enough to incorporate—do not overmix, to prevent the almonds from breaking.

Scoop about 1 cup (150 g) of the biscotti dough onto a clean, floured surface and roll into a flattened log about 1 inch (2.5 cm) wide. Place the log on a prepared baking sheet and repeat with the remaining dough.

Brush the biscotti logs with the egg wash and bake for 8 minutes, or until firm to the touch.

Remove from the oven and cool on wire racks for 15 minutes, then slice each log on an angle into ½-inch (12-mm) pieces.

Return the biscotti to the baking sheets and bake for 6 to 8 minutes more, until golden in color.

Transfer the biscotti back to the wire racks and let cool completely.

To serve, set a glass of about ¼ cup (60 ml) of the vin santo alongside three or four biscotti.

MAKE-AHEAD/STORAGE
The biscotti can be made up to 3 days in advance; store in an airtight container at room temperature until ready to use.

were still gelling, we were both obsessed with the idea of a "happening" that was there one minute, created a big splash, then disappeared the next minute, leaving the guests chattering about *what just happened*?!

"Wouldn't it be fun," we thought, "if two waiters walked into the middle of a crowded room with a long rope that stretched across the party? Then a chef would pull out hot pretzels from a suitcase and start hanging them on the rope! It would stimulate conversation and create a buzz . . . even if you were in another part of the event and didn't get a pretzel." We brought this idea to life at the Pinch Food Design opening party, albeit with coiled copper tubing instead of a rope.

Emboldened by seeing all our guests crowding around the pretzel pop-up, we realized that this was the element missing in so many cocktail parties of the time. There were traditional one-bite passed hors d'oeuvres and passed plates, but this was something a little more provocative. Handheld, limited-edition, mobile—it mirrored the first wave of pop-up shops and food trucks just starting to dot the Manhattan landscape. We loved the way these ephemeral moments could create such memorable experiences.

In your home, a pop-up isn't just a way to surprise and delight your guests; it's a way to get a more substantial item on the menu. The food in a pop-up dish is typically a bit larger than a single hors d'oeuvre—about four or five bites' worth—and its substantial size helps fill bellies quickly without resorting to an expensive multicourse meal or entire buffet of hors d'oeuvres. We like to stagger them throughout the night as a way to calm a hungry crowd; like good magic tricks, pop-ups use the power of distraction to cleverly manage your guests—and your budget.

In the following pages, you'll find ways to serve your food that will make your guests gasp and recipes that bring each Pinch pop-up to life (although they can stand deliciously on their own in a more standard presentation). We've suggested a single recipe for each pop-up, but as always, the sky's the limit for the food you can dish up on these easy, crowd-pleasing serving pieces. Use them with a new recipe or serve an old favorite!

A PARADE OF PRETZELS LOOPED ONTO COPPER PIPES OR CURTAIN RODS IS ALWAYS A PARTY PLEASER. DON'T FORGET

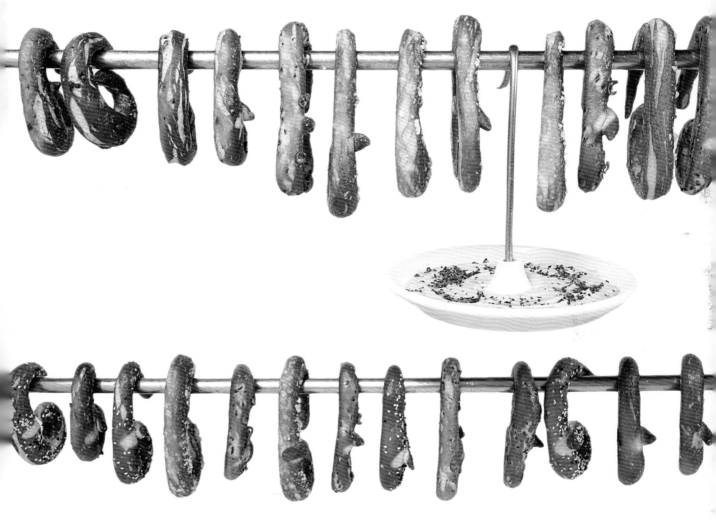

{BRANCH}

The idea for the Pinch branch display had been on the back burner for a really long time. We'd been hoarding some lovely hexagonal resin cups that had potential but no permanent home in our workshop, and when we needed an additional pop-up option for our in-house Peep Show (our annual showcase held in our studio), the idea took shape. Since we like to mix the natural and the industrial, attaching the cups to a gorgeous birch branch seemed, well, organic.

We organized the resin cups in a loose honeycomb pattern along the length of the branch to create a linear display of individual food receptacles. Each resin nook contains a bite and often a dipping sauce to go with the food. The natural, muted palette of birch and white resin creates a neutral canvas on which colorful bites—like a bundle of golden shoestring-fry "tater tots"—can really stand out and be grabbed easily.

Plus, there's the practical consideration that no one wants to dip his or her bite into someone else's sauce. (Think of George Costanza's infamous double-dip incident!) From pot stickers to spring rolls to crudités, the branch is tailor-made for serving any item that usually comes with a dipping sauce.

TO MAKE YOUR OWN NATURE-INSPIRED PIECE, YOU'LL NEED A LARGE, THICK BRANCH WITHOUT MANY EXTRA LIMBS, THOUGH A FEW SMALLER BRANCHES THAT STOP THE MAIN STRUCTURE FROM ROLLING WHEN PLACED ON A TABLE ARE QUITE HELPFUL. MAKE SURE ITS BARK ISN'T PEELING OR FLAKING OFF IN LARGE CHUNKS, EITHER–A VISUALLY APPEALING BRANCH IS PARAMOUNT.

FOR A DISPOSABLE POP-UP BRANCH DISPLAY, PLAIN WHITE PAPER ESPRESSO CUPS MAKE IDEAL DIPPING AND PRESENTING CUPS, AND THEY CAN BE ATTACHED TO THE BRANCH WITH FLAT-HEAD THUMBTACKS. WHEN THE PARTY'S OVER, CLEANUP IS EASY: REMOVE THE TACKS FROM THE PAPER CUPS AND COMPOST THE REST! FOR A MORE PERMANENT STATION, USE A GLUE GUN OR FLAT-HEAD NAILS TO ATTACH SMALL BAMBOO OR WOODEN BOWLS TO YOUR BRANCH OF CHOICE. DO A TEST DRIVE WHEN PIERCING THE BOWL WITH A NAIL TO MAKE SURE IT DOESN'T SPLIT DOWN THE MIDDLE. AFTER USE, THESE BOWLS CAN BE WIPED OUT WITH A SOAPY WASHCLOTH, THEN RINSED AND AIR-DRIED.

FOR EITHER SETUP, ATTACH THE CUPS OR BOWLS IN A RANDOMLY SPACED LINE ALONG ONE SIDE OF THE BRANCH. MAKE SURE TO KEEP THEM FAIRLY UPRIGHT SO THE DIPPING SAUCES WON'T SPILL OUT OF EACH CUP, AND ONLY USE THICK DIPPING SAUCES SUCH AS KETCHUP OR MAYONNAISE WITH YOUR DIY BRANCH BOWLS; THINNER SAUCES LIKE AU JUS OR MIGNONETTE MAY LEAK OUT.

Salt-and-Vinegar Tater Bundles

These potato bundles are basically an excuse to eat French fries in a party setting. We're using what nature gave us—the starch in the potatoes—to bind them together haphazardly; when assembled and fried, each bundle should have the spiky look of a handful of uncooked spaghetti.

YIELD: Serves 12
SPECIAL EQUIPMENT: mandoline or julienne slicer, steamer basket, electric deep-fryer or deep-fry thermometer, branch (optional)

2 medium shallots, minced
2 large russet potatoes (about 1 pound/
455 g total)
2 tablespoons potato starch (such as Bob's
Red Mill brand)
1 tablespoon kosher salt
½ teaspoon red pepper flakes
2 quarts (2 L) canola oil
1 tablespoon Maldon sea salt
1 tablespoon white vinegar powder

Place the shallots in a small bowl, add warm water to cover, and soak for 2 minutes, then drain. Set the shallots aside.

Peel the potatoes and either cut them by hand or use a mandoline or julienne slicer to slice them into long strips about ⅛ inch (3 mm) thick (about the width of shoestring fries).

Place the potato strips in a 4-quart (3.8-L) stockpot and add enough cold water to cover, or place the potatoes in a steamer basket over a pot of water. Cover and bring to a boil, and cook or steam the potatoes for 2 minutes. The strips will soften slightly but should not cook through.

Drain the potatoes in a colander; they'll leach some starch and begin sticking together.

In a large bowl, toss the potatoes with the shallots, potato starch, salt, and red pepper flakes. While they are still warm, group the potatoes in little batches, with all the sticks facing the same way, but slightly shuffled so the potatoes form a "bouquet" with pieces sticking out at different lengths. Each potato bundle should be about

8 inches (20 cm) long—we will be cutting these in half later.

Wrap a 2-inch (5-cm) piece of foil around the middle of each potato bunch and place the bunches on a rimmed baking sheet. Freeze for at least 1 hour.

In an electric deep-fryer or large, high-sided pot, heat the oil until it registers 350°F (175°C) on a deep-fry thermometer. Line a baking sheet with paper towels.

Remove the foil from the frozen potato bundles and fry them in batches until golden brown; timing will vary depending on your equipment, but it should take no longer than 4 minutes.

Remove each fried bundle from the oil with tongs and transfer to the prepared baking sheet. Cut each bundle in half to make two 4-inch (10-cm) bundles.

Sprinkle each bundle with salt and vinegar powder and serve immediately.

MAKE-AHEAD/STORAGE
The unfried potato strip bundles can be frozen for up to 1 week before frying and serving. Remove the foil and fry the frozen bundles as noted above.

{BALLOON}

As movies like *The Red Balloon* and *Up* prove, we're all fascinated by the idea of floating through the air via a handful of helium orbs. And though it might take a lot of effort to get a human or an entire house into the clouds, it's pretty easy to get your food flying—or at least floating.

One of our favorite party tricks is to gently steer balloon trays above guests' heads, then guide them down into the middle of a crowd. It's not as difficult as it sounds, though we do recommend "driving" the balloons around your house a few times to get the hang of it.

If you've got a fun party theme, it's almost too easy to play it up with balloons—they come in a rainbow of colors and can be labeled. We usually serve dessert on the balloons when the party's winding down and needs a little kick in the pants. Make our Brookies with "Milk" (see page 150) or miniaturize your favorite cookies for this presentation.

DIY

LIGHTWEIGHT ¼-INCH (6-MM) FOAM CORE FROM THE CRAFT STORE MAKES AN IDEAL TRAY FOR THIS PIECE. WE RECOMMEND COVERING THE FOAM WITH CONTACT PAPER ON ONE SIDE TO GIVE YOU A WORKABLE SURFACE. USE AN X-ACTO KNIFE TO CUT YOUR FOAM CORE INTO A 2-BY-3-FOOT (61-BY-91-CM) TRAY IN YOUR PREFERRED SHAPE—WE MAKE OURS INTO FREE-FORM "CLOUDS," BUT A REGULAR CIRCLE OR RECTANGLE IS FINE TOO! CUT A HOLE IN EACH CORNER OF THE TRAY WITH THE X-ACTO KNIFE OR WITH A GROMMETING TOOL, AVAILABLE AT FABRIC OR HARDWARE STORES.

CUT TWO 15-FOOT (5-YARD/4.5-METER) PIECES OF BUTCHER'S TWINE OR DECORATIVE STRING. LOOP ONE END OF ONE STRING THROUGH A TRAY HOLE, GOING FROM THE TOPSIDE TO THE UNDERSIDE, AND RUN IT DIAGONALLY ACROSS THE UNDERSIDE OF THE TRAY TO BRING IT OUT THROUGH THE OPPOSITE HOLE. REPEAT WITH THE SECOND PIECE OF STRING SO YOU END UP WITH A CRISSCROSS OF STRING CENTERED ON THE UNDERSIDE OF THE TRAY.

PULL THE ENDS OF THE STRINGS SO THEY MEET EVENLY AND THE TRAY BALANCES LEVEL. TIE THE ENDS OF THE STRINGS INTO A SLIPKNOT, THEN SECURE WITH A REGULAR KNOT. SLIP THE LOOP ONTO AN OPEN 3-INCH (7.5-CM) BINDER RING, THEN SNAP IT CLOSED. KEEP THE EXTRA STRING AS YOUR "GUIDE" TO STEER THE TRAY THROUGH THE PARTY. ON THE UNDERSIDE OF THE TRAY WHERE THE TWO STRINGS CROSS, SECURE THE STRING IN PLACE WITH A STICKER OR PIECE OF TAPE.

TO CARRY 1 POUND (455 G) OF HORS D'OEUVRES ON THE TRAY, YOU'LL NEED FOUR 36-INCH (91-CM) BALLOONS (EACH WILL CARRY A LITTLE MORE THAN 4 OUNCES/115 G OF WEIGHT). WEIGH YOUR FINISHED BITES ON A KITCHEN SCALE TO DETERMINE HOW MANY BALLOONS YOU'LL NEED PER TRAY. OVERFILL THE TRAY AND YOU WON'T GET LIFTOFF! ODD NUMBERS OF BALLOONS ARE PREFERRED TO CREATE THE PERFECT ORB BOUQUET; OUR AVERAGE TRAY USES SEVEN BALLOONS.

GET PREFILLED HELIUM BALLOONS FROM YOUR LOCAL PARTY STORE AND SECURE THE BALLOONS TO THE BINDER RING BY PULLING THEIR STRINGS TOGETHER IN A BOUQUET, THEN ATTACHING THEM TO THE RING WITH A SLIPKNOT AND A REGULAR KNOT AS YOU DID WITH THE TRAY STRING.

Brookies and "Milk"

A brookie is a cookie with the texture of a brownie; or you could call it a brownie that's baked as a cookie. Filled with a creamy panna cotta that subs in for a glass of milk, it evokes that after-school nostalgic feeling—in a sophisticated new package.

YIELD: Serves 12
SPECIAL EQUIPMENT: balloon tray (optional)

For the brookies:
1 cup (125 g) all-purpose flour
½ cup (43 g) unsweetened cocoa powder
1 teaspoon kosher salt
¼ cup (115 g) unsalted butter
1¼ cups (250 g) granulated sugar
1 large egg yolk
1 tablespoon heavy cream
1 teaspoon vanilla extract

For the milk panna cotta:
1 sheet leaf gelatin
½ cup (240 ml) whole milk
½ cup (240 ml) heavy cream
2 tablespoons granulated sugar

Make the brookies: Preheat the oven to 325°F (165°C) and line a large baking sheet with parchment paper or a nonstick baking mat.

In a medium bowl, whisk together the flour, cocoa powder, and salt and set aside.

In the bowl of a stand mixer fitted with the paddle attachment or with an electric hand mixer, beat the butter and ⅔ cup (135 g) of the sugar together on medium speed for 2 minutes, or until the butter is fluffy and light.

Reduce the mixer speed to low and stir in the egg yolk until fully incorporated, then stir in the cream and vanilla.

Add the flour mixture in increments, stirring just until the dry ingredients are incorporated into a soft dough.

Place the remaining sugar in a small bowl.

Roll the dough into 1½-inch (4-cm) balls between the palms of your hands, then roll the balls lightly in the bowl of sugar.

Place the balls about 1 inch (2.5 cm) apart on the prepared baking sheet, then gently press each ball with your palm into a disc about half its original height.

Press your thumb into the middle of each disc until you almost touch the baking sheet. The cookie might crack a bit, but that lends to the charm of this classic kiddie favorite.

Bake for 8 minutes, then transfer the cookies to a wire cooling rack and cool to room temperature.

Make the panna cotta: Snap the gelatin sheet in half and place both pieces in a small bowl. Cover with cold water and soak the gelatin sheets for 5 to 10 minutes, until they soften.

In a small saucepan, stir together the milk, cream, and sugar and warm over low heat, stirring constantly, until the liquid is warm and the sugar has dissolved. Do not bring to a boil. Remove from the heat.

Gently squeeze the softened gelatin sheets between your fingers to remove excess water and add the gelatin to the milk. Stir until the gelatin dissolves.

Assemble the dish: Line a large rimmed baking sheet with waxed paper.

Spoon the panna cotta into the indentation of each brookie and place on the prepared baking sheet. Refrigerate for at least 2 hours, until the centers are set.

MAKE-AHEAD/STORAGE
The brookies can be made up to 1 day in advance and stored in an airtight container in the refrigerator until ready to serve.

{ U M B R E L L A }

Looking at food from a different vantage point stimulates the senses, as we've discovered through our entirely unscientific observations. Something about seeing what you're about to eat from an unexpected angle makes you curious—*so* curious that you can't resist reaching out to grab whatever it is. After the success of the balloon pop-up, we'd been dying to do a similar up-in-the-air serving structure. With the umbrellas, we finally have our next "wow moment."

We use delicate Asian-style wooden parasols with see-through panels for our pop-up umbrellas. The umbrellas themselves, which we buy from the company Brelli, are eco-friendly and designed to biodegrade in less than five years, and their vinyl panels don't block sight lines or interrupt the visual flow of the party at all; in fact, they let the party happen around them.

DIY

WHILE WE DON'T RECOMMEND USING THE OLD UMBRELLA FROM THE FLOOR OF YOUR CAR, ANY COOL PARASOL WILL WORK FOR THIS PRESENTATION. A GROMMETING TOOL, WHICH YOU CAN BUY AT YOUR LOCAL FABRIC OR HARDWARE STORE, MAKES NEAT LITTLE METAL-EDGED HOLES. STAMP OUT HOLES IN EACH PANEL OF THE UMBRELLA; YOU'LL WANT TO GROMMET THEM FOR THE EXTRA REINFORCEMENT IN THE FABRIC TO PREVENT TEARS.

IT MAY TAKE A BIT OF TRIAL AND ERROR TO FIND THE RIGHT HOOK TO HOLD YOUR HANGING BITES. WE USE CURVED BAMBOO TOOTHPICKS—HELD IN PLACE BY MINI FINGERLING POTATOES, OF ALL THINGS!—BUT YOU CAN USE EVERYTHING FROM S-HOOKS TO PEGBOARD HOOKS TO SCREW-IN HOOKS (LIKE YOU'D INSTALL FOR HANGING PLANTS OR PAPER LANTERNS) TO UNUSUAL PAPER CLIPS, ALL HELD IN PLACE WITH LEFTOVER WINE CORKS.

As a nod to the traditional food-cart vendors seen at street fairs and on urban corners, we love to hang our umbrellas with traditional "street foods" like churros, cotton candy, and soft pretzels. It's a balancing act, quite literally, to find the kind of bites that will hang beautifully without dripping or shaking anything onto people's heads. (Hint: Egg rolls don't work!)

As with all of our pop-ups, the umbrella itself is designed to look good whether it's completely stocked with food, half full, or even completely picked off and empty. As opposed to the last few forlorn pieces of shrimp sitting on a tray, the sculptural look of the umbrella makes it seem like any number of bites dangling from its ribs is the right number.

Maple Sugar Churros

Maple sugar solves the problem of ensuring that nothing falls onto your guests' noggins when you're serving from an umbrella. It's stickier than regular granulated or confectioners' sugar, so it adheres to the churro more strongly.

YIELD: Serves 15
SPECIAL EQUIPMENT: large pastry bag fitted with a large star tip, electric deep-fryer or deep-fry thermometer, umbrella, hooks (optional)

2 cups (480 ml) water
1 cup (230 g) unsalted butter
¼ cup (50 g) granulated sugar
1 teaspoon kosher salt
Zest of 1 orange
2 cups (250 g) all-purpose flour
2 large eggs
1 quart (960 ml) canola oil
½ cup (110 g) maple sugar

In a 1- to 2-quart (960-ml- to 2-L) high-sided saucepan, combine the water, butter, sugar, salt, and orange zest and bring to a boil over medium heat until the butter is fully melted and the sugar has dissolved.

Using a silicone spatula or a wooden spoon, stir in the flour and cook, stirring constantly, until a ball of dough forms and pulls away from the sides of the pan.

Scrape the dough into the bowl of a stand mixer fitted with the paddle attachment. With the mixer on low speed, add the eggs to the dough, one at a time.

Cut fifteen 6-inch (15-cm) squares of parchment paper and line them up on a clean work surface or large baking sheet. Scrape the dough into a large pastry bag fitted with a large star tip, and onto each piece of parchment paper pipe the dough into 4- to 5-inch (10- to 12-cm) circles with a cross or plus-sign "handle" on one side.

In an electric deep-fryer or large, high-sided pot, heat the canola oil until it registers 375°F (190°C) on a deep-fry thermometer. Line a baking sheet with paper towels.

Gently slide the churros and their paper into the oil, one or two at a time, paper side up. The oil will separate the paper from the churro; use a pair of heatproof tongs to grab and carefully discard the half-fried paper.

Fry the churros until golden; timing will vary depending on your equipment, but it should take no longer than 5 minutes.

Use tongs to transfer the churros to the prepared baking sheet to cool slightly.

Place half of the maple sugar in a large zip-top bag, then add half of the fried churros. Seal and toss gently to coat, then repeat with the remaining maple sugar and churros. Serve warm.

MAKE-AHEAD/STORAGE
The churros can be fried a few hours in advance and stored at room temperature on a baking sheet. Reheat the churros in a 350°F (175°C) oven, then toss them with the maple sugar and serve.

{HINGE}

Inspired by the classic architectural ruler that unfolds from a compact bundle into a long, orderly line, the Hinge appears to be a simple walnut cutting board—but is so much more.

As we present the Hinge, two servers walk into the middle of the party holding the chunky square board between them. When they start walking away from each other, the piece starts to unhinge into a striking 9-foot- (3-m-) long board. Instead of crowding around one poor server and his small tray of hors d'oeuvres, ravenous party guests have a room's length of serving space in which to approach and take a taste. Burgers small enough to eat in one gulp or any single-bite, self-contained hors d'oeuvres from pages 44 to 61 work well here. Or purchase bites such as sushi as an easy way to fill up your Hinge.

DIY

GRAB A GORGEOUS TWO-BY-FOUR IN THE WOOD OF YOUR CHOICE, BUT MAKE SURE IT'S NOT CHEMICALLY TREATED IN ANY WAY, SINCE YOU'LL BE PUTTING FOOD DIRECTLY ON ITS SURFACE. SALAD BOWL FINISH OR CERTAIN PAINTS WORK WELL AS FOOD-SAFE TOPCOATS FOR THE WOOD. IF A GLOSSIER LOOK IS DESIRED, YOU CAN ALSO FIND A FOOD-SAFE POLYURETHANE SEALANT. (ASK WHICH PAINTS, STAINS, AND SEALANTS ARE MEANT FOR DINING ROOM TABLES IF YOU AREN'T SURE WHICH ONES TO USE.) IF YOU DON'T FEEL COMFORTABLE DOING IT YOURSELF, HAVE THE HARDWARE STORE CUT THE WOOD INTO 2-FOOT (61-CM) PIECES. USE DOOR HINGES TO ATTACH EACH PIECE TO THE NEXT, MAKING SURE TO HINGE ON ONE SIDE, THEN THE OTHER, AS YOU GO ALONG SO THE WOOD WILL FOLD OVER ONTO ITSELF. (WE ROUT OUT TROUGHS TO INLAY BOAT HINGES FOR OUR MODEL SO THE PIECE FOLDS FLUSH, BUT THAT'S AN EXTRA STEP YOU DON'T HAVE TO TAKE.) WHEN PRESENTING THE HINGE TO YOUR GUESTS, WE ENCOURAGE YOU TO FIND A WILLING PARTNER TO GIVE THE MOMENT OF UNFOLDING ITS PROPER IMPACT.

TUNA ROLLS TOPPED WITH JAPANESE GUACAMOLE OR ANY OTHER SINGLE BITE LOOKS GREAT ON A HINGE.

ATTACH HINGES ON ALTERNATING SIDES SO IT UNFOLDS BEAUTIFULLY.

Veggie Sliders with Red Pepper Ketchup and Fennel Slaw

Sliders, like cupcakes, are one of those mini food trends whose fifteen minutes of fame have stretched on and on and on . . . but these bite-size foods are popular for good reason. They pack a lot of nostalgic deliciousness into a small bite, and it's easy to create infinite flavor variations. Here, we mix things up with an all-veggie slider and homemade ketchup.

YIELD: 24 sliders
SPECIAL EQUIPMENT: mandoline, electric deep-fryer or deep-fry thermometer, Hinge (optional)

For the red pepper ketchup:
1 red bell pepper, stemmed, seeded,
    and roughly chopped
1 medium shallot, roughly chopped
1 cup (240 ml) water
2 tablespoons red wine vinegar
3 tablespoons granulated sugar
1 teaspoon kosher salt
1 teaspoon red pepper flakes

For the veggie sliders:
1 small red beet, scrubbed
3 cups (720 ml) water
¾ cup (105 g) bulgur
½ cup (110 g) French lentils
3 tablespoons finely chopped scallions
2 tablespoons freshly ground black pepper
1½ teaspoons kosher salt
½ teaspoon red pepper flakes

For the fennel slaw:
1 small fennel bulb, stems and fronds removed
1 tablespoon extra-virgin olive oil
Maldon sea salt and freshly ground black pepper

To assemble:
2 quarts (2 L) canola oil
24 small potato rolls or slider buns, toasted until brown
24 thin cucumber slices
Mayonnaise

Make the red pepper ketchup: Place all the ingredients in a 1-quart (960-ml) saucepan and bring to a simmer over medium-low heat. Cook for 20 minutes, stirring occasionally, until the pepper is very soft and almost dissolved into the sauce.

Transfer the liquid to a blender or food processor, taking care not to scald yourself, and puree until smooth.

Refrigerate in a lidded container for up to 2 weeks.

Make the veggie sliders: Preheat the oven to 400°F (205°C).

Trim the root and tip from the beet and wrap in foil. Roast for 30 to 45 minutes, until the beet is tender when pierced with a knife. Allow the beet to cool until you can handle it easily, then rub the beet with a paper towel to remove the skin.

Grate the beet with the fine side of a box grater to get ½ cup (45 g) of grated cooked beet. Reserve at room temperature.

While the beet roasts, in a 1-quart (960-ml) saucepan, bring 2 cups (480 ml) of the water to a boil and add the bulgur. Cook, stirring occasionally, until the bulgur has soaked up all the water and is fluffy and tender, about 15 minutes.

In a separate saucepan, bring the remaining 1 cup (240 ml) water to a boil and add the lentils. Cook, stirring occasionally, until the lentils are tender, about 15 minutes. Drain any excess water from the bulgur and lentils.

Pulse the cooked bulgur and lentils in a food processor until the mixture starts to form a ball, but is still coarse and grainy. Transfer to a large bowl and add the grated beet, scallions, black pepper, salt, and red pepper flakes. The color of the mixture should look like that of ground beef.

Line a rimmed baking sheet with waxed paper.

Shape the mixture into 24 burger patties the same size as your buns, since the veggie sliders do not shrink as they cook, and place on the prepared baking sheet. Freeze for at least 1 hour, until solid.

Make the fennel slaw: Slice the fennel on a mandoline or thinly by hand, then cut it into thin strips. In a bowl, toss with the oil and salt and pepper. Reserve in the bowl.

Assemble the dish: Heat an electric deep-fryer or large, high-sided pot filled with the oil to 350˚F (175˚).

Line a baking sheet with paper towels.

Fry the frozen burger patties until golden; timing will vary depending on your equipment, but should take no longer than 5 minutes. Use tongs to transfer the burgers to the prepared baking sheet to cool slightly.

Lay the buns out and spread the red pepper ketchup on both sides. Place a small handful of fennel slaw on the bottom bun, then top with a patty, then a slice of cucumber, and some mayonnaise. Finish by closing it up with the top bun.

Serve immediately.

MAKE-AHEAD/STORAGE
The burgers can be made up to 1 week in advance and stored in an airtight container in the freezer; they can be fried frozen. The ketchup can be made up to 1 week in advance and stored in an airtight container in the refrigerator. The slaw can be made up to 6 hours in advance and stored in an airtight container in the refrigerator.

{ CLÔCHE }

"What's inside the glass?" Revealing the tasty bites tucked under a glass clôche is one of the quintessential Pinch pop-up moments, combining the element of surprise with an over-the-top theatrical effect. Three servers wheel pedestals onto the floor, topped with glass clôches mysteriously filled with smoke. Simultaneously, they whisk the clôches off to release gentle billows of applewood smoke and display different smoked dishes—pork belly, cheese, and tuna, all skewered on breadsticks—on the pedestals.

It's a moment that routinely elicits gasps—not because the guests can't breathe, thankfully, but because it's just so cool. Even if not everyone at the party witnesses the unveiling, they most certainly can smell the aromatic wood smoke wafting throughout the room. Clôches make us think of elegant, ritzy dinners; inspired by the grandeur of classic restaurant service, we like to turn that idea upside-down by using them for a tongue-in-cheek presentation. What was formal becomes a fun conversation starter.

It's easy to make smoke at home with a simple gadget, as the following recipe reveals. (Talk about another conversation piece!) You don't have to use three clôches as we do for the high-end dramatic effect—one is plenty.

Pork Belly Breadstick Spikes

How do you get the scent and taste of smoked foods without a bulky outdoor smoker? You use a cool contraption called a Smoking Gun. It pipes small amounts of aromatic hardwood smoke into the container of your choice, infusing everything from meats and fish to cheese and butter with the tantalizing aroma of the outdoors.

YIELD: 24 breadsticks
SPECIAL EQUIPMENT: Smoking Gun, clôche

For the breadstick spikes:
1¼ cups (300 ml) warm (110°F/43°C to 115°F/46°C) water
2 teaspoons granulated sugar
1 tablespoon (about 1½ packets) active dry yeast
2 cups (250 g) unbleached all-purpose flour
1¾ cups (210 g) whole-wheat flour
¼ cup (60 ml) olive oil
1½ teaspoons kosher salt

For the pork belly:
1 quart (960 ml) water
1 cup (240 ml) honey
¼ cup (60 ml) soy sauce
2 medium shallots, roughly chopped
2 tablespoons chopped peeled fresh ginger
2 tablespoons coriander seeds
1 pound (455 g) pork belly, skin removed

To assemble:
Maldon sea salt

Make the breadstick spikes: Preheat the oven to 375°F (190°C) and line two large baking sheets with parchment paper or nonstick baking mats.

Pour the warm water into a small bowl and sprinkle in the sugar and yeast evenly. Stir gently and let rest for 10 minutes, or until the yeast is bubbling and the liquid is cloudy.

Put the liquid, both flours, the oil, and salt in a large bowl or the bowl of a stand mixer fitted with the dough hook. Stir until a shaggy dough forms, then knead by hand or with the mixer on low speed until smooth, 6 to 7 minutes.

Transfer the dough to a clean, floured surface (if you've kneaded it with the stand mixer) and divide it into 24 equal pieces. Use the palms of your hands to roll each piece into a log approximately 10 inches (25 cm) long and as thick as a pencil, with an elongated pointed tip.

Transfer the breadsticks to the prepared baking sheets and bake for about 12 minutes, until lightly toasted. Remove the baking sheets from the oven; transfer the breadsticks to a wire rack to cool.

Make the pork belly: In a 3-quart (2.8-L) sauté pan or Dutch oven, stir together the water, honey, soy sauce, shallots, ginger, and coriander seeds. Bring to a simmer over low heat and add the pork belly. Cover and cook for 3 hours.

Use tongs to remove the pork belly from the simmering liquid and transfer to a rimmed baking sheet. Cover loosely with foil or plastic wrap and refrigerate until cool.

Strain the liquid into a 1-quart (960-ml) saucepan. Bring to a simmer over medium heat and cook until reduced to a syrup, about 20 minutes. Reserve, covered, at room temperature.

Once the pork belly is cool, cut the meat into 1-inch (2.5-cm) cubes and use a paring knife to poke a hole through each cube's center. Brush each pork belly cube with the reserved syrup and "stab" it with a breadstick. Sprinkle the pork belly with salt, then place on a serving plate under a glass clôche, cheese dome, or overturned glass bowl.

Use a Smoking Gun to pipe smoke into the clôche, trapping it underneath the dome. To serve, lift the clôche dramatically in front of your guests.

MAKE-AHEAD/STORAGE
The pork belly can be prepared up to 1 week in advance and stored in an airtight container in the freezer. The glaze can be made up to 3 weeks in advance and stored in an airtight container in the refrigerator. The breadsticks can be made up to 1 day in advance and stored in an airtight container at room temperature.

{HOLESOME}

After hanging food from strings and dangling it from hooks, we came up with the idea of displaying food in cubbyholes. Not only would this give us a new plane to play with—going horizontal instead of vertical and designing bites that lay flat—but also the idea of separating each piece of food appealed to us.

The Holesome is a full 360-degree experience, with clusters of white round tubes framed by sumptuous walnut that gracefully holds the tubes in place. The honeycomblike arrangement of the tubes looks delicate, but can hold quite a bit of food. There's something amusingly proprietary about it, harkening back to the days of cubbyholes in elementary school, or those amazing pigeonhole desks at old hotels.

This stacked cubby structure—think Connect Four, but elongated—gives us the chance to have fun making food that mirrors the tube shape, like éclairs, bread pudding sticks, baguette sandwiches, and hot dogs. Guests can approach the Holesome from both sides and pull food out of the cubbies as they desire—a true grab-and-go experience. We serve all our pop-ups at eye level or above, and bring them out so guests can grab and snack from a temporary buffet. Though we have two servers holding the Holesome's frame on either side, so the entire display is able to move throughout our events, a stationary cubby that can be covered with a tablecloth until it's ready to be revealed could also do the trick. And making your own is easier than you think.

DIY

CLEAN ALUMINUM CANS, ARCHITECTURAL MAILING TUBES, OR EVEN CERTAIN WINE RACKS MAKE TERRIFIC OPTIONS FOR A DIY HOLESOME. IF YOU'RE USING CANS, OPEN THEM ON BOTH ENDS WITH A SAFETY-EDGE CAN OPENER THAT DOESN'T LEAVE SHARP EDGES. THE CANS OR TUBES CAN BE GLUE-GUNNED TO EACH OTHER HORIZONTALLY IN FREE-FORM ORGANIC STACKS, GLUED TO FOUND WOOD BEAMS OR ONE-BY-THREE WOOD PLANKS FROM THE LUMBERYARD, OR EVEN PLACED IN AN OPEN-SIDED WINE RACK AS SHOWN HERE WITH A WINE RACK PURCHASED AT IKEA.

WE STAGGER THE FOOD THROUGHOUT THE HOLES TO CREATE A VISUAL EQUILIBRIUM BETWEEN FILLED AND OPEN TUBES, BALANCING NEGATIVE AND POSITIVE SPACE WITHIN THE DISPLAY. EXPERIMENT TO FIND WHAT LOOKS BEST IN YOUR AT-HOME HOLESOME.

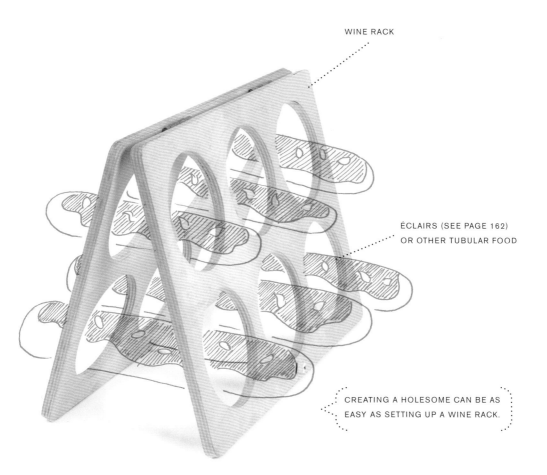

WINE RACK

ÉCLAIRS (SEE PAGE 162)
OR OTHER TUBULAR FOOD

CREATING A HOLESOME CAN BE AS
EASY AS SETTING UP A WINE RACK.

Almond Éclairs

We love the way the shape of the éclair mimics the tubular structure of the Holesome. If you've got guests with nut allergies, feel free to substitute vanilla or another flavor of extract for the almond in this recipe and omit the sliced almonds.

YIELD: Serves 12
SPECIAL EQUIPMENT: pastry bag fitted with a large round piping tip, Holesome (optional)

For the pâte à choux:
½ cup (120 ml) water
2 tablespoons unsalted butter, at room temperature
½ teaspoon kosher salt
⅔ cup (80 g) unbleached all-purpose flour
3 large eggs

For the pastry cream:
4 large egg yolks
½ cup (100 g) granulated sugar
1 tablespoon cornstarch
1 tablespoon unbleached all-purpose flour
1 vanilla bean
1 cup milk
1 teaspoon almond extract

To assemble:
¼ cup (20 g) almond slices
⅔ cup (90 g) coarsely chopped semisweet chocolate
1 tablespoon unsalted butter

Make the pâte à choux: Preheat the oven to 400°F (205°C). Line a large baking sheet with parchment paper or a nonstick baking mat.

In a 1-quart (960-ml) high-sided saucepan, combine the water, butter, and salt and bring to a boil over medium heat until the butter is fully melted.

Using a silicone spatula or a wooden spoon, stir in the flour and cook, stirring constantly, until a ball of dough forms and pulls away from the sides of the pan.

Scrape the dough into the bowl of a stand mixer fitted with the paddle attachment and, with the mixer on low speed, add the eggs to the dough, one at a time, allowing each to incorporate before adding the next.

Scrape the dough into a pastry bag fitted with a large round piping tip and pipe thin 4- to 5-inch (10- to 12-cm) strips

of dough onto the prepared baking sheet. Bake for 15 to 20 minutes, until the pastry is puffed and golden brown. Be careful not to underbake the pastry or it will deflate when removed from the oven. Safeguard against this by turning off the oven when you think the pastry is done and leaving it in the oven for a few minutes more, then piercing each pastry with a toothpick or chopstick before cooling completely on a rack.

Make the pastry cream: In the bowl of a stand mixer fitted with the paddle attachment, or with a hand mixer, beat the egg yolks and sugar together until the eggs are pale and thickened and drip in a thick ribbon from the beaters.

Sift the cornstarch and flour over the egg yolks and use a silicone spatula to fold them into the mixture.

Halve the vanilla bean lengthwise and scrape out the seeds. Place the seeds and the milk in a small saucepan and cook over medium heat, stirring frequently, until the milk starts to bubble around the edges. Pour the milk into the egg yolks in a slow, steady stream, whisking constantly to combine.

Return the milk and eggs to the saucepan and cook over low heat, stirring constantly with a silicone spatula, just until the mixture thickens and the spatula starts to skid across the bottom of the pan.

Strain through a fine-mesh sieve into a clean bowl and stir in the almond extract. Refrigerate overnight.

Assemble the dish: In a small skillet, toast the almonds over medium-low heat, just until their fragrance fills the kitchen and they start to tan a bit. Remove them from the heat; they will continue to toast as they cool.

Pour the pastry cream into a pastry bag fitted with a large round piping tip. Poke a hole in one end of each éclair and insert the piping tip, squeezing gently but firmly to fill the hollow center of each pastry.

Place the chocolate and butter in a microwave-safe bowl and microwave in 10-second intervals, stirring after each round, until the chocolate is melted into a glaze.

Using an offset spatula or a small silicone spatula, spread the chocolate glaze across the top of each filled éclair; transfer to a clean baking sheet and sprinkle with the almond slices. Allow the glaze to set for at least 1 hour before serving.

The pastry shells can be made up to 1 week in advance and stored in an airtight container in the freezer. The pastry cream can be made up to 3 days in advance and stored in an airtight container in the refrigerator. The éclairs can be filled and decorated earlier in the day, about 6 hours before serving. Store at room temperature until ready to serve.

{ WHEELBARROW }

If you're anything like us, you can slurp down a plate of oysters in the same time it takes you to blink. But who wants to buy and shuck dozens upon dozens of oysters for a simple backyard party? The wheelbarrow raw bar makes it whimsical and memorable—though you only need to stock it once and the overall quantity will be less, guests don't feel like they've been deprived of oysters. In fact, they feel like you've added something decadent and luxurious to the menu, but your wallet won't suffer. The same goes for shrimp, crab legs, clams, scallops, or any favorite raw seafood preparation typically served on ice.

To announce the arrival of the wheelbarrow in style, not to mention alert a crowd of seven hundred people when we're on the move, we attached a copper bicycle bell to one of the wheelbarrow handles. It's like the jingle of an ice cream truck, but for adults!

DIY

YOU DON'T NEED TO BUILD YOUR OWN SPECIAL WHEELBARROW LIKE WE DID, BUT A FEW TRICKS WILL MAKE THE BARROW YOU ALREADY OWN INTO A PERFECT SERVING VESSEL. TO KEEP THE WHEELBARROW WEIGHT MANAGEABLE, CREATE A FALSE BOTTOM BY PLACING A LARGE PLASTIC PUNCH BOWL OR STORAGE BIN UPSIDE-DOWN IN THE WHEELBARROW TO FORM A DOME. COVER IT WITH ICE; YOU WON'T NEED TO USE AS MANY BAGS TO FILL THE WHEELBARROW AND THE WATER WILL CONVENIENTLY DRAIN AWAY AS IT MELTS INSTEAD OF MAKING A COLD SLURRY. AT THE END OF THE NIGHT, DUMP THE WHOLE THING INTO THE GARDEN.

CREATE A CONVENIENT SHELL DISPOSAL SYSTEM FOR GUESTS—BECAUSE NO ONE WANTS TO WALK AROUND THE PARTY WITH A PILE OF OYSTER SHELLS IN THEIR PURSE—BY TAKING AN OLD-SCHOOL METAL MAILBOX AND HANGING IT ON THE SIDE OF THE WHEELBARROW. ADD A DECORATIVE KNOB SO GUESTS CAN EASILY OPEN AND CLOSE THE LID OF THE SHELL DIS-POSAL BOX. IF DRILLING THROUGH METAL ISN'T YOUR THING, A RETRO ALUMINIZED BUCKET OR SAND PAIL HAS THE RIGHT NAUTICAL FLAIR.

AS A FINAL TOUCH, MAKE THE WHOLE THING JUST A BIT MORE DRAMATIC BY LIGHTING THE ICE: PLACE LED LIGHTS IN PLAS-TIC SANDWICH BAGS TO KEEP THEM FROM GETTING WATERLOGGED WHILE ADDING A COOL GLOW TO THE WHOLE PRESEN-TATION. YOU CAN EASILY FIND BATTERY-OPERATED LEDS INTENDED FOR ILLUMINATING DARK CLOSETS, OR SNAG A FEW OF YOUR KIDS' GLOW STICKS. THEY WON'T MIND.

IF A WHEELBARROW SEEMS A LITTLE CUMBERSOME FOR YOUR EVENT SPACE, A FUN ALTERNATIVE PRESENTATION IS TO FILL A CANTILEVERED TOOLBOX INSTEAD (SEE OPPOSITE)!

USING A VINTAGE DRAFTING ART SUPPLY BOX LIKE THIS OR ANY TOOL BOX IS A FUN WAY TO SERVE CHILLED SEAFOOD. STRATEGIZE WHEN AND WHERE TO REVEAL TO GUESTS FOR THE MOST IMPACT AND VISIBILITY.

FILL WITH ICE AND OYSTERS OR ANY CHILLED SURPRISE.

A CANTILEVERED OPENING IS KEY.

Fresh Oysters with Cucumber Ponzu

Don't want to shuck oysters on the spot? Shuck them in advance and serve on the half-shell, or turn this bite into a quick-assembly oyster shooter, placing pre-shucked oyster bellies and their liquor into shot glasses or disposable glasses. You can add a little salted water to increase the liquid, then spoon the sauce over the oysters before tucking them into the ice.

YIELD: 20 oysters
SPECIAL EQUIPMENT: oyster-shucking knife and protective mesh glove for shucking, wheelbarrow or other presentation vessel to hold ice

1 tablespoon chopped peeled fresh ginger
1 small clove garlic
3 tablespoons unseasoned rice vinegar
1 tablespoon soy sauce
1 tablespoon fresh lime juice
½ small cucumber
20 large oysters, such as Wellfleet

In a blender, puree the ginger, garlic, rice vinegar, soy sauce, and lime juice until smooth.

Peel and seed the cucumber, then dice into very small cubes no larger than ¼ inch (6 mm); you should have about ½ cup (65 g) of dice. Add the cucumber bits to the sauce.

Shuck the oysters and place on a bed of ice in a wheelbarrow or other presentation vessel. Spoon the sauce over each oyster and serve cold.

MAKE-AHEAD/STORAGE
The sauce can be made up to 3 weeks in advance and stored in an airtight container in the refrigerator; add the cucumber the day of serving.

We're not enamored of the word "buffet," which conjures up images of silver chafing dishes and wicker baskets, so we decided to turn the idea of the buffet upside-down—almost literally in some cases. With the rebirth comes a new name: Interactions. And it is this current adaptation that defines the look of a Pinch event.

At Pinch, our Interactions are a lot closer to art installations than sideboards. It was a natural progression from displaying food in tabletop vessels to making the whole table part of the display. We call it "food furniture." Our Interactions are pieces designed to be fun and functional from the ground up, able to be wiped down and reused time and again. Many are thin or nearly see-through, so they don't interrupt the flow of the party happening around them.

With each Interaction, guests get to touch their food and see it in a way they haven't before. Half the experience is discovering how to serve yourself (or have a chef serve you) and the other half is taking the time to enjoy the experience itself. We want guests to feel they can linger at the Interactions, to hang out with the food and with one another.

And because people-watching is also a big part of why parties are so much fun (otherwise we'd all be showing up in sweats instead of stilettos), it's a built-in bonus to see how partygoers respond to each Interaction. It's almost a personality test: There are always people who dive in right away, and others who hang back to let others try before they do. Are you the kind of person who jumps off the high dive, culinarily speaking, or do you wait in the shallow end of the pool? The Interaction might tell you more about your character than any psychological quiz could!

Party guests take more pictures of our Interactions than of anything else we do. Of all our inventive ways to serve and feed our guests, they require the most intensive collaboration among all members of the team and represent the baseline of what Pinch does. Designing an Interaction takes a lot of patience and imagination. Our brainstorms are often initiated by a party need or a fun food experience we've had or fantasized about. We visualize how a guest will see it for the first time, how it will hold up to the onslaught of two hundred or more hungry people, and how we'll be able to install it and replenish it over the course of an evening.

But never fear: In your kitchen, you can rely on our years of research and development until you're ready to fly on your own. With the DIY suggestions in the following pages, even the most timid host will feel empowered, more

{ N E W   W A V E }

The New Wave is a crowning achievement—no, really. We cut up and reconstruct crown moldings to create a pattern of peaks and valleys: They're perfect for serving tacos, falafel, burritos, or anything that benefits from being nestled and compartmentalized into a concave surface.

On one side of the wave, chefs are heating tortillas on a griddle and plating tacos; on the other, guests are topping their fresh, warm tacos with all the condiments their hearts desire from bowls placed in front of the New Wave. Use your own serving pieces or seek out terra-cotta bowls or vibrant options at flea markets or from one of the fun vendors listed in the Toolbox chapter.

DIY

TO MAKE YOUR OWN NEW WAVE SERVING PIECE, SAW A LONG PIECE OF CROWN MOLDING INTO 6-INCH-LONG (15-CM-LONG) STRIPS. KEEPING EACH PIECE FLAT SIDE DOWN, TURN THEM 90 DEGREES, SO THAT THE UNCUT EDGES ARE ALL TOUCHING BOTTOM-TO-BOTTOM, THEN TOP-TO-TOP. GLUE THE PIECES ONTO A TRIMMABLE MATERIAL LIKE MUSEUM- OR PARTICLEBOARD. IF YOU HAVE ACCESS TO MORE HEAVY-DUTY POWER TOOLS, A STRONGER MASONITE OR THIN PLYWOOD IS BETTER. MAKE SURE ALL THE CUT EDGES ARE FLUSH WHEN GLUING DOWN TO CREATE A WAVE PATTERN.

AFTER THE GLUE DRIES, TRIM THE BOTTOM MATERIAL SO IT IS FLUSH WITH THE EDGE OF THE MOLDING, THEN SAND THE CUT SURFACES UNTIL THEY'RE SMOOTH, AND COAT WITH GLOSSY FOOD-SAFE PAINT IN WHITE OR ANY COLOR YOU CHOOSE. THE GLOSSY FOOD-SAFE FINISH WILL MAKE IT EASIER TO WIPE AND KEEP CLEAN FOR LONG-TERM USE.

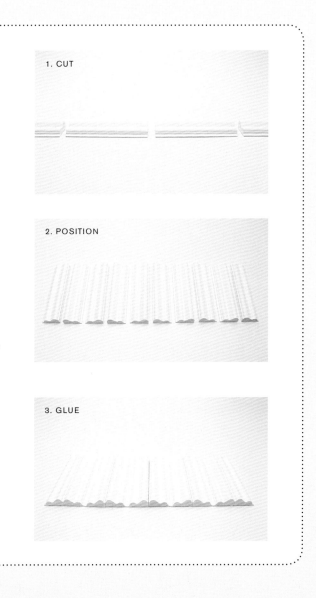

1. CUT

2. POSITION

3. GLUE

Pork Belly and Hanger Steak Tacos

We make our tacos with 4½-inch (11-cm) corn tortillas from Tortilleria Nixtamal, just across the river in Queens; they're organic and freshly pressed, and arrive warm at our doorstep. We know we're lucky to have such a treasure here in New York, so if you use refrigerated or thawed soft corn tortillas, just warm them in a dry cast-iron pan for a few seconds to soften them.

YIELD: Serves 12
SPECIAL EQUIPMENT: mandoline or Japanese slicer, meat thermometer, New Wave tray (optional)

For the guajillo sauce:
2 cups (480 ml) water
3 plum tomatoes
6 dried guajillo chiles, stemmed, seeded, and de-ribbed
1 large clove garlic
1 small yellow onion, roughly chopped
1 teaspoon kosher salt

For the roasted pineapple salsa:
1 tablespoon vegetable oil
2 tablespoons minced shallots
½ ripe pineapple
1 tablespoon smoked paprika
1 teaspoon Maldon sea salt
¼ cup (15 g) chopped fresh cilantro leaves and stems

For the radish salsa:
1 pound (455 g) red radishes
1 medium Spanish onion
3 jalapeño peppers
¼ cup (60 ml) fresh lime juice
1 teaspoon Maldon sea salt
¼ cup (15 g) chopped fresh cilantro leaves and stems

For the tomatillo salsa:
8 medium tomatillos, husked and rinsed
3 jalapeño peppers, halved and seeded
1 small white onion, sliced into ½-inch (12-mm) rounds
3 cloves garlic
¼ cup (15 g) chopped fresh cilantro leaves and stems
1 teaspoon kosher salt

For the guacamole:
4 Hass avocados, halved and pitted
3 tablespoons fresh lime juice
2 large plum tomatoes, peeled, seeded, and diced into ½-inch (12-mm) cubes (see the guajillo sauce instructions for peeling tomatoes)

1 large or 2 small jalapeño peppers, seeded and minced
1 large shallot, minced
¼ cup (15 g) chopped fresh cilantro leaves and stems
Kosher salt and freshly ground black pepper

For the pork belly:
1 pound (455 g) pork belly, hard skin removed

For the hanger steak:
2 tablespoons fresh lime juice
1 tablespoon vegetable oil
3 tablespoons roughly chopped fresh oregano leaves
2 cloves garlic, minced
1 teaspoon kosher salt
½ teaspoon freshly ground black pepper
1 pound (455 g) hanger steak

To assemble:
2 packages 4½-inch (11-cm) corn tortillas

Make the guajillo sauce: In a large stockpot, bring the water to a boil over medium-high heat. Fill a medium bowl with ice water. Cut an X into both ends of each tomato and drop the tomatoes into the boiling water. Cook for 30 to 45 seconds, until the skin starts to peel back; use a skimmer or a slotted spoon to remove the tomatoes and drop them into the ice water to halt cooking. Keep the water in the stockpot at a boil.

Peel the skins off the tomatoes, scoop out the seeds, and chop roughly. Add the chopped tomatoes, chiles, garlic, onion, and salt to the boiling water and reduce the heat to a simmer. Cook for 30 minutes.

Pour the sauce into a fine-mesh sieve set over a large bowl to reserve the liquid. Puree the softened tomatoes, chiles, garlic, and onion in a blender or food processor along with 1 cup (240 ml) of the reserved liquid.

Save 3 tablespoons of the sauce for the pork belly recipe below. Refrigerate the remaining sauce in a Mason jar or other lidded container for another use.

Make the roasted pineapple salsa: In a 2-quart (2-L) sauté pan or wide skillet, heat the oil over medium-low heat. Add the shallots and cook for 8 to 10 minutes, until they are soft but not completely mushy.

While the shallots cook, peel and core the pineapple and dice it into ¼-inch (6-mm) cubes.

Raise the heat under the pan to medium-high and add the pineapple, paprika, and salt. Cook, stirring occasionally, until the pineapple starts to caramelize.

Transfer to a bowl and let cool to room temperature. Stir in the cilantro just before serving.

Make the radish salsa: Slice the radishes paper-thin on a mandoline or Japanese slicer.

Remove the root and stem ends of the onion, then slice into quarters. Slice each quarter into thin strips lengthwise along the grain of the onion.

Slice the jalapeños into paper-thin half-moons.

In a medium bowl, toss the radishes, onion, and jalapeños with the lime juice and salt. Let the vegetables marinate for 30 minutes, then stir in the cilantro just before serving.

Make the tomatillo salsa: Heat a large sauté pan or wide skillet over medium-low heat. Add the tomatillos, jalapeños, onion, and garlic and cook for about 15 minutes, turning occasionally, until the vegetables are very soft and charred.

Transfer the vegetables and their juices to a clean, lidded bowl and refrigerate until chilled, at least 2 hours.

Transfer to a blender or food processor, add the cilantro and salt, and blend to a chunky puree.

Make the guacamole: Scoop the avocado flesh into a large bowl and mix with the lime juice, keeping the texture a little chunky. Add the tomatoes, jalapeños, shallots, and cilantro. Season with salt and pepper.

Make the pork belly: Preheat the oven to 300°F (150°C).

Place a large sheet of parchment paper on a clean work surface. Rub the pork belly with the reserved 3 tablespoons guajillo sauce, then place on the parchment paper. Wrap tightly, using a second sheet if necessary, then wrap again in foil, making sure no paper is exposed.

Place on a rimmed baking sheet and cook for 1½ hours, or until the belly is very tender.

Carefully remove the pork belly from its foil and paper cocoon and cool until it's easy to handle. Chop roughly into bite-size pieces. Refrigerate in a lidded container until needed. Sear the pork bites in a hot skillet to reheat before serving.

Make the hanger steak: In a small bowl, whisk the lime juice, oil, oregano, garlic, salt, and pepper together, then transfer to a large zip-top bag. Add the steak and seal the bag tightly, pushing out all the air so the marinade coats the meat completely. Marinate the steak in the refrigerator for at least 4 hours or overnight.

Remove the steak from the bag and pat dry, discarding the marinade. Heat a cast-iron or other heavy-bottomed skillet over medium-high heat until a drop of water sizzles in the pan. Add the steak and cook until a meat thermometer registers 135°F (57°C). Let the steak rest on a cutting board or plate for 5 minutes before slicing into bite-size pieces.

Assemble the dish: Place all the ingredients, including the tortillas, in separate serving bowls or on platters and allow guests to assemble tacos at their convenience.

MAKE-AHEAD/STORAGE
The guajillo sauce, roasted pineapple salsa, and tomatillo salsa can be made up to 3 weeks in advance and stored in separate airtight containers in the refrigerator. The pork belly can be made up to 3 days in advance and stored in an airtight container in the refrigerator. The hanger steak can be marinated 1 day in advance. The radish salsa and the guacamole can be made up to 12 hours in advance and stored in airtight containers in the refrigerator. Adding a teaspoon of vitamin C powder (found at health food stores) to the guacamole will ensure that it stays green.

{PLATEAU}

Have you noticed how many restaurants now have their kitchens right out in the open? The idea of dinner as theater is nothing groundbreaking, but in the past decade restaurant designers have taken it to new levels, and we applaud the move. We love watching plates being set on the pass—that high shelf that separates the kitchen from the dining room—before they're whisked away to each table.

The Plateau is our way of bringing the kitchen pass into the party. Just as if they were getting a dish straight from a restaurant kitchen, we're cooking to order in front of our guests' eyes, assembling each dish and letting them take it away. It's a step beyond the Chef's Table, which brings the idea of plating to the people—but this time, we're bringing the stovetop, too.

In typical Pinch fashion, the name *Plateau* has two meanings: It refers to the flat-topped pedestals of various heights that create a landscaped horizon on which dishes can rest, but it's also the French word for "tray."

Our Plateau sports a high-gloss façade, reminiscent of the white porcelain plates that are restaurant staples, while the circular white penny-tiled counter echoes the round form of each plate. In case our obsession with white, shiny elements wasn't enough here, we use vintage white enamel Dansk serving ware. This clean, bright surface is a neutral palette for the multicomponent tapas-size portions we're churning out.

Our Bread Pudding with Butterscotch Sauce, Pears, and Pecans is shown opposite (see recipe on page 175). This dish is a great fit for the Plateau because we can either leave pre-plated dishes on the risers or allow guests to add toppings to the bread pudding themselves. The toppings are simply arranged in attractive bowls around the central dish.

FINISHED PLATES OF FOOD
FOR GUESTS TO ENJOY

PLACE YOUR PEDESTALS ON A COUNTER OR TABLE
TO CREATE A VISUALLY APPEALING PLATEAU FOR
SERVING ANY KIND OF SMALL PLATE.

VINTAGE TABLE LEGS

DIY

THE COOK, PLATE, AND SERVE STYLE OF THE PLATEAU MAKES THIS INTERACTION A WORTHY SETUP AT A BARBECUE STATION, KITCHEN ISLAND, OR ANYWHERE YOU CAN ASSEMBLE FRESHLY COOKED FOOD IN FRONT OF YOUR GUESTS. MAKE A PRESENTATION STATION BY STACKING PLATES ON TOP OF VINTAGE WOODEN TABLE LEGS, PILED BOOKS, UPSIDE-DOWN CHAMPAGNE BUCKETS, HATBOXES, OR EVEN OLD-TIMEY KITCHEN SCALES–ANYTHING THAT CREATES A BORDERLINE OF VARYING LEVELS.

AS FOR WHAT TO SERVE ON YOUR PLATEAU? ANY OF THE RECIPES FROM THE SMALL PLATES CHAPTER, SUCH AS THE FRIED POLENTA (SEE PAGE 120) OR BREAD PUDDING (SEE OPPOSITE), WORK EQUALLY WELL HERE. ASSEMBLE YOUR DISH ON THE TOP PLATE OF THE STACK AND LET YOUR GUESTS WHISK IT AWAY.

Bread Pudding with Butterscotch Sauce, Pears, and Pecans

This dish is the cousin to French toast with maple syrup. It's a bit more work to prepare, but well worth it for its versatility: It can be made in advance, then refrigerated or frozen, and the sauce will keep for up to a month. You can even pre-plate to serve it warm, not hot, and your guests will still line up for more.

YIELD: Serves 12

For the bread pudding:
2 cups (480 ml) whole milk
2 cups (480 ml) heavy cream
⅔ cup (135 g) granulated sugar
½ teaspoon kosher salt
1 vanilla bean
½ pound (225 g) challah bread, cut into 1-inch (2.5-cm) cubes and toasted
3 large egg yolks

For the butterscotch sauce:
¼ cup (60 g) unsalted butter
1 cup (220 g) packed dark brown sugar
¾ cup (180 ml) heavy cream
1 tablespoon vanilla extract
1 teaspoon kosher salt

To assemble:
½ cup (55 g) pecan pieces
1 pear

Make the bread pudding: In a 2-quart (2-L) heavy-bottomed saucepan, combine the milk, cream, sugar, and salt. Halve the vanilla bean lengthwise, scrape out the seeds, and add the seeds and pod to the pan with the milk mixture. Bring to a boil over medium-low heat, stirring constantly so the milk doesn't burn. Remove from the heat, cover, and let steep for 5 minutes to infuse the vanilla flavor into the milk.

Preheat the oven to 325°F (165°C). Place the toasted bread cubes in a 9-by-13-inch (23-by-33-cm) baking dish.

Remove the vanilla bean pod from the milk mixture. Whisk the egg yolks into the warm milk, then strain the liquid through a fine-mesh sieve over the bread cubes. Toss gently to make sure each cube is evenly coated, then press tightly into the pan.

Bake for about 20 minutes, until the pudding is puffed and golden brown on the edges, rotating the pan after 10 minutes to ensure even baking.

Remove the pan from the oven and cool completely on a wire rack. Cut the bread pudding into 2-inch (5-cm) squares and reserve at room temperature or cover and refrigerate overnight.

Make the butterscotch sauce: In a 1-quart (960-ml) heavy-bottomed saucepan, melt the butter over medium-low heat. Add the brown sugar and stir until dissolved; continue to stir for 3 to 5 minutes more as the liquid starts to bubble and take on a shiny consistency; it will look like lava.

Carefully whisk in the cream; the liquid will steam and bubble up. Reduce the heat to low and cook, stirring frequently, for 10 minutes more.

Remove from the heat and let cool for 2 minutes, then add the vanilla and salt.

Reserve at room temperature or pour into a heatproof container and refrigerate if not using immediately.

Assemble the dish: Bring the bread pudding and the butterscotch sauce, if necessary, back to room temperature.

In a skillet, toast the pecan pieces over medium heat until they are fragrant and just starting to brown; they'll continue to cook a bit once removed from the heat.

Core and dice the pear.

Place a cube of bread pudding in the center of each plate, generously spoon butterscotch sauce on top, and sprinkle with the pecans and diced pear. Serve immediately.

MAKE-AHEAD/STORAGE
The bread pudding can be made up to 3 days in advance; cut into squares and store in an airtight container in the refrigerator until ready to use. The butterscotch sauce can be made up to 1 month in advance; store in an airtight container in the refrigerator until ready to use. Bring both components to room temperature before assembling and serving.

{ MARBLEOUS }

A decade ago, during a visit to the famous droog design studio in Amsterdam, TJ became entranced with their "Come a little bit closer" bench, which uses marbles and seating plates to help you slide closer to or farther away from the people sitting next to you. The brief moment of interaction with the bench left a lasting impression—as she says, "It's the kind of memorable experience we're trying to create at our parties, so I had to borrow it."

The idea of sliding plates from place to place, using marbles as ball bearings, merged with our memories of the kitschy floating sushi boats or conveyor belts found at old-school sushi bars. The Marbleous takes these concepts of food and movement to create a tactile, interactive plating station. White marbles in a large white trough are topped with small appetizer plates. A large, custom-shaped vacu-formed lazy Susan acts as the chef's *mise en place* for doling out sashimi, salads, and other chilly items to party guests.

Though sushi is one of our favorite dishes to serve, anything cold—from ice cream to gazpacho—makes a great edible subject for this cool, clean Interaction. We use all-white marbles to match our smooth, glossy plates, but feel free to choose a color that matches your party décor and theme.

DIY

LINE A ROW OF MARBLE-FILLED TRAYS NEXT TO EACH OTHER ON A TABLE, OR MAKE A BORDER ON ANY TABLE BY PLACING PAINTED PIECES OF WOOD OR THICK MUSEUM BOARD AROUND THE EDGES TO FRAME IT OUT. MAKE SURE TO SECURE THE FRAME WITH CLAMPS, OR FOR A CLEANER LOOK, LOOP DUCT OR GORILLA TAPE OR EXTRA-STRONG DOUBLE-STICK TAPE AND PLACE BETWEEN THE FRAME AND THE TABLE. THIS IS SO YOUR GUESTS DON'T ACCIDENTALLY MOVE THE BORDER, BECAUSE THEN YOU'LL HAVE A NEW PARTY GAME TO PLAY!

AFTER THE FRAME IS SECURELY ATTACHED TO THE TABLE, PLACE A LAZY SUSAN RIGHT ONTO THE TABLE. IF THERE IS LESS THAN AN INCH FROM THE TABLETOP TO THE BOTTOM OF THE SPINNING SURFACE, PLACE THE LAZY SUSAN ON A THIN PIECE OF PLEXIGLAS OR FOAM CORE, ELEVATING IT JUST ENOUGH TO CLEAR THE MARBLES AND SPIN.

FINALLY, POUR YOUR MARBLES INTO THE BORDERED SPACE. THIS TECHNIQUE CAN ALSO BE USED TO CREATE A THIN TABLE RUNNER–STYLE MARBLEOUS, ALLOWING GUESTS TO SLIDE FOODS FAMILY-STYLE UP AND DOWN THE MIDDLE OF THE TABLE FOR A SIT-DOWN DINNER.

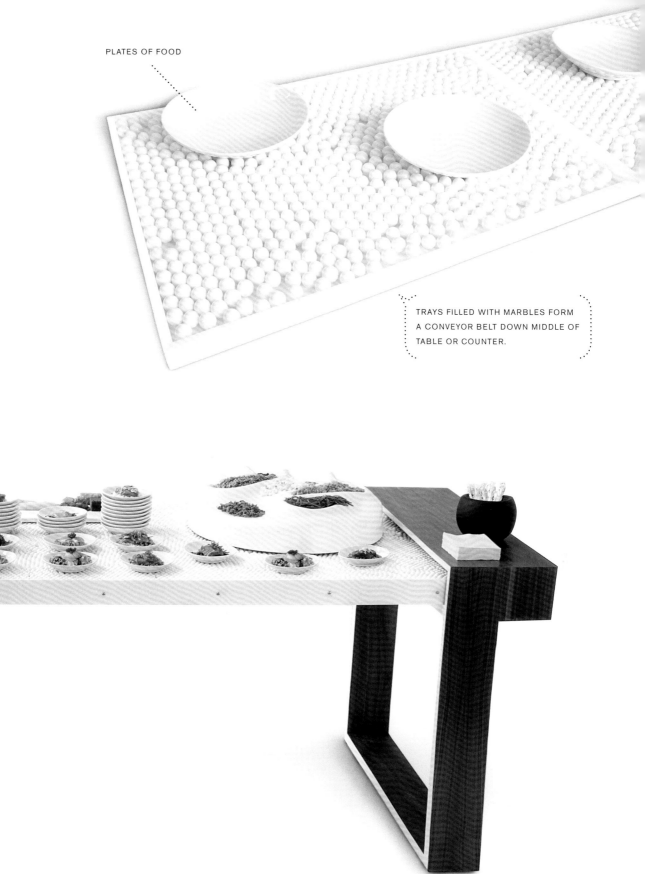

PLATES OF FOOD

TRAYS FILLED WITH MARBLES FORM
A CONVEYOR BELT DOWN MIDDLE OF
TABLE OR COUNTER.

Crudas and Grains

Italian and Japanese cuisines are similar in that many traditional dishes use minimal ingredients—like pasta and sauce or fish and rice—and this dish mixes both of those influences, pairing healthy grains with sushi, sashimi, tartare, or carpaccio.

YIELD: Serves 12

For the ponzu sauce:
3 tablespoons soy sauce
1½ tablespoons mirin
1 teaspoon fresh lemon juice
2 teaspoons finely grated peeled fresh ginger
1 medium clove garlic, coarsely chopped

For the yuzu sauce:
½ cup (120 ml) water
3 tablespoons granulated sugar
1 tablespoon saffron threads
1 tablespoon fresh lemon zest
2 teaspoons fresh lemon juice
¼ cup (60 ml) yuzu juice
¼ cup (30 g) roughly chopped peeled daikon

For the miso quinoa:
1½ cups (255 g) quinoa
2 teaspoons yellow miso
1 tablespoon unseasoned rice vinegar
1 tablespoon honey
1 tablespoon vegetable oil
2 tablespoons minced scallions

For the herbed farro:
1½ cups (225 g) farro
2 tablespoons extra-virgin olive oil
1 tablespoon white balsamic vinegar
1 tablespoon minced fresh basil
1 tablespoon minced fresh thyme
1 tablespoon minced fresh flat-leaf parsley
1 teaspoon kosher salt
½ teaspoon freshly ground black pepper

For the sushi rice:
2 cups (200 g) jasmine or short-grain sushi rice
¼ cup (60 ml) unseasoned rice vinegar
1 tablespoon mirin
2 tablespoons granulated sugar
1 teaspoon kosher salt

For the sesame snow peas:
1 pound (455 g) fresh snow peas, trimmed
1 tablespoon tahini
2 teaspoons unseasoned rice vinegar
1 teaspoon fish sauce
1 teaspoon vegetable oil
1 teaspoon sesame oil
2 tablespoons sesame seeds, toasted
1 teaspoon finely grated peeled fresh ginger

To assemble:
½ pound (225 g) sushi-grade yellowfin tuna
½ pound (225 g) sushi-grade salmon
½ pound (225 g) sushi-grade fluke

Make the ponzu sauce: In a mini food processor or with an immersion blender, pulse all the ingredients until well blended. Cover and refrigerate or reserve at room temperature for up to 1 hour before serving.

Make the yuzu sauce: In a small saucepan, combine the water, sugar, saffron, lemon zest, and lemon juice and bring to a boil over medium heat, stirring until the sugar has dissolved. Transfer to a clean, lidded bowl and chill for at least 1 hour.

Strain through a fine-mesh sieve into a blender or food processor. Add the yuzu juice and daikon and puree until well blended. Cover and refrigerate or reserve at room temperature for up to 1 hour before serving.

Make the miso quinoa: In a stockpot, bring 3 quarts (2.8 L) water to a boil over medium-high heat, then add the quinoa. Reduce the heat to a simmer and cook for 10 to 15 minutes, until the quinoa is tender. Drain the quinoa in a fine-mesh sieve, then transfer to a large bowl and cool to room temperature.

In a small bowl, whisk the miso, vinegar, and honey together. Vigorously whisk in the oil to make a dressing, then add the dressing to the quinoa and toss well. Gently stir in the scallions. Cover and refrigerate or reserve at room temperature for up to 1 hour before serving.

Make the herbed farro: In a stockpot, bring 3 quarts (2.8 L) water to a boil over medium-high heat, then add the farro. Reduce the heat to a simmer and cook for 30 minutes, or until the farro is tender. Drain the farro in a fine-mesh sieve, then transfer to a large bowl and cool to room temperature.

In a small bowl, whisk together the oil, vinegar, herbs, salt, and pepper to make a dressing. Add the dressing to the farro and toss well. Cover and refrigerate or reserve at room temperature for up to 1 hour before serving.

Make the sushi rice: Rinse the rice in a fine-mesh sieve set into a large bowl under running water until the water runs clear, then drain fully and repeat.

In a stockpot, bring 3 quarts (2.8 L) water to a boil over medium-high heat, then add the rice. Reduce the heat to a simmer, cover, and cook for 20 minutes, or until the rice is tender. Drain the rice in a fine-mesh sieve, then transfer to a large bowl and cool to room temperature.

In a small bowl, whisk together the vinegar, mirin, sugar, and salt until the sugar and salt are dissolved. Add to the rice and toss well. Cover and refrigerate or reserve at room temperature for up to 1 hour before serving.

Make the sesame snow peas: Julienne the snow peas lengthwise into matchstick-thin strands.

In a medium bowl, whisk together the tahini, vinegar, fish sauce, vegetable oil, and sesame oil, then stir in the sesame seeds and ginger. Add the snow peas to the bowl and toss well. Cover and refrigerate or reserve at room temperature for up to 1 hour before serving.

Assemble the dish: Slice the fish into paper-thin bite-size pieces. Scoop your choice of one or two grains or snow peas onto a plate in a small pile, then layer your choice of fish. Drizzle the yuzu and/or ponzu sauces over the fish and serve.

MAKE-AHEAD/STORAGE
The ponzu sauce and yuzu sauce can be made up to 3 weeks in advance and stored in airtight containers in the refrigerator. The farro and quinoa can be cooked up to 1 day in advance and stored in airtight containers in the refrigerator, then dressed on event day.

Buttermilk Panna Cotta with Cantaloupe Jus and Rice Noodles

A mash-up of different textures delights the tongue in this dessert. The panna cotta is rich and creamy, the jus is refreshingly light, and crunchy nuts, crispy rice noodles, and fruit make eating this simple dish a lot of fun.

YIELD: Serves 12
SPECIAL EQUIPMENT: small, shallow silicone molds (about ½-cup/120-ml capacity) in fun shapes; chinois or cheesecloth

For the buttermilk panna cotta:
6 leaf gelatin sheets
1 vanilla bean
1½ cups (360 ml) heavy cream
¼ cup (50 g) plus 3 tablespoons granulated sugar
2 cups (480 ml) plus 3 tablespoons cold buttermilk

For the cantaloupe jus:
2 cantaloupes, peeled, seeded, and cut into chunks
1 cup (240 ml) water
2 tablespoons granulated sugar
Zest and juice of 2 limes
2 kaffir lime leaves

For the rice noodles:
1 cup (240 ml) vegetable oil
1 small handful vermicelli rice noodles
2 teaspoons confectioners' sugar

For the sugared walnuts:
½ cup (50 g) walnut halves
1 tablespoon confectioners' sugar

To assemble:
½ cup (85 g) peeled, seeded honeydew melon,
   cut into ½-inch (12-mm) cubes
½ cup (85 g) peeled mango, cut into ½-inch (12-mm)
   cubes
½ cup (85 g) pineapple, cut into ½-inch (12-mm) cubes
½ cup (75 g) seedless grapes, quartered
½ cup (70 g) blackberries, halved or quartered,
   depending on size

Make the buttermilk panna cotta: Place the gelatin in a wide, shallow bowl and add enough cold water to cover. Let the gelatin rest in the water for about 5 minutes, until softened.

Halve the vanilla bean lengthwise and scrape out the seeds. Place the seeds and pod in a small saucepan along with the cream and sugar and cook over medium-low heat, stirring until the sugar has dissolved.

When the cream is warm to the touch, remove the gelatin from the water and squeeze to remove excess water. Add the gelatin to the cream and stir until it dissolves.

Stir in the buttermilk, then strain through a fine-mesh sieve to remove the vanilla bean and any undissolved gelatin bits. Pour into the mold(s) of your choice and refrigerate for at least 8 hours, until firm.

Make the cantaloupe jus: Puree all the ingredients in a blender, then strain through a chinois or a cheesecloth-lined fine-mesh sieve into a clean bowl. Refrigerate until needed.

Make the rice noodles: Line a baking sheet with paper towels.

In a small, high-sided saucepan, heat the vegetable oil until a small piece of rice noodle thrown into the pot sizzles and turns golden brown.

Add the handful of rice noodles and fry until golden brown, then use tongs or a skimmer to transfer the noodles to the prepared baking sheet. Let cool completely.

In a medium bowl, toss the fried noodles with the confectioners' sugar. Reserve at room temperature.

Make the sugared walnuts: In a small bowl, toss the walnuts and confectioners' sugar together to coat well.

Heat a small skillet over medium heat and add the walnuts. Toast until just starting to brown, then transfer to a clean plate or small cutting board and cool completely.

Assemble the dish: Place each type of fruit, the noodles, and the walnuts in individual serving bowls. Pour the cantaloupe jus into a small serving pitcher.

Unmold the panna cottas onto serving plates, then allow guests to top them with spoonfuls of fruit, sprinkle with noodles and walnuts, and drizzle with cantaloupe jus.

MAKE-AHEAD/STORAGE
The panna cotta can be made up to 3 days in advance and stored in an airtight container in the refrigerator. The walnuts and noodles can be made 1 day in advance and stored in airtight containers at room temperature.

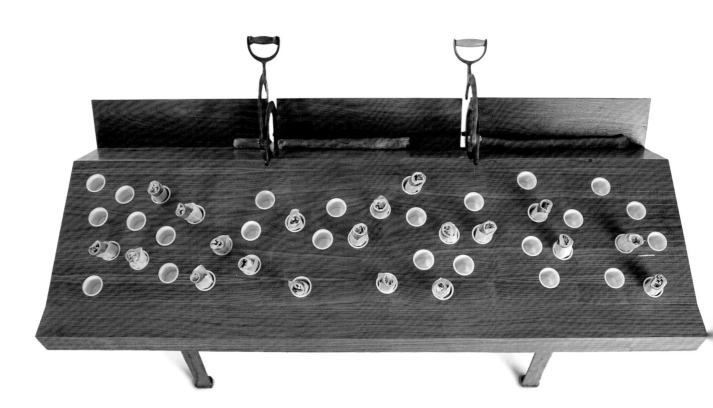

{SLICER}

We have shared a lifelong love affair with bread and sandwiches. TJ grew up with an old-fashioned bread slicer in her home, and Bob can make a sandwich out of anything he finds in the fridge. Our discovery of a super-cool vintage Raadvad slicer from Denmark inspired us to create this Interaction and slice sandwiches in a whole new way.

Before stumbling upon the Raadvad, we were trying to figure out how to get warm grab-and-go sandwiches into a lot of people's hands very quickly. Originally, the idea was to put on a show and slice multiple pieces at a time with multiple blades, but we fell in love with these vintage slicers. Freshly sliced *anything* is better, and we place each custom-sliced sandwich in a waxed bag that can be personalized for each party with stickers, labels, or even simply a permanent marker. It's a great setup for picnic-style get-togethers or for kids' birthdays, since you can customize the sizes of the sandwiches to your guests' exact specifications.

EBAY IS A TREMENDOUS RESOURCE FOR VINTAGE BREAD SLICERS (INCLUDING RAADVADS!) AT AFFORDABLE PRICES, BUT A SHARP SERRATED KNIFE AND AN ARTISANAL CUTTING BOARD WORK EQUALLY WELL. SERVE SLICED CYLINDERS OF STROMBOLI OR CAKE IN A SELECTION OF MIX-AND-MATCH CUPS—ANYTHING FROM MASON JARS TO PVC TUBES. EVEN CARDBOARD MAILING TUBES COVERED IN DECORATIVE PAPER OR WASHI TAPE MAKE FOR A STUNNING BUT ACCESSIBLE PRESENTATION. DON'T FORGET TO LINE THE TUBES WITH PARCHMENT PAPER OR NAPKINS FOR EASY GRAB-AND-GO. THE PAPER CAN BE BRANDED WITH A MONOGRAM OR A MENU.

JARS LINED WITH
PARCHMENT PAPER

IF YOU DON'T HAVE AN OLD-SCHOOL
BREAD SLICER, A WOOD BOARD AND
SHARP SERRATED KNIFE ARE ALL YOU
NEED FOR CUTTING SANDWICHES.

Wild Mushroom, Caramelized Onion, and Goat Cheese Stromboli

A stromboli is a great way to be creative with leftovers; last night's risotto or meatloaf becomes a whole new meal. Making these strombolis thin and long—more baguette-shape as opposed to loaf-shape—is harder to do, but it's this tubular shape that makes them great for eating standing up at a party. Chef Petilu, who makes all our bread at Pinch, tinkered with this dough so it would stay moist when baked in advance.

YIELD: Serves 12
SPECIAL EQUIPMENT: meat thermometer, pizza or pastry cutter, slicer (optional)

For the caramelized onions:
2 medium Spanish onions
1 cup (240 ml) water
2 tablespoons unsalted butter
2 tablespoons balsamic vinegar
1 teaspoon kosher salt

For the wild mushrooms:
3 portobello mushrooms, stems removed
½ teaspoon kosher salt
¼ teaspoon freshly ground black pepper
¼ teaspoon red pepper flakes
1½ tablespoons extra-virgin olive oil

For the stromboli dough:
6 cups (840 g) bread flour
1 tablespoon kosher salt
1 teaspoon active dry yeast
3 cups (720 ml) warm water

To assemble:
2 (4-ounce/115-g) goat cheese logs, like Montrachet, each cut into 6 strips about ½ inch (12 mm) wide
2 tablespoons extra-virgin olive oil

Make the caramelized onions: Slice off the root and stem ends of the onions, peel, and cut into halves lengthwise. Slice lengthwise, with the grain of the onion, into paper-thin strips.

In a high-sided 2-quart (2-L) sauté pan or skillet, bring the water, butter, and vinegar to a boil over medium heat. Add the onions and salt and continue to boil until the liquid is nearly evaporated. Reduce the heat and continue to cook for about 20 minutes, until the onions are deeply caramelized.

Transfer to a clean, lidded bowl and refrigerate.

Make the wild mushrooms: Preheat the oven to 400°F (205°C). Line a baking sheet with parchment paper or a nonstick baking mat.

Place the mushrooms, gills facing up, on the prepared baking sheet and sprinkle with the salt, black pepper, red pepper flakes, and oil.

Roast for 15 minutes, or until glistening and slightly shriveled.

Transfer to a clean, lidded bowl and refrigerate.

Make the stromboli dough: In a large bowl, whisk together the flour, salt, and yeast. Add the water and mix by hand for about 2 minutes, until a shaggy, tacky dough forms.

Cover the bowl with plastic wrap and set it in a warm place for about 2 hours, until the dough doubles in size.

Transfer the dough to a clean, floured surface and roll into a rectangle about 12 by 18 inches (30.5 by 46 cm), and no more than ⅛ inch (3 mm) thick. Slice the dough into long rectangles, each 3 inches (7.5 cm) wide. (You'll be rolling them up to about the diameter of a thick broomstick.)

Assemble the stromboli: Preheat the oven to 400°F (205°C). Line a large rimmed baking sheet with parchment paper or a nonstick baking mat.

Cut the prepared wild mushrooms into ½-inch (12-mm) strips. Stack some of the caramelized onions, mushrooms, and goat cheese along the long end of each dough strip, leaving about ½ inch (12 mm) of dough at the end before you place the stack. Use the exposed flap of dough to start rolling the stromboli into a tube. Press the seam of the dough to seal.

Place each rolled stromboli on the prepared baking sheet and let rest at room temperature for 30 minutes.

Brush the stromboli with the oil and bake for 25 minutes, or until golden brown and bubbling.

Let cool for 5 minutes, then slice into 3-inch (7.5-cm) pieces and serve.

MAKE-AHEAD/STORAGE

The caramelized onions and wild mushrooms can be made up to 1 day in advance and stored in separate airtight containers in the refrigerator until ready to assemble and bake into the stromboli.

Galette des Rois

Although most people are fond of this traditional king's cake because of the hidden prize baked inside, we just love it for its basic flavor profile. The key is browning both the butter pastry and the almonds to give it that extra dimension of nuttiness. We roll these into the same shape as the strombolis so we can transition the slicer from dinner to dessert easily.

YIELD: Serves 12
SPECIAL EQUIPMENT: pastry bag with large round piping tip, slicer (optional)

For the cake:
½ cup (115 g) unsalted butter
½ cup (100 g) granulated sugar
1 cup (140 g) almond flour, such as Bob's Red Mill
1 tablespoon cornstarch
½ teaspoon kosher salt
2 large eggs
1 teaspoon almond extract
1 sheet thawed frozen puff pastry

For the topping:
1 large egg, whisked with 1 tablespoon water to make an
   egg wash
1 cup (90 g) sliced almonds
2 tablespoons confectioners' sugar

Make the cake: Preheat the oven to 350°F (175°C). Line a baking sheet with parchment paper.

In the bowl of a stand mixer fitted with the paddle attachment, beat the butter on medium speed until pale, fluffy, and smooth. Add the sugar, almond flour, cornstarch, and salt and beat until incorporated.

Reduce the mixer speed to low and add the eggs, one at a time, making sure the first is completely incorporated before adding the second. Add the almond extract and stir for 15 seconds more.

Scoop the filling into a pastry bag fitted with a large round piping tip.

On a clean, lightly floured surface, roll the puff pastry into a 16-by-8-inch (40.5-by-20-cm) rectangle.

Pipe a log the thickness of a hot dog down the long edge of each puff pastry. Slice the pastry in half lengthwise, so you have two 16-by-4-inch (40.5-by-10-cm) rectangles, each with a log of filling. Roll each rectangle, starting with the side

with filling, into a log with the seam on the bottom. Transfer each carefully to the prepared baking sheet.

Make the topping: Brush the logs with the egg wash and liberally sprinkle sliced almonds and confectioners' sugar over the top.

Bake for 20 minutes, or until the logs are a deep, rich brown, then transfer to a wire rack to cool completely.

When cooled, slice into bite-size pieces and serve.

MAKE-AHEAD/STORAGE
The cakes can be made up to 1 day in advance and stored in an airtight container in the refrigerator.

{CLIPBOARD}

We are constantly searching for a replacement for the plate or cocktail napkin to hold food at a stand-up cocktail party. Serving on parchment paper as they do at a butcher shop or salumeria was an obvious choice. We wanted to stack pre-portioned combinations much like guests would make for themselves, but we would give them the perfect balance. Using a clipboard to hold the paper that holds the food was the perfect marriage of form and function—plus it's funny.

Once we had these clipboards filled with charcuterie, we needed to display them so guests could easily pick one up and add edible garnishes like pickles or berries. We tested how far you could tilt a food-filled clipboard before the food slid off—it was much more vertical than we thought. Using angles, spacing, and gravity, we created a display that looks plentiful and inviting, and lets guests experience a new way of eating.

CLIPBOARDS LEND THEMSELVES TO AN ARRAY OF DISPLAYS: INSTEAD OF LINING THEM UP FLAT, LIKE PLACE CARDS ON A TABLE, WE LOVE THE IDEA OF HANGING THEM OFF CORKBOARDS OR PEGBOARDS TO CREATE A VERTICAL WALL OF CHARCUTERIE AND CHEESE. PLATE STANDS (ESPECIALLY THOSE THAT LET YOU STACK MULTIPLE PLATES IN A ROW), STAND-UP FILE FOLDERS, AND EASELS MAKE IT EASY TO STACK THE CLIPBOARDS AND LET GUESTS GRAB FROM ANY ANGLE.

BECAUSE YOU ARE SERVING ON PAPER, YOU HAVE THE ABILITY TO PRINT THE MENU RIGHT ON THE "PLATE." GIVE A SHOUT-OUT TO THE LOCAL CHEESE FARMERS AND ARTISANAL SALUMERIAS SO GUESTS CAN KNOW MORE ABOUT EACH BITE THEY ARE TASTING. BUILDING MENU LABELING INTO THE DESIGN MAKES THE PRESENTATION MORE FLUID AND CREATES THE IMPRESSION OF A PERSONAL BUFFET.

ADD CORK TO THE BOTTOM OF EACH CLIPBOARD AS INSTRUCTED IN THE SMALL PLATES CHAPTER (PAGE 117) SO THAT GUESTS CAN EASILY REST THE CLIPBOARDS ON TOP OF THEIR WINE GLASSES WHILE CHATTING AND MANEUVERING AROUND THE PARTY. IT'S AN EXTRA STEP THAT'S NOT EXACTLY NECESSARY BUT IS A NICE TOUCH.

WE ALSO ADDED PEDESTAL BOWLS THAT WE MAKE FROM RECLAIMED WOODEN FARM-TABLE LEGS TO HOUSE THE TASTY ADD-ONS. A TRIP TO THE ANTIQUE MALL CAN PROVIDE ALL THE PROPS YOU NEED FOR YOUR OWN PERSONAL PICKLE PEDESTALS. TAKE A LOOK AT THE EXAMPLES ON PAGE 174. STURDY TABLE OR CHAIR LEGS CAN BE SAWN OFF ABANDONED FURNITURE, WITH MISMATCHED BOWLS GLUED TO THEIR BASES.

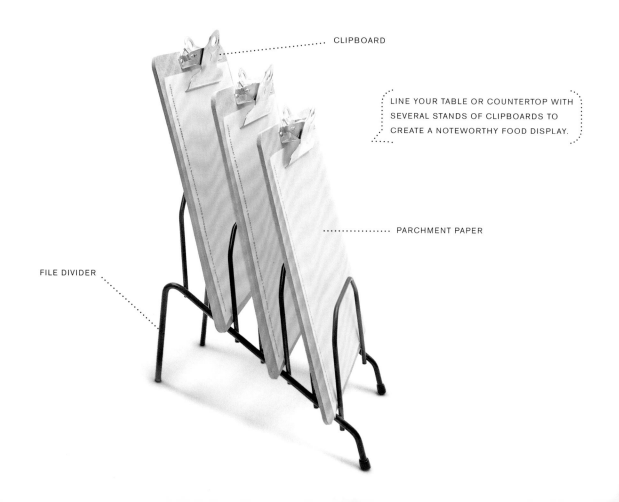

CLIPBOARD

LINE YOUR TABLE OR COUNTERTOP WITH SEVERAL STANDS OF CLIPBOARDS TO CREATE A NOTEWORTHY FOOD DISPLAY.

PARCHMENT PAPER

FILE DIVIDER

Antipasti with Italian Pickles

With so many local salami and cheese producers, remembering what you're eating takes concentration. That's why it's nice to label the serving paper, which should have a presentation reminiscent of the antipasti wrappers you would get from an Italian salumeria. How else are you going to memorize the names of cheeses like Fuzzy Wheel from Twig Farm or O' My Heart from Lazy Lady Farm, and salamis like *finocchiona* from Salumeria Biellese or *salame vinotto* from Salumeria Rosi?

YIELD: Serves 12
SPECIAL EQUIPMENT: Mason jars (optional), clipboards

For the Italian pickles:
2 cups (480 ml) white balsamic vinegar
½ cup (100 g) granulated sugar
2 poblano peppers, cut into ⅛-inch (3-mm) rings
2 large carrots, sliced on an angle into ⅛-inch (3-mm) coins
2 celery stalks, cut into 3-by-½-inch (7.5-cm-by-12-mm) pieces
½ head cauliflower, cut into small florets no more than 1 inch (2.5 cm) wide
2 large cloves garlic, thinly sliced

To assemble:
1 slice per person of:
Sliced fennel salami or another soft salami
Parma prosciutto, sliced paper-thin
Local cheese similar to Italian fontina
Smoked mozzarella
Whole-grain bread

Make the Italian pickles: In a small bowl, whisk the vinegar and sugar together until the sugar has completely dissolved.

In a large, nonreactive bowl (stainless steel, glass, or ceramic), toss the vegetables and garlic together, then pour the vinegar mixture over the vegetables.

Cover and refrigerate for at least 24 hours and up to 2 weeks. (If storing for longer than 24 hours, you can refrigerator-pickle the vegetables: Divide them between two 1-quart/960-ml Mason jars and pour 1 cup/240 ml of the vinegar mixture over each.)

Strain the vegetables from the pickling liquid before serving.

Assemble the dish: Snap twelve pieces of parchment paper onto twelve clipboards. Arrange the meats and cheeses on the parchment paper. Layer a slice of bread across one of the charcuterie slices so it "sticks" to the meat and doesn't fall off the board.

Serve with pickles on the side.

MAKE-AHEAD/STORAGE
The Italian pickles can be made up to 2 weeks in advance and stored in airtight containers in the refrigerator.

coffee caramel | pink peppercorn cookie | butterscotch poached pineapple | mocha chip

Dessert au Papiotte

We use coffee caramel to make little shelves for the pink peppercorn cookie, the pineapple, and the mocha chip, so that everything sticks to the paper.

YIELD: Serves 12
SPECIAL EQUIPMENT: candy thermometer, pizza cutter, pastry bag with large round piping tip, kitchen/crème brûlée torch, clipboards

For the coffee caramel:
½ cup (120 ml) heavy cream
½ cup (115 g) unsalted butter
1 teaspoon instant coffee powder
1 teaspoon coffee extract
½ cup (100 g) granulated sugar
2 teaspoons glucose or light corn syrup
2 tablespoons water

For the pink peppercorn cookies:
¼ cup (60 g) unsalted butter
¼ cup (50 g) granulated sugar
½ cup (65 g) all-purpose flour
2 large egg whites
1 tablespoon pink peppercorns

For the mocha chip:
1 pound (455 g) semisweet chocolate (about 60 percent cacao), roughly chopped

1½ tablespoons freshly ground coffee
1 teaspoon Maldon sea salt

To assemble:
Caramel-Poached pineapple (see page 214) tossed in
   granulated sugar

Make the coffee caramel: Line a rimmed baking sheet
with waxed paper.

In a small saucepan, bring the cream and butter to a boil
over medium heat. Whisk in the coffee powder and coffee
extract and set aside.

In a high-sided 2-quart (2-L) saucepan, stir together the
sugar, glucose, and water over medium heat until the sugar
dissolves. Stop stirring and clip a candy thermometer to
the pan. Cook until the mixture registers 293°F (145°C) on
the thermometer.

Add the cream mixture to the sugar and stir to combine.
Continue to cook until the temperature rises again to 250°F
(120°C).

Pour the caramel onto the prepared baking sheet and let set
for at least 3 hours at room temperature.

Flip the paper out onto a cutting board and use an oiled pizza
cutter or long knife to slice the caramel into ½-by-2-inch
(12-mm-by-5-cm) strips.

Make the pink peppercorn cookies: Preheat the oven to
350°F (175°C). Line a baking sheet with parchment paper or
a nonstick baking mat.

In the bowl of a stand mixer fitted with the paddle attachment,
beat the butter and sugar together on medium speed for 2 to
3 minutes, until the butter is pale and fluffy.

Reduce the mixer speed to low and add half of the flour, then
one egg white, making sure each is incorporated before adding
the next. Repeat with the remaining flour and egg white.

Add the peppercorns and stir for 15 seconds more.

Scoop the batter into a pastry bag fitted with a large round
piping tip and pipe marble-size dots onto the prepared baking
sheet, spacing them 1 inch (2.5 cm) apart.

Bake for 18 minutes, then carefully transfer to a wire rack to
cool completely.

Make the mocha chip: Line a large baking sheet with
parchment paper or a nonstick baking liner.

In a heatproof bowl, microwave the chocolate on 50 percent
power for 1 minute. Stir, then continue cooking in 30-second
intervals, stirring after each, until the chocolate is melted.

Stir 1 tablespoon of the coffee into the melted chocolate,
then pour it onto the lined baking sheet. Spread the
chocolate into an even layer with a silicone spatula.

Sprinkle the chocolate with the remaining coffee and Maldon
salt. Let cool for at least 20 minutes until the chocolate
hardens. Break into irregular pieces roughly 1½ to 2 inches
(4 to 5 cm) wide.

Assemble the dish: Snap twelve pieces of parchment paper
onto clipboards. Lay 3 strips of the coffee caramel on the
paper. Place a piece of mocha chip on one piece, pineapple
on the second, and a cookie on the third. Serve immediately.

MAKE-AHEAD/STORAGE
The coffee caramel can be made up to 1 week in advance
and stored in an airtight container in the refrigerator. The
cookies can be made 1 day in advance and stored in airtight
containers at room temperature. The mocha chip can be
made up to 1 week in advance; store in an airtight container
at room temperature.

{FRAME}

The most stripped-down design of all the Pinch Interactions, this minimalist station is nothing but an inch-thick walnut frame elevated by sawhorse legs with gripping teeth, requiring no screws or nails to attach. Holes drilled into the frame let us stick in skewers or hooks at our convenience, allowing food to hang from the top like stalactites or rise up from the bottom like stalagmites. It's strikingly thin, but light, since it's mostly made of air.

See-through is a key concept with this one: Hanging clear plastic pastry bags filled with a rainbow of sauces lets guests see what they're squeezing; thin-cut, translucent purple, orange, and yellow chips stuck on toothpick-width skewers appear to float in midair. And because the bulk of the Interaction is actually the empty space within the frame itself, it's not a cumbersome piece: You can nosh your way down the frame, talking to a friend on the other side the whole time.

We use clear disposable pastry bags for holding and hanging our sauces, available at any kitchen or baking supply store. Once the bags are filled, we tie them shut, then attach them to spring rope by looping the springs through holes punched into the tied-off ends of the bags or attaching the springs to bulldog clips. This method lets guests gently pull the sauces away from the frame to their plates. (We leave drip bowls below each sauce for any errant leaks, and make sure not to snip too much off the tip of each pastry bag, leaving just a small hole for squeezing out sauce!)

Stacks of cocktail napkins peeking out of envelopes interspersed with the hanging sauce bags make a practical but unexpected way to let guests grab and go. Also, it's always nice to label the sauces: We use round black stickers with white paint pens to mimic the chalkboard feeling that this piece of food furniture evokes.

DIY

CREATE YOUR OWN FRAME FROM AN OVERSIZE WOODEN PICTURE FRAME PURCHASED FROM A FLEA MARKET OR CRAFT STORE; IT SHOULD BE THIN ENOUGH TO GIVE THE EFFECT OF TRANSPARENCY BUT AT LEAST 1 INCH (2.5 CM) THICK SO YOU CAN DRILL INTO IT. SCREW EYE HOOKS INTO THE INTERIOR OF THE TOP SIDE AT REGULAR INTERVALS AND DRILL HOLES WIDE ENOUGH TO FIT BAMBOO SKEWERS ALONG THE INTERIOR OF THE BOTTOM. SO THAT IT WILL STAND UPRIGHT, BRACE THE FRAME WITH GRIPPING SAWHORSE LEGS IF YOU HAVE THEM, OR HOLD THE FRAME IN PLACE ON A BUFFET TABLE WITH STACKS OF BOOKS OR OTHER HEAVY HOUSEHOLD OBJECTS, OR CREATE A STAND OF YOUR OWN DESIGN IF YOU'RE HANDY.

SHOULD YOU NOT WANT TO HAMMER TOGETHER YOUR OWN FRAME, THE SAME BASIC EFFECT CAN BE REPLICATED AT HOME BY LINING UP A ROW OF VINTAGE THREAD OR YARN SPOOLS (FOUND AT ANTIQUE STORES, HOME GOODS STORES, OR ON ETSY) ON YOUR COUNTER. THE HOLES IN EACH SPOOL PROVIDE A BUILT-IN STAND FOR SKEWERS. ADD A VINTAGE KITCHEN SCALE, WINE CRATE, OR OTHER FLAT-TOPPED OBJECT, SUCH AS A STACK OF BOOKS, TO MAKE A SERVING STAND FOR SQUEEZE BOTTLES FILLED WITH DIPPING SAUCES.

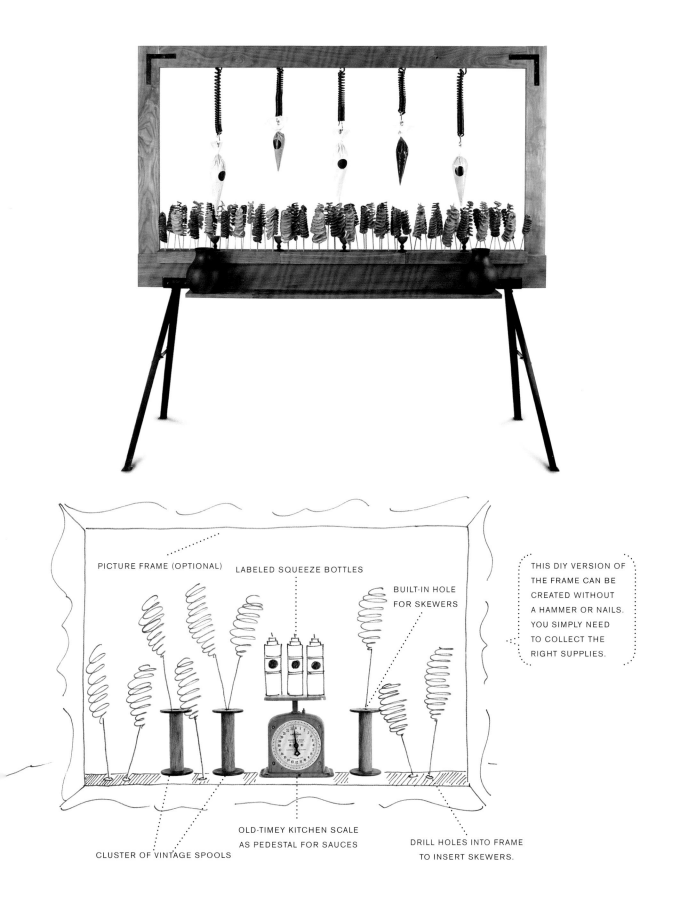

PICTURE FRAME (OPTIONAL)   LABELED SQUEEZE BOTTLES

BUILT-IN HOLE
FOR SKEWERS

THIS DIY VERSION OF
THE FRAME CAN BE
CREATED WITHOUT
A HAMMER OR NAILS.
YOU SIMPLY NEED
TO COLLECT THE
RIGHT SUPPLIES.

OLD-TIMEY KITCHEN SCALE
AS PEDESTAL FOR SAUCES

DRILL HOLES INTO FRAME
TO INSERT SKEWERS.

CLUSTER OF VINTAGE SPOOLS

Chips and Dip

These chips were inspired by a street food we found in Colombia—the showstopping potatoes look like a floral arrangement. We use a specialty spiral vegetable slicer to make thin spiral rounds of potato for this recipe. It's a fun and inexpensive tool, but you can also create spiral-cut strips of potatoes with an old-time metal apple peeler-corer-slicer. The Taleggio fondue, truffle mayo, red pepper ketchup, kimchi gastrique, and tomatillo salsa take the idea of chips and dip to another level.

YIELD: Serves 12
SPECIAL EQUIPMENT: spiral slicer (recommended) or mandoline/Japanese slicer, electric deep-fryer or deep-fry thermometer, bamboo skewers, clear disposable pastry bags, circular stickers for labeling, frame (optional)

For the chips:
12 purple or Yukon gold potatoes (½ potato per skewer)
2 quarts (2 L) vegetable oil
Kosher salt

For the Taleggio fondue:
2 tablespoons unsalted butter
1 tablespoon all-purpose flour
1½ cups (360 ml) whole milk
1 cup (250 g) Taleggio cheese, cut into pieces,
   rind and all

For the truffle mayo:
2 large egg yolks
2 teaspoons fresh lemon juice
1 teaspoon Dijon mustard
½ teaspoon kosher salt
¼ teaspoon cayenne pepper
⅓ cup (60 ml) olive oil
⅓ cup (60 ml) vegetable oil
1 tablespoon white truffle oil

To assemble:
Red pepper ketchup (see page 156)
Kimchi gastrique (see page 100)
Tomatillo salsa (see page 170)

Make the chips: Slice the potatoes into spiral rounds using a spiral vegetable slicer, or into paper-thin rounds using a mandoline or Japanese slicer.

In an electric deep-fryer or large, high-sided pot, heat the vegetable oil until it registers 350°F (175°C) on a deep-fry thermometer. Line a baking sheet with paper towels.

Fry the potatoes in batches until golden brown; timing will vary depending on your equipment, but it should take no longer than 4 minutes.

Use tongs to remove the chips from the oil and transfer them to the prepared baking sheet to cool slightly. Then thread each chip onto a bamboo skewer. Sprinkle the chips with salt while still warm.

Make the Taleggio fondue: In a 2-quart saucepan, heat the butter over medium-low heat until melted. Whisk in the flour to make a roux and cook, whisking constantly, until the roux starts to turn pale.

Whisk in the milk in a steady stream, continuing to whisk constantly to break up any lumps. Continue to cook and stir until the sauce starts to quiver and one or two bubbles break the surface.

Add the cheese and cook, whisking constantly, until fully incorporated into the sauce.

Make the truffle mayo: In a blender or food processor, pulse the egg yolks, lemon juice, mustard, salt, and cayenne to combine.

Add the oils in a slow, steady stream until the sauce thickens and forms an emulsion. Taste for seasoning and add more salt as needed.

Assemble the dish: Spoon each sauce into a clear pastry bag and tie each bag shut. Using stickers, create handwritten labels that can be placed on the bags, so guests can easily identify the sauces.

Hang the sauces from your frame, placing a bowl under each sauce so there will be a "drip cup" when you snip the tip off each bag.

Serve with the skewered potato chips.

MAKE-AHEAD/STORAGE
The truffle mayo, Taleggio fondue, red pepper ketchup, kimchi gastrique, and tomatillo salsa can be made up to 3 days in advance and stored in separate airtight containers in the refrigerator.

{SUSPENSION}

The copper pots and baking molds that hung in TJ's childhood kitchen inspired this Interaction of copper pipes extending at different latitudes and longitudes.

Because it's always important for us to create pieces that let the party swirl around them instead of blocking the flow of conversation, we use copper pipe that's only ½ inch (12 mm) in diameter, which makes the station almost see-through. It's a beautifully simple design, with the reed-thin pipes and swaying food making you feel like you've stepped into an Alexander Calder mobile. You have the opportunity to catch other guests' eyes, start conversations, and congregate around and within the piece.

The amount of food that can fit on the Suspension is staggering—if we placed the number of pizzas we hang from its hooks on a buffet table, it would likely stretch the length of the room. But because we change the vantage point, letting guests look up and see their food, it's far more pleasing to the senses than shuffling up to a table. And because the Suspension is thin and modular, we can make it as long as we want without sacrificing too much floor space.

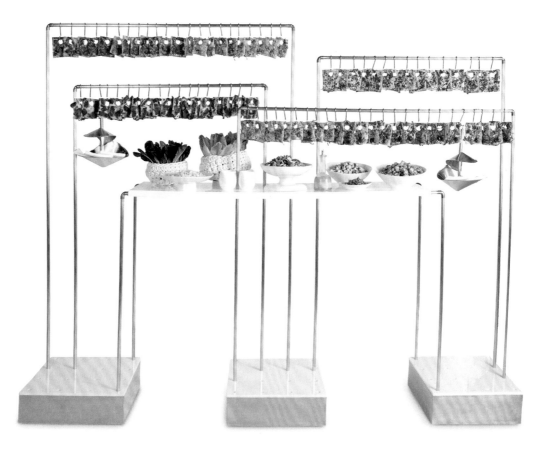

AT HOME, A SUSPENSION IS ANYTHING ON WHICH YOU'RE ABLE TO HANG ITEMS: A SHELF, EXPOSED PIPES, HOOKS THAT NORMALLY HOLD HANGING PLANTS AND BASKETS. FOR MORE DRAMATIC GATHERINGS, RENT A ROLLING RACK LIKE THE FASHION STYLISTS DO AND WHEEL YOUR EDIBLES OUT INTO THE PARTY FOR CONSUMPTION.

OR YOU CAN GO ALL OUT WITH A JUNGLE GYM–STYLE COPPER PIPE INTERACTION LIKE WE USE. FOR EACH COPPER ARCH, YOU'LL NEED TWO PIPES TO SERVE AS THE VERTICAL BARS, ONE PIPE TO SERVE AS THE HORIZONTAL HANGING BAR, AND TWO ELBOW FITTINGS TO CONNECT THEM. FOR EACH VERTICAL YOU WILL NEED A POT OR PLANTER FILLED WITH DENSE 4-INCH (10-CM) STYROFOAM ROUNDS LIKE THOSE YOU FIND IN CAKE OR CRAFT STORES. STABILIZE THE PIPES BY SECURING THEM INTO THE FOAM, WHICH YOU THEN CAN WEIGH DOWN WITH ROCKS AND COVER IN FLORAL MOSS.

FOR A MORE PERMANENT SOLUTION, DRILL HOLES INTO BLOCKS OF WOOD SO YOU CAN SLIDE THE PIPES IN AND OUT MORE EASILY. IF YOU'RE HOSTING YOUR PARTY OUTDOORS, YOU CAN SPIKE THE PIPES DIRECTLY INTO THE GROUND À LA TIKI TORCHES. ONCE YOUR SUSPENSION IS IN PLACE, ATTACH COPPER S-HOOKS TO THE HORIZONTAL BAR TO HANG FOOD AND LET IT DANGLE.

WE LIKE TO INCLUDE A FLOATING SHELF BELOW OUR SUSPENSION BARS, WHICH ALLOWS US TO SERVE ACCOUTREMENTS ALONG WITH THE ITEMS HANGING FROM THE HOOKS ABOVE. CREATE YOUR OWN SERVING SHELF BY BUILDING TWO COUNTER-HEIGHT BAR ARCHES AND PLACING THEM PARALLEL TO EACH OTHER, ANYWHERE FROM 1 TO 3 FEET (30.5 TO 91 CM) APART, DEPENDING ON THE SIZE OF YOUR SHELF. PLACE LARGE SERVING PLATTERS, PIECES OF WOOD, OR WHATEVER FLAT SURFACE FITS THE THEME OF YOUR PARTY ACROSS THE BOARDS SO PEOPLE CAN SERVE THEMSELVES FROM A COMFORTABLE HEIGHT. THEN GET READY FOR YOUR GUESTS TO DO THE LIMBO.

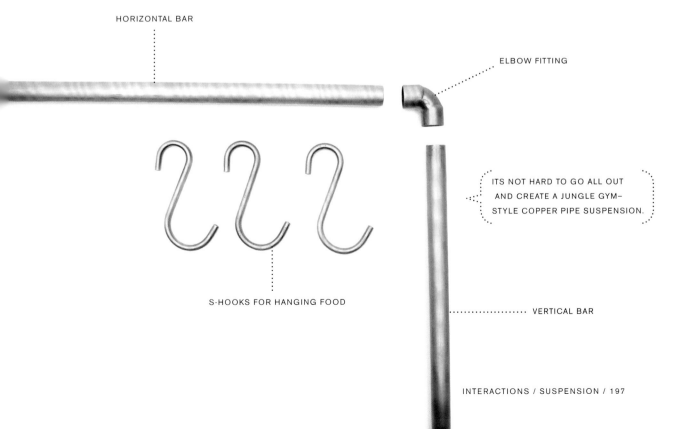

HORIZONTAL BAR

ELBOW FITTING

ITS NOT HARD TO GO ALL OUT AND CREATE A JUNGLE GYM– STYLE COPPER PIPE SUSPENSION.

S-HOOKS FOR HANGING FOOD

VERTICAL BAR

Hanging Pizzas with Deconstructed Caesar Salad

The secret to hanging a pizza on its side is to be generous with the cheese. It acts as the tasty glue that holds all the toppings on the dough. We love olive oil on our pies, and the first time we tried this Interaction a pool of the oil was left on the floor, so we had to change the proportions a bit—the recipe below includes the perfect amount of oil for a hanging pie!

YIELD: Serves 12
SPECIAL EQUIPMENT: cheese plane, pizza cutter, potato masher, Suspension (optional)

For the butternut squash, sage, and Pecorino pizza:
1 pound (455 g) butternut squash, peeled, seeded, and
   cut into 1-inch (2.5-cm) cubes
½ recipe stromboli dough (see page 185)
3 tablespoons roughly chopped fresh sage leaves
3 ounces (85 g) Pecorino cheese, sliced paper-thin with
   a cheese plane
1 tablespoon extra-virgin olive oil
½ teaspoon Maldon sea salt
½ teaspoon freshly ground black pepper

For the gorgonzola and frisée pizza:
1 head frisée, roughly chopped
1 tablespoon extra-virgin olive oil
1 teaspoon Maldon sea salt
½ teaspoon freshly ground black pepper
½ recipe stromboli dough (see page 185)
3 ounces (85 g) gorgonzola dolce

For the Caesar dressing:
2 large eggs
1 tablespoon Dijon mustard
2 tablespoons fresh lemon juice
2 tablespoons unseasoned rice vinegar
1 teaspoon Worcestershire sauce
1 clove garlic, pressed
2 anchovy fillets, mashed
½ teaspoon freshly ground black pepper
½ cup (120 ml) vegetable oil

For the croutons:
1 (4-inch/10-cm) piece baguette
2 tablespoons unsalted butter

To assemble:
1 cup (140 g) shredded leftover cooked chicken
½ cup (50 g) Parmigiano-Reggiano cheese,
   grated in strips
2 heads romaine lettuce

Make the butternut squash, sage, and Pecorino pizza:
Preheat the oven to 400°F (205°C). Line a baking sheet with parchment paper or a nonstick baking mat.

Place the squash on the prepared baking sheet and roast for 15 minutes, or until tender enough to pierce with a fork. Leave the oven on.

Transfer the squash to a large bowl and mash roughly with a potato masher.

Line a large rimmed baking sheet with parchment paper. On a clean, floured surface, roll the dough out into a rectangle approximately ⅜ inch (1 cm) thick and the size of the rimmed baking sheet. Transfer the dough to the parchment paper.

Generously sprinkle half the sage leaves over the dough, then toss the cheese slices on haphazardly. Don't cover the dough completely with the cheese. Leave a few open areas scattered across the surface of the pie.

Randomly scatter butternut squash over some of the cheese, but try to fill any areas not covered with cheese on the dough. Drizzle the dough with the olive oil and season with the salt and pepper.

Cut the dough with a pizza cutter into 2-by-4-inch (5-by-10-cm) rectangles. Use your finger to poke a hole about the size of a dime toward the top of each rectangle.

Bake for 15 minutes, or until bubbling and golden brown. Sprinkle the pizza with the remaining sage. Hang the pizzas from the hooks and serve while warm.

Make the gorgonzola and frisée pizza: Preheat the oven to 400°F (205°C).

In a small bowl, toss the frisée with the oil, half the salt, and half the pepper.

Line a large rimmed baking sheet with parchment paper. On a clean, floured surface, roll the dough out into a rectangle approximately ⅜ inch (1 cm) thick and the size of the rimmed baking sheet. Transfer the dough to the parchment paper.

Generously spread the cheese over the dough, cover with the frisée, and season with the remaining salt and pepper.

Cut the dough with a pizza cutter into 2-by-4-inch (5-by-10-cm) rectangles. Use your finger to poke a hole about the size of a dime toward the top of each rectangle.

Bake for 15 minutes, or until bubbling and golden brown. Hang the pizzas from the hooks and serve while warm.

Make the Caesar dressing: In a large bowl, using a fork, whisk together the eggs, mustard, lemon juice, vinegar, Worcestershire sauce, garlic, anchovies, and pepper. Add the oil slowly, whisking constantly to create an emulsion. This should be pourable for your guests, but not too runny— somewhere between mayonnaise and heavy cream.

The dressing can be made up to 2 days in advance and stored in an airtight container in the refrigerator. Bring to room temperature before serving.

Make the croutons: Tear the baguette into bite-size pieces.

In a large skillet, melt the butter over medium heat. Add the baguette pieces and cook for 3 to 5 minutes, stirring occasionally, until brown and crispy.

Assemble the dish: Place the croutons, chicken, and cheese in separate bowls and the dressing in a pouring vessel.

Arrange the sturdy inside leaves of the romaine in a large bowl or on a plate. Serve with the pizzas.

MAKE-AHEAD/STORAGE
The butternut squash and Caesar dressing can be made up to 1 day in advance and stored in airtight containers in the refrigerator. The croutons can be made up to 2 days in advance and stored in an airtight container at room temperature.

The pizzas can be baked up to 4 hours in advance, and reheated in a 350°F (175°C) oven for 5 to 10 minutes until the cheese melts and bubbles. Store, covered, at room temperature until needed.

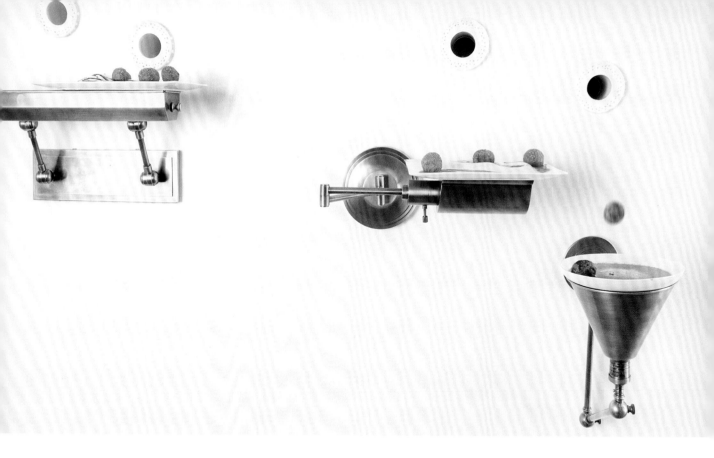

{ LITE BITE }

Whether you're lining up for churros at a street fair, anticipating a bag of beignets at New Orleans' famous Café du Monde, or waiting for the "Hot Now!" neon sign to light up at Krispy Kreme, the pleasures of freshly fried dough are undeniable. It's this desire to sink our teeth into a crunchy-on-the-outside, fluffy-on-the-inside pastry that inspired the Lite Bite—one of our most theatrical presentations.

The Lite Bite appears deceptively simple: a bunch of sconces on a wall, almost blending into the background of the party. But, like the curtain of Oz the Great and Powerful, the wall hides a frying station that lets us make fritters and beignets to order. A Mouse Trap–like series of PVC pipes slides them down to guests through holes in the wall.

A fritter shoots out of the wall, arcing into a warm dish of honey securely placed on one of the mounted sconces. The sticky sauce makes the flying fritter stop short like a golf ball hitting a sand trap. Needless to say, the crowd gathers quickly around this one.

Because we use a hidden camera to keep tabs on when the freshly fried fritters are picked up, we don't make too many at once. It looks automated, but the Interaction is really just cleverly disguised manual labor.

WE DON'T EXPECT ANYONE TO BUILD AN ENTIRE WALL WITH INSET PVC PIPES AND A MINI FRYING STATION FOR HIS OR HER NEXT PARTY, BUT THERE ARE EQUALLY INTRIGUING WAYS TO CAPTIVATE YOUR CROWD WITH FRESHLY FRIED DOUGH. LEAVE IT TO THE BRITS TO COME UP WITH AN ADORABLE CONTRAPTION CALLED AN EGG SKELTER: ESSENTIALLY A SPIRAL SLIDE FOR STORING EGGS, THIS METAL ACCESSORY CAN EASILY BE ADAPTED TO ACT AS A FRITTER SLIDE AS WELL!

SAW OFF THE METAL BAR THAT PREVENTS EGGS FROM SLIDING OFF THE END OF THE SKELTER, THEN ELEVATE THE MODIFIED SLIDE ON A TABLE IN FRONT OF A WIDE, SHALLOW DISH OF HONEY. ALTERNATIVELY, A LARGE, THIN PIECE OF WHITE PLEXI-GLAS HELD UP BY TWO BOOK EASELS BECOMES AN EASY SLIDE FOR SENDING FRITTERS AND BEIGNETS DOWN INTO A LONG TROUGH (OR PLATTER) OF DIP.

FRITTERS ON PARADE: TASTY BITES ROLL DOWN THE SPIRAL INTO A POOL OF HONEY.

EGG SKELTER (IF NECESSARY, ELEVATE ON AN UPSIDE-DOWN BOWL TO RAISE THE END OF THE SKELTER ABOVE PLATE OF HONEY)

CUT OFF THE EDGE WITH A HACKSAW SO YOU CAN ROLL THE BEIGNETS OFF.

FLAVORED HONEY

Prosciutto Beignets with Chile Honey

These beignets are best eaten as soon as they come out of the fryer. Though you can bake this dough like a gougère, frying makes the beignets roll through a tube more easily. How often do you get to say that about a food item? You can substitute many different flavored honeys, such as orange blossom or walnut.

YIELD: Serves 12
SPECIAL EQUIPMENT: spice grinder, electric deep-fryer or deep-fry thermometer, egg skelter (optional)

For the chile honey:
3 tablespoons red pepper flakes
1½ cups (360 ml) honey

For the prosciutto beignets:
2 cups (480 ml) water
½ cup (115 g) unsalted butter
1 teaspoon kosher salt
2 cups (250 g) all-purpose flour
2 large eggs
1 (4-ounce/115-g) chunk prosciutto, diced into ⅛-inch
    (3-mm) cubes
2 cups (200 g) grated fontina cheese
1 cup (100 g) grated Parmigiano-Reggiano cheese
2 quarts (2 L) vegetable oil

Make the chile honey: In a spice grinder, coarsely grind the red pepper flakes, then whisk them into the honey. Let sit for at least 2 hours to allow the chile to infuse the honey.

Make the prosciutto beignets: In a 3- to 4-quart (2.8- to 3.8-L) stockpot, bring the water, butter, and salt to a boil over medium heat. Add the flour and cook, stirring, until a ball of dough forms and pulls away from the sides of the pot.

Transfer the dough to the bowl of a stand mixer fitted with the paddle attachment and mix on low speed. Add the eggs, one at a time, making sure the first is fully incorporated before adding the second.

Stir in the prosciutto, fontina, and Parmigiano-Reggiano.

In an electric deep-fryer or a heavy, high-sided stockpot or Dutch oven, heat the oil until it registers 375°F (190°C) on a deep-fry thermometer. Line a baking sheet with paper towels.

Scoop golf ball–size rounds of the dough into the deep-fryer and cook until golden brown. Use a skimmer or tongs to transfer the beignets to the prepared baking sheet for a few seconds to drain off excess oil.

Place the honey in a wide, shallow serving bowl and slide the beignets into the honey via the egg skelter, or simply serve the honey alongside.

MAKE-AHEAD/STORAGE
The honey can be made up to 2 weeks in advance and stored in an airtight container at room temperature. The beignet batter can be made up to 1 day in advance and stored in an airtight container in the refrigerator. Let come to room temperature before frying.

INTERCOURSES

SURPRISING DISHES FOR SIT-DOWN DINNERS

Intercourses, or interactive seated courses, are a brand-new concept for the Pinch team. Passed hors d'oeuvres and stand-up bites were our bread and butter, so to speak, but it took us a long time to figure out how we could transmit that sense of playfulness to a sit-down meal. A nine-foot-long hinged board of sliders is great when it appears in the middle of a party for fifteen minutes, but we didn't want to occupy the table with an unwieldy centerpiece or other presentation that would interrupt the flow of an event.

During our first two years, we declined sit-down-dinner requests until we could come up with a way to Pinch them up. Finally, after many sleepless nights, it dawned on us that the key to our approach has always been creating interactivity—and with seated dinners it was no different. Each of our Intercourses involves guest participation: dipping, seasoning, assembling, and generally taking action.

As with many of our concepts, we're bringing a bit of the kitchen out to the party, and offering up a little jolt of surprise—guests aren't completely sure what's going to happen when the next course appears. We're not forcing guests to completely reconstruct their meals; we're just giving them a clever activity that helps them complete the dish and hopefully stimulate conversation and warmth. Their contribution—snipping herbs, squeezing sauces, pouring chocolate—makes each course tastier and a little more fun.

The name evokes the playful and provocative nature of these dishes. And we hope it makes our guests smile or strike up a conversation with their tablemates.

PINCH	BREAK	UNWRAP/REVEAL	SPRAY	POUR
CUT	SLIDE	GRATE	MIX/TOSS	BRUSH
SKEWER	SLICE	DROP	SQUEEZE	DUST/SHAKE

Raw Bar with Sesame Hijiki Salad and Red Pepper Cocktail Tube

Just as we did for large cocktail parties with our wheelbarrow pop-up (see page 164), this raw bar Intercourse is our way of serving pricey, luxe seafood at a seated dinner on a manageable budget. You can deliver a specific amount of gorgeously presented oysters and oversize shrimp to each guest without having to supply unending quantities. We pair the seafood with a briny seaweed salad and the classic raw bar accompaniments: mignonette, cocktail sauce, and a spritz of lemon.

But, this being Pinch, we can't just serve a wedge of lemon and a ramekin of mignonette and be done with it. Our from-scratch accoutrements are served in unexpected vessels—an eyedropper, a tiny tube, and a fun spritzer—that let guests squeeze their way to raw bar nirvana. Spritz a little, squeeze a lot: It's totally up to you.

YIELD: Serves 12
SPECIAL EQUIPMENT: eyedroppers or pipettes, ½-ounce (15-g) squeezable tubes, lemon sprayer nozzles or small spritzer bottles

For the mignonette:
1 shallot, roughly chopped
1 teaspoon freshly ground black pepper
¼ cup (60 ml) red wine vinegar
1 tablespoon fresh lemon juice
1 tablespoon soy sauce

For the red pepper cocktail tube:
½ cup (120 ml) red pepper ketchup (see page 156)
2 tablespoons grated fresh horseradish
1 tablespoon fresh lemon juice
1 teaspoon hot sauce, such as Tabasco

For the sesame hijiki salad:
4 ounces (115 g) dried hijiki seaweed
2 tablespoons unseasoned rice wine vinegar
1 teaspoon granulated sugar
¼ teaspoon kosher salt
2 teaspoons sesame oil
2 heads frisée lettuce, white parts only
2 tablespoons finely chopped scallion, green parts only

For the giant shrimp:
12 extra or super colossal shrimp (10–12 count)
  or 24 extra jumbo shrimp (16–20 count)

To assemble:
24 oysters
12 small lemons, or ½ cup (120 ml) fresh lemon juice
  (from about 2 lemons)

Make the mignonette: In a medium bowl, mix all the ingredients together and let sit for 30 minutes to 1 hour.

Transfer to a blender and puree until smooth, then fill twelve (½-ounce/15-g) squeezable tubes with the liquid. Reserve at room temperature until ready to serve.

Make the red pepper cocktail tube: In a blender or food processor, puree all the ingredients until smooth, then fill twelve eyedroppers or pipettes with the sauce. Refrigerate until ready to serve.

Make the sesame hijiki salad: In a large bowl filled with just enough water to cover, rehydrate the seaweed for 2 to 3 minutes, until softened.

In a small bowl, whisk together the vinegar, sugar, and salt until the sugar and salt dissolve, then whisk in the sesame oil.

Rinse and dry the frisée, and drain the softened seaweed.

Toss the frisée, seaweed, and scallions with the dressing just before serving.

Make the giant shrimp: In a small saucepan, bring 2 cups (480 ml) water to a bare simmer, just until bubbles start to form on the bottom and around the edges of the pan. Fill a large bowl with an ice water bath.

Poach the shrimp for about 3 minutes, just until cooked through, then transfer to the ice water to stop the cooking. Peel and devein the cooled shrimp. Refrigerate until ready to serve.

Assemble the dish: Shuck the oysters, leaving them in a half shell for presentation.

Insert sprayer nozzles directly into twelve lemons, or fill twelve small spritzer bottles with lemon juice.

Plate the dish by placing one colossal or two jumbo shrimp on each plate, along with two shucked oysters on the half shell, a small bowl of hijiki salad, a pipette of mignonette, a tube of cocktail sauce, and a lemon or lemon spritzer bottle.

Serve immediately.

MAKE-AHEAD/STORAGE
The mignonette and red pepper cocktail sauce can be made up to 3 days in advance and stored in airtight containers in the refrigerator.

Tin of Tuna Sashimi, Roasted Beets, and Trimmable Shiso

Chances are if you ask a gourmet to tell you his or her favorite fish, the answer won't be canned tuna. Even though tins of white boquerones from Spain and Italian salt-packed sardines are revered and delicious, the tins from the supermarket shelves are barely anyone's idea of high-end eats.

It's precisely that attitude toward tinned seafood that inspired this Intercourse, which turns the typical notion about canned seafood on its head: sushi-grade raw tuna and sweet, earthy roasted beets packed into a sardine can. The ingredients haven't been preserved or canned in any way—they're fresh, bursting with flavor, and top-quality. The subtle variations in color between the beets and tuna offer a visual playfulness as well.

The vinaigrette is in the tin with the tuna and beets, but it's up to each guest to snip his or her own greens and finish the dish. So, after they peel open the lid of the can, we place tiny embroidery scissors next to a sake cup filled with micro shiso to give guests another level of interaction.

YIELD: Serves 12
SPECIAL EQUIPMENT: 12 clean sardine or tuna tins, 12 sake cups, 12 pairs of embroidery scissors

For the roasted beets:
2 large beets (about 1½ pounds/680 g total)
2 teaspoons extra-virgin olive oil
1 teaspoon kosher salt
½ teaspoon freshly ground black pepper

For the ginger dressing:
2 tablespoons chopped pickled ginger
1 tablespoon minced shallot
2 tablespoons extra-virgin olive oil
1 tablespoon soy sauce
1 tablespoon unseasoned rice wine vinegar
2 teaspoons fresh lemon juice
1 tablespoon finely chopped scallion, green parts only

To assemble:
1½ pounds (680 g) sushi-quality center-cut yellowfin
    tuna, cut into perfect 1-inch (2.5-cm) cubes
Micro shiso or other miniature salad greens that look like
    a plant

Make the roasted beets: Preheat the oven to 300°F (150°C).

Scrub the beets of any dirt and pat dry, then rub the beets with oil. Place each beet on a large piece of foil and season with salt and pepper, then wrap the beets tightly in the foil.

Roast for about 1 hour, until a knife stabbed into the beet meets no resistance. Let the beets cool to room temperature,

then scrape the skins off with a knife or rub them off with a paper towel.

Dice the beets into perfect 1-inch (2.5-cm) cubes.

Make the ginger dressing: In a blender or food processor, combine the ginger, shallot, oil, soy sauce, vinegar, and lemon juice and puree until smooth.

Transfer to a medium bowl and stir in the scallions. Reserve at room temperature until ready to serve.

Assemble the dish: Toss the beets and tuna in the ginger dressing. Fill each sardine tin with tuna and beet cubes in a checkerboard pattern.

Fill twelve sake cups with a handful of micro shiso so that the cups look like small planters.

Plate each dish with a tin, a sake cup, and a pair of embroidery scissors for snipping the shiso.

MAKE-AHEAD/STORAGE
The beets can be roasted and cubed up to 2 days in advance; store in an airtight container in the refrigerator. Bring to room temperature before serving. The dressing can be made up to a week in advance; store in an airtight container in the refrigerator. Bring to room temperature before serving.

Acorn Clôche over Lamb Loin and Mint Gelée

At Pinch, we've played around with clôches before, using them to present dramatically smoky snacks in our pop-ups (see page 158). In this version, we've taken them a step further, moving from using premade serving pieces to making them ourselves. We scoop out acorn squashes and fit the hollowed rinds with decorative cabinet knobs. The anticipation of discovering what's under the clôche—and then the happy moment of revelation—make the course that much more memorable.

In this lamb dish, we transform the oozy green jelly that is the meat's traditional accompaniment into fun, textural cubes of mint gelée to avoid the problem of sauce leaking out from under the clôche. The layers of acorn squash "risotto" and tender kale echo the colorful green and orange striations on the squash rind.

YIELD: Serves 6
SPECIAL EQUIPMENT: candy thermometer, 6 decorative knobs, cookie cutter or ring mold, meat thermometer

For the mint gelée:
1 cup (40 g) fresh mint leaves
2 tablespoons fresh lemon juice
½ cup (100 g) granulated sugar
½ cup (120 ml) apple juice concentrate
2 tablespoons light corn syrup
2 ounces (55 g) liquid fruit pectin

For the stewed kale:
2 tablespoons extra-virgin olive oil
3 cloves garlic, minced
1 cup (240 ml) white wine
3 pounds (1.4 kg) kale, de-stemmed
Maldon sea salt
Freshly ground black pepper

For the acorn squash "risotto":
6 whole acorn squash
2 tablespoons kosher salt, plus more as needed
3 tablespoons extra-virgin olive oil
3 tablespoons minced shallots
2 tablespoons finely grated Parmigiano-Reggiano
  cheese
½ teaspoon freshly ground black pepper

For the lamb:
2 boneless single lamb loin roasts (12 to 14 ounces/340
  to 400 g each), trimmed
1 tablespoon extra-virgin olive oil
1 teaspoon kosher salt
½ teaspoon freshly ground black pepper
Pinch of red pepper flakes

Make the mint gelée: Bring a small pan of water to a boil. Fill a large bowl with ice water.

Add the mint leaves to the boiling water and cook for 10 seconds, then use a slotted spoon or metal strainer to remove the leaves and transfer to the ice water bath to stop the cooking process.

In a blender, puree the mint with the lemon juice until smooth. Set aside.

In a small pan, combine the sugar, apple juice, and corn syrup. Clip a candy thermometer to the pan. Bring the mixture to a boil and cook for about 6 minutes, until the mixture registers 225°F (110°C) on the thermometer.

Add the pectin and boil for 1 minute more.

Remove from the heat and stir the mint puree into the jelly liquid.

Pour into a clean square or oblong plastic container and let set at room temperature for at least 1 hour, until firm. Cut the mint gelée into ½-inch (12-mm) cubes.

Make the stewed kale: In a large skillet, heat the oil over medium-low heat, then add the garlic and cook, stirring, just until it starts to brown.

Add the wine, then the kale. Cover and cook for about 10 minutes, until the kale is wilted. Season with salt and pepper.

Make the acorn squash "risotto": Cut about one-quarter off the top of each squash and discard the seeds. Scoop out the flesh of the squash, reserving the flesh on a cutting board, until about a ½-inch (12-mm) exterior "wall" remains. Screw a decorative knob into the base of each squash to form clôches.

Roughly chop the scooped squash flesh into rice-size pieces and toss in a large bowl with a healthy pinch of salt. Let sit at room temperature for 30 minutes. Squeeze the juice from the flesh and discard the juice.

In a skillet or sauté pan, heat the oil over medium-low heat, then add the shallots. Cook for about 5 minutes, until the shallots are softened, then add 4 cups (960 g) of the reserved squash flesh. Cook for 10 to 15 minutes more, until the squash is tender.

Add the cheese and season with the pepper and salt. Reserve at room temperature until ready to serve.

Make the lamb: Rub the lamb loin with the oil and sprinkle with the salt, pepper, and red pepper flakes.

Heat a cast-iron or heavy-bottomed stainless-steel skillet over high heat and add the lamb to the pan. Cook, turning, until all sides are browned and a meat thermometer registers 130°F (54°C). Let the lamb rest for 5 minutes, then slice into bite-size pieces. Start assembly of the dish immediately, while the lamb is warm.

Assemble the dish: Place a ring mold that is smaller than the interior opening of the squash clôches on a plate and stack the risotto and kale inside. Fan out slices of lamb on top of the kale and top with cubes of mint gelée.

Remove the ring mold and cover the stack with a squash clôche. Repeat with the remaining plates and squash clôches.

MAKE-AHEAD/STORAGE
The mint gelée can be made up to 2 weeks in advance and stored in an airtight container in the refrigerator. The kale and risotto can be made up to 1 day in advance and stored overnight in separate airtight containers in the refrigerator; reheat each gently in a skillet before serving.

Hot Rocks with Beef Filet and Two Sauces

Sizzling-hot river rocks, thrown in the oven and heated up as if they were pizza stones, keep slices of tender filet mignon (or the meat of your choice) warm without overcooking; the beef is started in the oven and finished at the table, "grilled" on the rocks. We use bamboo tongs as utensils with this dish. They're visually striking, giving guests the impression that they are selecting meat from their own little robata barbecues.

Stop the rocks from sliding around the plate by placing them on translucently thin slices of raw ginger. The heat of the rock releases the rhizome's zippy aroma, and the ginger works as a natural trivet to keep the rock in place. Find large polished river rocks at any garden center or floral store and give them a good wash in the sink before using. Any dishwasher-safe ceramic or porcelain plate works well, as do flat pieces of slate, but it's best to avoid glass and plastic for this presentation.

YIELD: Serves 6
SPECIAL EQUIPMENT: mandoline or Japanese slicer, large river rocks, small bamboo tongs

For the raisin steak sauce:
1 tablespoon extra-virgin olive oil
¼ cup (40 g) minced onion
1 cup (140 g) raisins
2 cups (480 ml) water
½ cup (120 ml) balsamic vinegar
1 teaspoon mustard powder
1 tablespoon kosher salt
½ teaspoon freshly ground black pepper

For the Brussels sprouts:
1 pound (455 g) Brussels sprouts
2 tablespoons extra-virgin olive oil
2 cloves garlic, sliced paper-thin
½ teaspoon red pepper flakes
½ teaspoon Maldon sea salt
4 hard twists freshly ground black pepper

For the gratinéed potatoes:
3 pounds (1.4 kg) Yukon gold potatoes
2 tablespoons unsalted butter
6 cloves garlic, cut into thirds
2 cups (480 ml) half-and-half
2 teaspoons kosher salt
2 tablespoons finely grated Parmigiano-Reggiano cheese
Freshly ground black pepper

To assemble:
1 large, thick chunk unpeeled fresh ginger
6 (7-ounce/200-g) filets mignons, each cut into ¾-inch (2-cm) cubes
2 tablespoons extra-virgin olive oil

1 tablespoon Maldon sea salt
1 teaspoon freshly ground black pepper
6 tablespoons (90 ml) béarnaise sauce (see page 159)

Make the raisin steak sauce: In a skillet or high-sided sauté pan, heat the oil over medium heat, then add the onion and cook for about 10 minutes, until softened and browned.

Add the raisins, water, vinegar, mustard powder, salt, and pepper and bring to a boil. Reduce the heat and simmer for 10 minutes, or until the sauce has thickened slightly.

Transfer the sauce to a blender or food processor and puree until smooth. Refrigerate until ready to serve.

Make the Brussels sprouts: Slice the root end off each Brussels sprout, then peel away as many leaves as you can from the sprout until you hit the cabbagey center. Slice each center thinly.

In a high-sided sauté pan heat the oil over medium heat, then add the garlic slices and stir until they just start to brown.

Stir in the red pepper flakes, then add the leaves and sliced centers of the Brussels sprouts. Cook for 2 to 3 minutes, until they begin to soften, then season with the salt and pepper.

Make the gratinéed potatoes: Preheat the oven to 350°F (175°C).

Peel the potatoes and slice into ⅛-inch (3-mm) rounds with a mandoline or Japanese slicer. Set aside.

In a stockpot, heat the butter over medium-low heat until melted. Add the garlic and cook until it is just starting to brown.

Add the half-and-half and salt and raise the heat to medium until the half-and-half comes to a boil. Reduce the heat and simmer the half-and-half for 10 minutes to let the garlic flavor the cream.

Use a slotted spoon or metal strainer to remove the garlic pieces; discard them. Add the potatoes and cook for 10 minutes, or until tender but not falling apart.

Remove from the heat and stir in the cheese and pepper. Pour the potatoes and cream into a 9-by-13-inch (23-by-33-cm) baking dish, pressing them down until the liquid is squeezed to the top.

Bake for 30 minutes, then remove from the oven and cover with foil. Use a pot, flat meat tenderizer, or smaller pan to pack and compress the potato casserole. Remove the foil and let the casserole cool to room temperature.

Slice the casserole into 2-inch (5-cm) cubes. Reserve at room temperature until ready to serve, or refrigerate overnight in an airtight container and bring to room temperature before serving.

Assemble the dish: Preheat the oven to 400°F (205°C). Line a rimmed baking sheet with foil.

Slice the ginger into wide rounds, no more than ⅛ inch (3 mm) thick, that are large enough to use as "doilies" for the rocks. Place the ginger slices on the plates.

In a wide bowl, toss the steak cubes with the oil and season with the salt and pepper. Let sit at room temperature for 30 minutes. Place the rocks on the prepared baking sheet and heat in the oven while the steak rests.

Place the steak bites on the hot rocks and bake for 5 to 6 minutes.

While the steak cooks, plate the remaining ingredients: Place the potato cubes on the plate, cut side up so they can be easily grabbed with tongs. Toss the Brussels sprouts on top of and around the potato cubes.

Place the hot rocks with the steak on the ginger doilies and spoon the béarnaise sauce and steak sauce next to the rocks as a dipping sauce. Serve with tongs on each plate.

MAKE-AHEAD/STORAGE
The raisin steak sauce can be made up to 3 days in advance and stored in an airtight container in the refrigerator. The Brussels sprouts and gratinéed potatoes can be made up to 1 day in advance and stored in separate airtight containers in the refrigerator. Bring to room temperature before serving.

The Wood Block with Orange Terrine and Three Chocolates

We like to think of the wood block as a multipurpose stage of *amuse bouche*–style bites that open our imaginations to all sorts of tasty inventions. The excitement of interacting with the wood block comes from the choose-your-own-adventure act of combining flavors and bites any way you want. Pull off a magnetized fork, break off a piece of chilled chocolate bark, or slide a floating cookie out of its nook . . .

YIELD: Serves 12
SPECIAL EQUIPMENT: food-safe tile or marble slab, wood block (optional, see opposite page)

For the orange terrine:
4 large seedless oranges
1 vanilla bean
¼ cup (50 g) granulated sugar
1 (1-inch/2.5-cm) piece fresh ginger, peeled and
    thinly sliced
1 tablespoon triple sec
1 envelope (1 tablespoon/7 g) unflavored gelatin

For the chocolate mousse:
¼ cup (25 g) confectioners' sugar
2 tablespoons unsweetened cocoa powder
½ cup heavy cream

For the cocoa tuile:
¾ cup (95 g) all-purpose flour
3 tablespoons unsweetened cocoa powder
½ cup (115 g) unsalted butter, cut into ½-inch
    (12-mm) cubes
1 cup (100 g) confectioners' sugar

1 tablespoon glucose or light corn syrup

For the ginger-lavender chocolate bark
1⅓ cups (190 g) chopped bittersweet chocolate (at least
    70 percent cacao)
2 tablespoons finely chopped crystallized ginger
1 tablespoon pesticide-free dried lavender
2 teaspoons Maldon sea salt

Make the orange terrine: Using a sharp paring knife, slice off the peel and pith of each orange. Working over a bowl, cut between the membranes of each orange to make suprêmes, or pithless segments. Squeeze any remaining juice from the leftover membranes into the bowl, then strain the suprêmes through a fine-mesh sieve, reserving the suprêmes and juice separately.

Halve the vanilla bean lengthwise and scrape out the seeds. Place the seeds and pod in a small saucepan and add ½ cup (120 ml) of the orange juice, the sugar, ginger, and triple sec. Cook over low heat, stirring, until the sugar has dissolved, then remove from the heat. Cover and let sit for 2 hours.

Strain the orange juice mixture into a clean square or oblong plastic container, then stir in the gelatin and reserved suprêmes.

Refrigerate for 3 hours, or until firm, then cut the terrine into 1-inch (2.5-cm) cubes. Refrigerate until ready to serve.

Make the chocolate mousse:
Whisk the confectioners' sugar and cocoa powder together in a small bowl.

With an electric hand mixer or stand mixer fitted with the whisk attachment, whip the cream on medium speed until soft peaks form. Continue to whip the cream while adding the cocoa and sugar in a steady stream until fully incorporated.

Make the cocoa tuile: In a small bowl, whisk the flour and cocoa powder together.

In a stand mixer fitted with the paddle attachment, beat the butter and confectioners' sugar together on medium speed for 2 to 3 minutes, until the butter is light and fluffy.

Reduce the mixer speed to low and stir in the glucose, then add the flour and cocoa powder and stir until a soft dough forms. Pat the dough into a disc and wrap in plastic wrap. Refrigerate for at least 1 hour.

Preheat the oven to 350°F (175°C). Tear off two pieces of parchment paper, each the size of a large baking sheet. With a rolling pin, roll the chilled dough between the pieces of parchment paper until very thin, no more than ⅛ inch (3 mm) thick. Transfer to the baking sheet and remove the top piece of parchment paper. Bake for 6 minutes, or until crispy, then transfer to a wire rack to cool completely.

Break into chip-size pieces. Reserve at room temperature until ready to assemble.

Make the ginger-lavender chocolate bark: Chill a food-safe tile or marble slab in the refrigerator.

In a heatproof bowl, microwave the chocolate on 50 percent power for 1 minute. Stir, then continue cooking in 30-second intervals, stirring after each, until the chocolate is melted. Spread the chocolate on twelve chilled tiles and liberally sprinkle with the ginger, lavender, and salt. Reserve at room temperature until ready to assemble.

Assemble the dish: Stab the terrine cubes with magnetized forks and attach to the magnetized wood block. Pipe the chocolate mousse on top of the orange terrine. Place the chocolate bark tile on top of the wood block and secure the cocoa tuiles with inside the built-in groove.

If not using a wood block for presentation, place the chocolate bark on a large plate. Stab three terrine cubes with forks and place on the plate, then pipe chocolate mousse on top of the orange terrine. Place a cocoa tuile on the plate and serve.

MAKE-AHEAD/STORAGE
The orange terrine and the chocolate mousse can be made up to 3 days in advance and stored in airtight containers in the refrigerator. The cocoa tuile can be made 2 days in advance; break into pieces when cool and store in an airtight container at room temperature. The chocolate bark can be made 6 hours before serving and stored on the chilled tile in the refrigerator.

DIY

A GORGEOUS HARDWOOD BLOCK (6 BY 3 BY 2 INCHES/15 BY 7.5 BY 5 CM), SANDED AND SEALED WITH A BEESWAX SALAD-BOWL FINISH, EASILY BECOMES A UNIQUE SERVING PIECE. SAW A SLOT FOR PRESENTING THE COCOA TUILE ON THE SIDE, GLUE MAGNETS TO THE BACK, AND FIT A CERAMIC SUBWAY TILE OR MARBLE SLAB REMNANT ON TOP. OR TAKE ANY ONE OF THESE ELEMENTS AND PRESENT INDIVIDUALLY, SUCH AS PLACING A CHILLED TILE ON ONE OF YOUR EVERYDAY PLATES AND LETTING GUESTS POUR AND SEASON THEIR OWN CHOCOLATE BARK AT THE TABLE.

The Slide with Cardamom Beignets and Caramel-Poached Pineapple

Rube Goldberg devices, those quirky mechanisms where a single action starts an amusing (and often complex) chain reaction, have always been a favorite of ours. For this Intercourse, simply lift the fork and the warm beignets slide down the copper rails and roll into the sauce. The poached pineapple pieces act as a guardrail to stop the beignets from rolling off the board. Experiment with your own food combinations—savory gougères and cheese sauce, or meatballs and marinara, for example—or use recipes from other chapters, like prosciutto beignets (page 202) and blueberry jam.

YIELD: Serves 12
SPECIAL EQUIPMENT: electric deep-fryer or deep-fry thermometer, Slide (optional)

For the cardamom beignets:
2½ cups (315 g) all-purpose flour
1 tablespoon plus 1 teaspoon baking powder
6 large eggs
½ cup (100 g) granulated sugar
1 teaspoon vanilla extract
1 pound (455 g) fresh whole-milk ricotta
4 cups (960 ml) vegetable oil
¼ cup (50 g) granulated sugar
½ teaspoon cardamom

For the caramel-poached pineapple:
½ cup (100 g) granulated sugar
¼ cup (60 ml) water
1½ tablespoons unsalted butter
1 pineapple, peeled, cored, and cut into 1-inch (2.5-cm) cubes

To assemble:
Chocolate sauce (see page 112)
Honey

Make the cardamom beignets: In a medium bowl, whisk together the flour and baking powder.

Using a hand mixer in a large bowl or in a stand mixer fitted with the paddle attachment, beat the eggs, sugar, and vanilla together on medium-low speed for about 2 minutes, until thick and pale. Reduce the mixer speed to low and stir in the ricotta; mix until smooth, then add the flour mixture and stir just until combined.

In an electric deep-fryer or a heavy, high-sided stockpot or Dutch oven, heat the oil until it registers 375°F (190°C) on a deep-fry thermometer. Line a baking sheet with paper towels. Scoop golf ball–size rounds of the dough into the deep-fryer and cook for 3 to 4 minutes, until golden brown. Use a spider or flat metal strainer to transfer the beignets to the prepared baking sheet for a few seconds to drain off excess oil.

In a medium bowl, mix the sugar and cardamom. While the beignets are still hot, toss them in the sugar mix to coat.

Make the caramel-poached pineapple: In a small saucepan, stir together the sugar and water over medium-low heat until the sugar has the consistency of wet sand.

Once the sugar dissolves and starts to bubble, cook, without stirring, until the sugar is golden brown and caramelized, then remove from the heat and quickly and carefully whisk in the butter.

Add the pineapple and return the pan to the stove. Cook the pineapple over low heat for about 20 minutes, until soft.

Assemble the dish: Line a piece of wood or serving platter with parchment paper. Place three cubes of pineapple on one side of the paper, and thickly smear two lines of chocolate sauce and honey next to them.

Stab a beignet with a fork, then insert the fork and copper wire into the wood through the parchment paper or place the fork on the platter. Place two more beignets behind or next to the fork and serve immediately.

MAKE-AHEAD/STORAGE
The beignets are best served fresh, though they can be made up to 2 hours in advance and reserved at room temperature. The pineapple and the chocolate sauce can be made up to 3 days in advance and stored in airtight containers in the refrigerator. Reheat the pineapple and chocolate sauce before serving.

CUT BLOCKS OF PINE JUST A LITTLE LARGER THAN A SHEET OF PARCHMENT PAPER, SO THE PARCHMENT FITS SNUGLY ON TOP OF THE WOOD. PRE-DRILL HOLES INTO THE WOOD USING AN ⅛-INCH (3-MM) DRILL BIT. AS FOR THE FORK HOLES, THEIR SIZE WILL DEPEND ON THE DIAMETER OF YOUR FORK TINES. LOOK FOR ¾-BY-6-INCH (2-BY-15-CM) COPPER-PLATED WIRE PIPE HOOKS AT THE HARDWARE STORE FOR A PRE-BENT PIECE PERFECTLY SIZED TO HOLD FRESH BEIGNETS OR OTHER FRIED DOUGH. ANGLE THE FORK OR WIRE AT 45 DEGREES TO GET THE BEIGNETS TO SLIDE. PRINT THE MENU AND THE INSTRUCTIONS ON THE PARCHMENT PAPER TO HELP GUESTS ALONG.

QUICKLY PULL UP FORK TO BEGIN

DONUT SLIDE

warm cardamon donuts
honey + dark chocolate sauces
caramel poached fruit

TOOLBOX

OUR FAVORITE RESOURCES

Sometimes we know exactly what we are looking for and where to buy it. Other times, we'll be wandering the aisles of a hardware store in Istanbul, strolling through a farmers' market in Lucca, or just surfing the Internet when we see a bowl, vase, table, ingredient, or some other piece that gets our creative juices flowing.

We especially love it when we find something but have no idea what it is. Whether it's a special cutting tool or fruit, it lets us have a lightbulb moment, even if its intended purpose isn't what we end up using it for in the end. We encourage you do the same with any items you find while wandering your own hardware store aisles or exploring markets and stores: Pick it up, turn it upside down, taste it, smell it, try to hang it . . . think about all the possibilities! That's where the fun begins.

Below are just a few of our go-to places for materials and inspiration:

SPECIALTY SHOPS
Fishs Eddy: fishseddy.com
ABC Carpet & Home: abchome.com
Jamali Garden: jamaligarden.com
Moon River Chattel:
moonriverchattel.com
RePOP: repopny.com
City Foundry: cityfoundry.com
Flea Markets and Stoop Sales
Farmers' Markets

SPECIALTY WEBSITES
PackNWood: packnwood.com
BrewTensils: brewtensils.com
Europe2You: europe2you.com
Etsy: etsy.com
Cost Plus World Market:
worldmarket.com
Uline: uline.com
Quirky: quirky.com
Brelli: thebrelli.com

HARDWARE STORES
Prince Lumber: princelumber.com
KDM Hardware: kdmhardware.com
Garber Hardware: garberhardware.com
Home Depot: homedepot.com
Lowes: lowes.com

ART SUPPLY STORES
New York Central Art Supply:
nycentralart.com
The Compleat Sculptor: sculpt.com
Paper Presentation:
paperpresentation.com
Pearl Fine Art Supplies: pearlpaint.com
Utrecht Art Supplies: utrechtart.com

CULINARY SUPPLIES
Bowery Kitchen Supply:
bowerykitchens.com
Korin: korin.com
JB Prince: jbprince.com

The Meadow: atthemeadow.com
Albert Uster Imports: auiswiss.com
The Chef's Garden: chefs-garden.com
Kalustyan's: kalustyans.com
Terra Spice: terraspice.com
N.Y. Cake: nycake.com
Sur la Table: surlatable.com
Williams-Sonoma: williams-sonoma.com
Crate & Barrel: crateandbarrel.com
CB2: cb2.com
West Elm: westelm.com

WHEN ALL ELSE FAILS
The Container Store:
containerstore.com
Bed Bath & Beyond:
bedbathandbeyond.com
Amazon: amazon.com
eBay: ebay.com
Staples: staples.com

INDEX

ACKNOWLEDGMENTS

When we first started Pinch, we were truly a pinch of an organization, a small team aspiring to big things. We didn't know how fast Pinch was going to grow. Partners Karen Hillburn, Stella Rankin, and Chef Rideiby Pena believed in us enough to leave their cushy jobs to help build this company from its infancy. Now there's an amazing group of people who bring their own creative approaches to the company.

Like a spider web, the Pinch team is a delicate but intricately woven arrangement of people who grab ideas and won't let go. Each member of our staff—whether cooking, building, casting, or serving—is deeply invested in his or her work. We're constantly impressed by the way our colleagues approach tasks, projects, and challenges from their imaginative and thoughtful perspectives.

It's a cliché, but Pinch is a truly close-knit group of people. We're all veterans of the business who can look at catering and design in a fresh way, and we're always excited for the roller-coaster ride of creating something newer, cooler, and more unexpected each day.

Pinch would not be Pinch without the great Petilu, Pastry Chef Stacy (many of her recipes are in this book); Hugo, the Whiz Kid; the smartest person at Pinch, Amanda; Lead Fabricator Al, Junior, and his posse of EZ and Richard; casting director Crosby; Chef Lewis and Chef Wing; RJ the Terrible; Captain Marshall; Captain Jeremy; Do-it-all Trish; Erin the Planner; Steady Jorge; Sous Chef Jose; Pastry Chef Izzy; Orlando; Roy; Emily; and all the others who have walked through our doors. Kerri Brewer, thank you for your amazing photographs and for setting us up to take our own. A special thanks to Brandi Bowles for convincing us to write this book, and to all the lovely people at Abrams, especially Laura and John, for making it such an enjoyable process.

Our families have also been incredibly supportive and encouraging: Mary, Ricardo, Rogan, Lynn, Sarann, Jean-Louis, Justin, Herb, Alex, and Joan.

Viva la Pincha.

Published in 2014 by Stewart, Tabori & Chang
An imprint of ABRAMS

Text copyright © 2014 TJ Girard and Bob Spiegel
Photographs copyright © 2014 Pinch Food Design
Illustrations page 203 copyright © Heesang Lee

Library of Congress Control Number: 2014930932

ISBN: 978-1-61769-085-3

Editor: Laura Dozier
Designer: John Gall and Rachel Willey
Production Manager: Tina Cameron
Photographs by: TJ Girard and Kerri Brewer

The text of this book was composed in Berthold Akzidenz Grotesk.

Printed and bound in China

10 9 8 7 6 5 4 3 2 1

Stewart, Tabori & Chang books are available at special discounts when purchased in quantity for
premiums and promotions as well as fundraising or educational use. Special editions can also be created
to specification. For details, contact specialsales@abramsbooks.com or the address below.

THE ART OF BOOKS SINCE 1949
115 West 18th Street
New York, NY 10011
www.abramsbooks.com

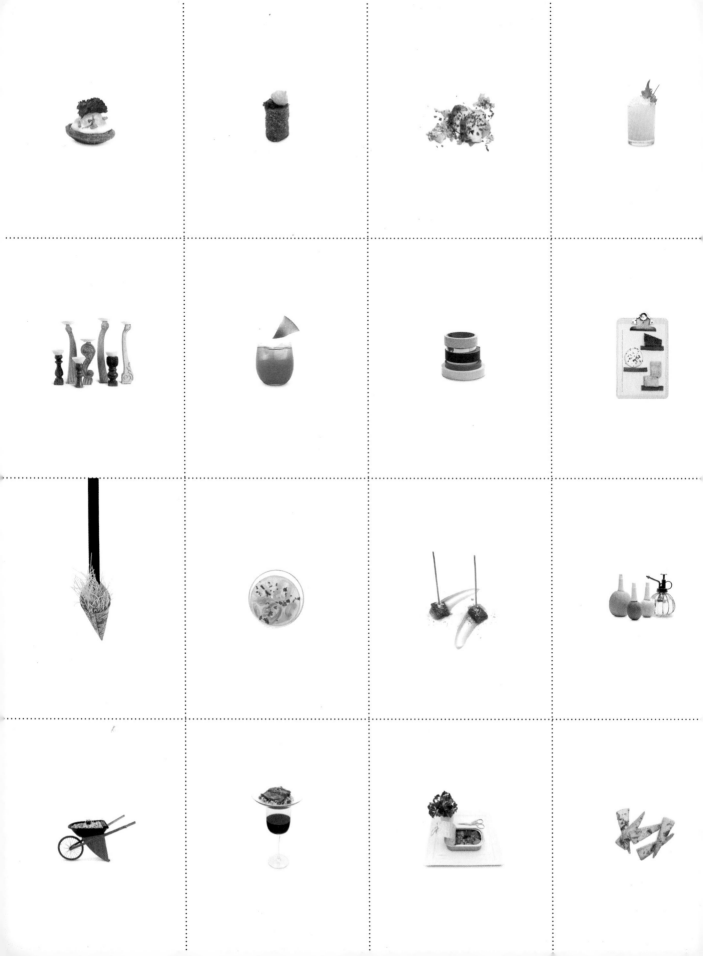